SHANGHAI JOURNAL

An Eyewitness Account of the Cultural Revolution

—— Neale Hunter ——

With a new Introduction by the Author

HONG KONG
OXFORD UNIVERSITY PRESS
OXFORD   NEW YORK
1988

Oxford University Press

Oxford   New York   Toronto
Petaling Jaya   Singapore   Hong Kong   Tokyo
Delhi   Bombay   Calcutta   Madras   Karachi
Nairobi   Dar es Salaam   Cape Town
Melbourne   Auckland

and associated companies in
Berlin   Ibadan

Shanghai Journal, An Eyewitness Account of the
Cultural Revolution, by Neale Hunter. Originally
published in the USA by Praeger Publishers, a
division of Greenwood Press, Inc., New York, NY, USA
Copyright © 1969 by Frederick A. Praeger, Inc.
Introduction © Oxford University Press 1988

This edition reprinted, with permission and
with the addition of an Introduction, in
Oxford Paperbacks 1988

ISBN 0 19 582710 4

Printed in Hong Kong by Golden Crown Printing Co. Ltd.
Published by Oxford University Press, Warwick House, Hong Kong

Introduction

Readers of *Shanghai Journal* should be warned at the outset that the fortunes of certain individuals mentioned in this book have changed dramatically.

Take Teng Hsiao-p'ing. At the time of the Red Guards, he was identified as a most dangerous 'revisionist', one of the few men capable of undoing the Chinese revolution. Today, he has more power than anyone.

Or take his worst enemies in those days — those who built the movement into a giant guillotine, which they set up over Teng's neck. Today, they are without power.

Four of them have been singled out by name — a compliment, in a way, an acknowledgement that they, at that time, presented the greatest threat. These four — Chang Ch'un-ch'iao, Yao Wenyuan, Wang Hung-wen, and Chiang Ch'ing (Mao's wife) — have in fact received the highest 'honour in reverse' that China can convey: they have been turned into *myth*. Dubbed the 'Gang of Four', they are kept as living negative-exemplars, their evil features distorted, like guardian statues in old Buddhist temples.

Shanghai Journal could not ignore these four, when they were

Note: The Wade-Giles system of romanization for Chinese personal and place names has been used in this Introduction to conform with usage in the original text. A glossary at the end of the Introduction gives both Wade-Giles and the putonghua pinyin forms of these names.

mortals; for they used Shanghai as base in their bid for power. A republished *Shanghai Journal* will still have to confront them *as humans* — human ideologues and human politicians, despite their promotion to myth.

Readers should also be advised that some of the policies pursued by China now are almost the reverse of those she espoused in the days of the Red Guards.

In those days, policy-makers bowed to political principles. Now, politics have become strangely quiet in China. The national commitment is to heal the sick economy.

In those days, China believed in self-reliance. Now, she can borrow vast sums from abroad, and make massive imports of foreign technology.

In those days, moral incentives outweighed material ones. Now, private enterprise — of a kind — is back, along with the profit motive; and individuals have the right to get rich.

In those days, lip-service, at least, was paid to collectives, and to the dream of a future '*commune*-ist' society. Now, the family is openly acknowledged as the basic unit of China's economy.

If some Red Guards had mastered the Taoist art of travelling through time on a cloud, and could simultaneously see the China of their day and China now, they might very well conclude that Teng Hsiao-p'ing was leading their country into the maw of capitalism.

Unfortunately, Taoist clouds no longer clutter China's air space. The Chinese have all had to live through the last twenty years. If you could ask a peasant — who has spent that time doing backbreaking work, with three thoughts out of every four on rivers and soil and crops — he might describe the ten years since Teng as 'a little less lean' than the ten years before.

Readers and writers of books are the only ones who can fly on magic clouds. We are the privileged, the 'outside observers', who can see points twenty years apart without having to live through the intervening time. We can say the changes are 'spectacular' — even that the new policies look 'pragmatic'. But the height, which makes it easy for us to see history, makes it hard for us to see into human motives. We cannot tell, from here, whether Teng Hsiao-

Introduction

p'ing is a *true rightist*, who really does want China to go on to capitalism. Or a *true leftist*, who is only tolerating 'pragmatic' policies until China is well enough to go on to communism. We can only speculate — or, in my case *hope* — that he is a *true moderate*, that he holds power by virtue of a truce that has been in force since the end of the Cultural Revolution, and that his main function is to keep the rabid left and right from each other's throats.

From this height, we can also see the whole span of Chinese political history. Pragmatism is more noticeable for its absence than for its presence. It seems that Chinese policy-makers — whether Communist or Confucian — have always been sticklers for principle, if not sometimes 'ideology-mad'. Edoarda Masi put this well:

> No other people has so absolute a need as do the Chinese to define its own form in order to recognize that it truly exists.
>
> (*China Winter* [New York, E. P. Dutton, 1982], pp. 40–1.)

We in the West invented pragmatism, so we naturally tend to welcome its occurrence in China. We say: 'The Chinese are seeing sense at last.' Which means: 'seeing as we do'. We forget that if the Chinese thought as we do, they would no longer be unique. They would be just another part of the Westernized world.

Whatever the significance of the changes in China, surely *Shanghai Journal* is a dated book. Like a pot-bound plant, its roots have been cramped by the shape of the period it describes. Transplanted into the present, how long will it survive?

One thing that might help it to make the transition is that it is not really a 'scholar's book' at all. It is not a completely objective study of a particular time and place. I admit it has that *appearance*. It purports to see China through the eyes of the Red Guards, to be a 'documentary'. It even bristles with appendices. But it is also an 'eyewitness account'. The author was involved — sometimes deeply — in the story he tells. This makes it a *personal* book — one that could be excused if it reflected, here and there, the author's views. In fact, it does more than that. There are several occasions when the author's *biases* show through quite clearly.

Introduction

One of these is so obvious that the original jacket blurb advertised the book as 'essentially sympathetic to the efforts of the Red-Guards to eradicate the creeping bureaucratization of Chinese society...'.

An equally arbitrary 'taking of sides' is shown in the treatment of Chang Ch'un-ch'iao. *Shanghai Journal*'s reaction to the seizure of power by his group, early in 1967, is one of mistrust, almost hostility. (A spokesman for Chang Ch'un-ch'iao was angry with the book for that reason. See below, pp. *xix–xxii*.) Since Chang Ch'un-ch'iao's group is precisely the one that has become the 'Gang of Four', does this not show extraordinary political acuity on my part? The answer is 'No'. The sides I took in the movement did not spring from any cool analysis of the situation. They were what are crudely known as 'gut reactions' — instinctive reactions — arising from parts of my 'character' formed long before I thought of going to China.

Since my personal preferences seem to have entered the book, I had better add a word of 'self-criticism'. I believe I went to China 'with an open mind'; but it is not cynical to point out that this phrase can mean an equally balanced load of preconceptions.

In my case, I can see three levels of these.

The deepest level — and the one which made me take the side of the Red Guards against the bureaucracy in general and against Chang Ch'un-ch'iao in particular — was formed in childhood. I grew up in Australia, where the average person tends to have a healthy disrespect for bureaucrats, who are derided as 'pen-pushers', and an ingrained antipathy to all authority, all 'powers that be', no matter how highly sanctioned. To be born in Australia is to acquire, as a birthright, a national hero who shot three policemen dead.

A shallower level of preconceptions is what could be called one's 'frame of mind' at any particular time. In my case, this had changed several times in the years before I went to China. My attitude to 'European values', for example, had fluctuated. I had been shocked by my first taste of life in Europe's cities, by what I saw as their ostentation and greed, and the alienation of people from reality and from each other. This dinted faith was restored by a year spent in Spain. The peasants I met there struck me as admirable — both as individuals, and as the class that did the hardest work for the least reward.

My shallowest level of preconceptions were those relating to China. I am sure I took at least my share of these when I went there.

I know I had *political* preconceptions. I entertained a 'hope against hope' that China would prove a better society than the picture of her painted in the West. I say 'hope against hope', because the picture was a gloomy one indeed. Those were the days of the United States in Vietnam, and most Western reports on China described her as an arrogant and unpredictable power — now armed with nuclear weapons — that acted as a kind of 'entropy factor', increasing the world's disorder. There was even talk by the United States 'hawks' of 'taking China out'.

They were also the days when the 'Godless communists' had turned the good Chinese into 'blue ants', forced them to live and eat communally in barracks, segregated the sexes, and so on.

I did not believe this picture. The proof that I did not *dis*believe it either is provided by the huge relief I felt when I found China was not a bad place at all. Certainly, it had sinophiles and xenophobes and dogmatists and some petty-minded bureaucrats. But the 'feel' was good. The people were energetic and optimistic. It was a society that had lifted itself, at great cost, out of an unpromising past, and managed to rejuvenate itself in the process. Its future seemed unlimited.

Some of my preconceptions were embarrassing, almost racist. They related to what sort of *humans* the Chinese would turn out to be. Anyway, I was pleased to find them as human as people elsewhere, and as different from each other as people elsewhere. This was clear from the start, but was made crystal-clear when I got to know my students and found that some were quick, some were diligent, some were witty, some were vain, and so on.

It was the realization that I had been wrong about China that first made me think of writing a book. It struck me as tragic that the United States and China, say, should be prepared to fight, with each side so royally ignorant of the other. I had in mind, not a *Shanghai Journal* then, but some minor antidote to world war.

Then the Cultural Revolution started. Before long, rival Red Guard groups — many including people I knew — were writing vituperative posters against each other. At that stage I had no idea that it would grow into a ten-year 'winter of discontent'. But I knew, from the appearance of widespread hate, that something was wrong in my estimation of China.

I started to collect materials, spasmodically at first, then more systematically, as more and more people I knew got hurt. This collection 'grew into' *Shanghai Journal* — which was the last type of book I had imagined writing. It started, not as an antidote to war, but as an antidote to my own confusion.

It was ironic. I had gone to China, half expecting it to be a land of hate, and found, to my intense relief, that it was not, that it was in many ways the opposite. Now the Cultural Revolution seemed to be sneering: 'Hi, sucker! Welcome to the Land of Hate!'

These disillusions were felt as emotions. They were not a part of my experience in China that I could observe with scholarly detachment or fit into political theories.

Emotions did not dictate my choice of sides. I would have supported the Red Guards anyway, against the bureaucracy and men like Chang Ch'un-ch'iao. The deepest part of my 'make-up' decided that. The effect of the emotional experience was to make me take sides more angrily and more openly — so openly, that I am afraid it shows in the book.

In a way, I am not sorry now. A book that takes sides on an important issue — that applauds an 'army of innocents', as it tackles the 'entrenched and cunning' Chinese bureaucracy — may last longer than a pure history book.

Some may find it disturbing that a writer on China should openly take sides. It might help to point out that I am by no means the first to do so. If anyone was the first, it was Marco Polo; for he started a 700-year-long tradition of Westerners going to China, living there for a time, and writing a book. And his book was so partial to China that few Europeans believed him!

Introduction

Since his day, every conceivable type of Westerner has gone to China: from pirates to missionaries, from sinologists to opium-peddlers, from Ambassadors Plenipotentiary to tourists.

And every conceivable type of book has appeared: from the learned and long-term studies of the Jesuits, to pot-boiler novels; from the dry, business-minded reports of British consuls, to books that were such a tissue of lies that even the Chinese texts in them were forged by the authors. It will be clear that if I include *Shanghai Journal* as a minuscule part of this tradition it is no compliment. For the literature has a common failing: it seems to have the greatest difficulty in being objective, especially where China is concerned. Most of it takes sides — sometimes subtly, sometimes outrageously — for or against China.

For most of the seven centuries, the literature has tended to flatter China. So the Jesuits, who wrote in about the middle of the period, sent home mainly positive descriptions of Chinese society. Certainly, that is the way in which their writings were received in Europe. French thinkers, for example, were so impressed by the accounts of China's social practices that they started demanding similar ones for France — a demand which led (indirectly) to the French Revolution.

It was only in the last two centuries — when China showed graphically that she had lost any lead she may have had over Europe — that the tendency to denigrate her became commonplace. Then British and other foreign nationals could write home that China was 'beyond reform', thus justifying intervention by their governments. In this way, much of China's economy fell under foreign control.

Since then, the successful revolution has made it possible to write books in praise of her again. But negative books are as numerous as ever.

How are we to explain this tendency of Westerners to react emotionally to China, to be either greatly impressed or greatly depressed by her? Surely the contrast in civilizations must be the main reason.

For most of the time since the thirteenth century, Chinese civilization has been at its most stable, most peaceful, most homogeneous, and most complacent; also at its least imaginative and least tolerant of change.

Europe during the same period has known nothing but change. The Renaissance saw a quantum leap in growth, a drastic expansion of trade, wealth, technical skills, and power; a new economic system, that lived on growth; a new philosophy, that put humans at the centre; new art; new politics; new science. Europe dreamed some of her strongest dreams in that time.

People travelling from these turbulent societies to China found a civilization that could not have been more opposite. It also presented itself as a real alternative. But, because of its very coherence, it presented itself as an entity, asking to be accepted or rejected as an entity.

Many Westerners have had great difficulty in deciding how much of China to accept, how much to reject. But the choice has to be made. Even today — for China is as different from the West today as she has ever been — the choice can be traumatic.

I am thinking of Edoarda Masi's choice, made in her book *China Winter*. Few Westerners know China as well as she, or can describe it with such haunting beauty and brilliant insight. Her book is a natural sequel to *Shanghai Journal*. She was teaching in Shanghai in 1976, the year when Chang Ch'un-ch'iao's group finally had their power taken away, and were turned into the 'Gang of Four'.

But the two books are natural opposites. She reacts emotionally, as I did, but her 'gut reaction', her instinct, is to grieve for Chang Ch'un-ch'iao and his friends, seeing their fall as a tragic fore-shortening of the Cultural Revolution. She makes her choice about China then, on the last page of her book:

> I could not remain in this country, but it is lacerating to leave it. The country rejects me because it wants to conquer me totally, to be the universal theater of human events, and to expand within me until it excludes everything else. To avoid that, I have to practice violence against myself.

Marco Polo, her fellow Italian from 700 years earlier, would have read that wide-eyed, his lips searching for the word 'paranoia' — which was probably only a medical term in his day, not yet needed by the general public. But he and Masi are not so different: he went to China and blithely accepted everything. She went, and because China did not fulfil her own political dream for it, she rejected everything.

Most of us 'observers' are caught in between. But we are all, at some stage, tempted to be a Marco Polo, or to be an Edoarda Masi.

Once an 'observer of China' has acquired strong views, it is extremely difficult to change them. It probably takes an *emotional* experience to change them. *Reading* about China — whether one reads what China says about herself, or what foreigners say about her — is unlikely to have much effect. Even *going* to China, to live or visit, will not necessarily change those views one iota. In my own case, I have been back three times since the days of *Shanghai Journal*, have learned different things each time, and nothing without effort.

To take the second and third trips first. In 1979, the early days of the Teng Hsiao-p'ing era, I took two China Travel Service 'pot-luck tours' in succession. I call them 'pot-luck' because, though one knows where one is going, one does not have the faintest idea who one's travelling companions will be. That is very democratic, and a sign of a new openness to foreigners on the part of the Chinese government. But it inevitably means that the foreigners spend more time studying each other than the country they are supposed to be touring.

I went to Canton with a group of Italian bankers, who were treating themselves and their wives to a Chinese holiday. Canton was delightful; but what I remember from the trip is the uncanny eloquence of Italian gestures, and the 'fact' that spaghetti was invented in Italy.

Then I spent ten days in Nanning and Kunming. They were delightful, too. I met an ex-Red Guard in Nanning, who said his group had shelled the city with artillery stolen from the PLA. But even he was 'upstaged' by the lanky English journalist in our group, who said he had been condemned to death by Idi Amin and that he had spent what he took to be the last night of his life sleeping on his suit on the stone floor of his cell, so as to look presentable at his execution!

On these second and third visits, I deliberately chose to go to China with the least possible fanfare, to flit in and out as a tourist, and to give places like Shanghai and Peking a wide berth.

This is because of what happened on my first trip back, which was in 1971. On that occasion I was actually *invited*: my whole family were 'honoured guests' or 'friends of China'. (To this day, I have not decided whether we were 'friends of China' or 'friends of the "Gang of Four"'.) We were made so welcome that there were times when the Hunters seemed the sole object of concern for two whole sections of the Chinese government: the Foreign Experts Bureau and the Association for Friendship with Foreign Countries. The 'mood' of the trip is shown by our being invited for two months, but staying three — including eleven precious days in Shanghai.

There is a double irony in this honoured status. One is that *Shanghai Journal* must have been among the reasons for it; yet that book was almost openly hostile to those who took power in Shanghai in 1967, and who still held power there in 1971.

The other irony is that, in order to write *Shanghai Journal* at all, I had been forced to bend, or break, one of the ground rules for foreigners in China during the Cultural Revolution: on leaving the country, they were obliged to submit all written and printed materials for inspection. When we left, however, the sheaf of Red Guard papers and leaflets, which was to form the basis of the book, was not presented for examination. The rest of our belongings were searched with a fine-toothed comb, for at that very time — because of fears that the Cultural Revolution was endangering China's security — the Customs had been placed under military control. I took a risk in this deception, for similar indiscretions by foreigners had landed some of them in Chinese jails for long periods.

Anyway, the 'honoured' Hunters toured the land in 1971. It sounds a perfect way to learn. In fact, the only member of the family who came away clearly knowing more than he did when he went in was my son Tim — then nearly four years old — who emerged speaking far better Chinese than his parents ever managed, complete with the coveted rolled 'r's of the Peking dialect. (He forgot it just as quickly.)

The rest of us, as we traipsed, with our little escort of Chinese, through hundreds of prime examples of the radical political line then in force, could hardly complain about the *quantity* of information. It took half a million words just to jot it down as notes! But the *quality* was indeed debatable. It came across like endless vegetables, served up to one craving meat: nutritious-looking stuff, all of it; but too bland to whet the appetite, let alone swallow.

I found myself almost nostalgic for the early stages of the Cultural Revolution. At least that plastered the walls with two — or even twenty-two — opinions or versions of each event.

The value of the 1971 trip is shown by the fact that the notebooks recording it have lain in a trunk from that day to this. My only reason for disturbing them is that I thought they might help with this new Introduction. I see now — but only in a retrospect of sixteen years — that I did learn something on that trip after all. Two things, two lessons, both in Shanghai. Trust the big city to provide any surprises!

One lesson was learned at the Foreign Languages Institute, which we revisited.

The other was learned during a criticism of *Shanghai Journal*, 'performed' — I use that word because it felt like surgery without anaesthetic — by a colleague of Chang Ch'un-ch'iao, a man who was as proud then to style himself 'spokesman for the Chairman of the Shanghai Revolutionary Committee', as he would have been appalled later to find himself 'lackey of the "Gang of Four"'.

I include these experiences here. They may seem unrelated, but they are not; for each, in a different way, continues the story of *Shanghai Journal*. Each also makes me angry — or renews an anger.

The Shanghai Foreign Languages Institute

The 'revolutionary committee' that received us at the Institute was also the main achievement of the Cultural Revolution: it embodied the new way in which power was to be *shared*. In theory, these committees were 70 per cent 'masses', 20 per cent cadres, and 10 per cent army or workers. That should have made them sprightly. Ours moved more like an elephant!

It consisted of all the old Party committee members who had survived criticism; plus representatives of the Red Guard groups that had survived; plus a 'Workers' "Mao Tse-tung Thought" Propaganda Team', sent in to stem factionalism; plus a 'PLA "Mao Tse-tung Thought" Propaganda Team', sent in to continue what the workers had left unfinished.

In theory, political peace now reigned. Only one Party member in the whole place had still not passed the test, was still classified as a 'capitalist-roader', and was 'doing manual labour under the supervision of the masses'. (Our friends told us he was making concrete bricks.) I was amazed when I heard his name; for this was the very man who had been suddenly hoisted to the top of the Institute's power structure just before we left Shanghai. (See *Shanghai Journal*, pp. 287–8.) He and the former Party Secretary had been opposite poles in a Chinese power-play for years, with now one, now the other, prevailing. I would wager that the period of Teng Hsiao-p'ing has restored him yet again to his 'rightful' position — if the years of concrete-making have left much of him.

While we were at the Institute, we asked to visit some of our Chinese friends in their homes. The request was granted; but the visits were disappointing. Our friends were still reserved, even when alone with us. I imagine that we put extra pressure on them, singling them out in this way.

In one case, the problem was logistical. The friend lived in the oldest, pre-European part of Shanghai. The appearance of a chauffeur-driven car, bearing foreigners through this maze of ancient lanes, caused 10,000 children to congregate and follow, creating a human traffic jam that deserves to be there still.

We learned that all of our former students had graduated and been assigned jobs — but only after a year spent working in the countryside. Many were middle-school teachers. Between them, they were spread all over China; however, from their letters and occasional trips home, the teachers at the Institute kept an accurate, but friendly, record of them all.

Introduction

I was keen to know whether there had been any discrimination in the assignment of jobs. My students had been notoriously conservative during the movement, while my wife's students had been leaders of the most radical wing. When I heard that my favourite student was in Sinkiang — a classic place of exile — I assumed that he had been sent there as punishment. Then I found that my wife's most red-ragging student was in Yunnan — not much closer to Shanghai. Perhaps they were both in exile. My wife's students had turned on Chang Ch'un-ch'iao at a critical point in the seizure of power in Shanghai. (See the next section, criticism of *Shanghai Journal*.)

The amazing thing about the Institute was that *everyone* had survived. The worst physical dislocation that they had had to endure was to spend one year at a cadre school. Teachers and Party members alike had to go there. The place seems to have combined the peasant's labour and life-style with prescribed doses of the 'correct ideology'.

Our Institute had its own cadre school, in a remote part of Anhui Province — so remote that the most frightening thing, for several of our friends, was 'to hear wolves howling at night'.

I mention this for those who imagine China is a carbon copy of the Soviet Union *at its worst*, that the Chinese liquidate each other physically as freely as the Russians have *at their worst*, and that China abounds, not just in real wolves to frighten people, but in the human wolves that populate the novels of Solzhenitsyn. Chinese conformity-making is tedious, humiliating, and disgracefully time-wasting. But rarely lethal.

My Institute, however, taken as a typical example of how Chinese society was organized in that year of 1971, had some truly alarming features.

For one thing, it was inexcusably *top-heavy*: a committee of several dozen, running a staff of several hundred, produced a student body totalling 32! I know, because I met them all personally — the 20 who were taking English and the 12 who were taking German. These new students, we were told, represented significant progress. They were from the working class, not from the bourgeoisie. Like so much in China that year, they were an improvement only *in theory*; *in practice*, they were clearly out of their depth in language study, and there was a tenseness to them, as if too much responsibility had been placed on their proletarian shoulders.

Another depressing aspect of the Institute was that there was no noticeable life, or liveliness, in it. After five years of 'struggle' — which was really the imposition of one political line on another — everyone had come through, but had come through *chastened*. To be sure, the place was politically 'pure' — it was run by China's 'leftists' on more or less 'leftist' lines. But the people there were not happy. There was no trace of the kind of atmosphere that would encourage creative thinking.

My Institute also looked like a disaster in terms of the Chinese economy.

Economies develop a logic, almost a mind of their own. Shanghai — even within the Chinese economy — has needs of her own. If they are met, she produces fantastic wealth. The city sits, after all, as San Francisco sits, at the mouth of one of the world's rich river systems. Even before the Second World War, Shanghai was ranked sixth of all ports in the world.

My Institute's product that year of 32 students — even with the 'correct' ideology — can hardly have delighted this economic Shanghai. They were not just an insult to an economy. They would bring any economy to its knees.

The ultimate aim of the Cultural Revolution was economic. The reason for asking the Chinese people to go through a second liberation — this time of the mind and spirit — was to recharge, even supercharge the economy into a second, hopefully perpetual, Great Leap Forward.

In this, it failed.

Criticism of Shanghai Journal *by a Member of*
Chang Ch'un-ch'iao's Staff

It was originally *my* idea to hear what the Chinese thought of *Shanghai Journal*; but I hardly expected this suggestion to result in a formal criticism session, that started one day in mid-afternoon, and continued after a break for the evening meal.

Introduction

Six hours of criticism for one book!

The encounter was held in Shanghai Mansions (pictured in *Shanghai Journal*, facing p. 91). The fact that I had once lived there did not make me sit more comfortably in my chair.

I could not describe this session, so I will have to quote from what my critic said. He spent much time surveying the course of the Cultural Revolution in Shanghai. I shall spare the reader this, for his account and *Shanghai Journal*'s — though differing diametrically in interpretation — largely agreed as to what were the main events, their chronology, and the people involved.

In the extract which follows — less than one-sixth of the original — I have focused on what he said about the *book itself*. I half wish it had been possible to separate this from what he said about *me*!

I admire three things about your *Shanghai Journal*:
— the courageous way you've set your own experience against the distorted picture of the Cultural Revolution presented by the Western press;
— the diligence of your study of events in China;
— the spirit which prompted you to say you may have made mistakes in the book, and would like it discussed.

The fact is, you were only here a short time, and you didn't really see very much. It's easy to get a false perspective.

To my mind, the main thing wrong with your book is that you haven't interpreted the Cultural Revolution as a fight between classes. That's the only way to see it — as a continuation of the struggle between the proletariat and the bourgeoisie, each trying to transform China according to its own world outlook. Your failure to see in these terms caused you to miss the simplest of points sometimes — despite the vast amount of stuff you read.

It also made your attempt to correct the bourgeois picture ineffective.

I'm sorry to be frank. I'm telling you this, as a friend, so you'll be more effective next time.

I know some of the main documents were not published until after you'd left. But look at the way you've used the materials you *had*: you went to all kinds of meetings, and you collected all sorts of Red Guard publications, but you paid them more attention than major documents, issued at critical points in the movement, by the Central

Committee itself, documents that were approved by Chairman Mao, that were *his own* instructions!

Your lack of class perspective also explains why the book is too soft on the overthrown Party leaders, Ts'ao Ti-ch'iu and Ch'en P'ei-hsien [see *Shanghai Journal, passim*]. Obviously, you did not hate them enough. We should hate class enemies. Lu Hsun knew that.

On the other hand, you were too hard on Chang Ch'un-ch'iao. You did not give him the credit he deserves.

These people are not just individuals. They represent different classes and different lines.

We feel Chang Ch'un-ch'iao and Yao Wen-yuan carried out Chairman Mao's revolutionary line, while Ts'ao Ti-ch'iu and Ch'en P'ei-hsien carried out Liu Shao-ch'i's revisionist line.

I think that what stopped you grasping the essence of the movement, and also distorted your view of specific events, was the influence of your wife's students. [Here he mentioned two by name.] They were leaders of the Field Army at your Institute, but they also belonged to the Shanghai-wide Red Guard group: the Red Revolutionaries. Your book badly misinterprets the part played by this group.

For one thing, you exaggerate their role in the early stages. You concentrate on a single incident — such as their occupation of the *Liberation Daily* — and you blow it out of all proportion. [See *Shanghai Journal*, Chapter 8.]

For another, you completely understate the serious situation the group caused, when it turned against Chang Ch'un-ch'iao in January 1967. [*Shanghai Journal*, Chapter 11.] Just as the revolutionary masses were on the point of taking power from the capitalist-roaders — when unity was of paramount importance — this group went and acted on its own behalf! On January 23, its members seized the Seals of Office from the old Municipal Party Committee, and from the ten Shanghai district committees as well. This was ludicrous! They imagined that was all there was to it: taking power was getting twenty seals in a bag!

Some of the leaders of the group then rang up some members of the Workers Headquarters. Another of your Institute people was in on this [name given].

'We've taken power!' they said.

It was an attempt to apply pressure.

There were three groups leading the movement at that time. One was the Workers Headquarters. One was my group: the Shanghai Administration Liaison Station, led by Hsü Ching-hsien (he's now a

Introduction

Vice-Chairman of the Revolutionary Committee). And one was the Peasants Headquarters. All these groups said the action of the Red Revolutionaries was against Chairman Mao's instructions. Chang Ch'un-ch'iao criticized them too. He said this was no time for unilateral action. They should maintain a Grand Alliance, and get ready for the formation of the Shanghai Commune.

They ignored this advice. Instead, they took further action, which only made things worse: they detained Hsü Ching-hsien at Futan University.

They also started to attack Chang Ch'un-ch'iao by name.

They coined two slogans:

— one was: 'Chang Ch'un-ch'iao is not synonymous with the Central Committee Cultural Revolution Group!'
— the other was: 'Chang Ch'un-ch'iao is a peach-picker!'

When I read the bit in your book about Chang Ch'un-ch'iao waiting for the fruits of victory to fall into his lap, I suspected they were not your words, but those of the Red Revolutionaries. For 'peach-picker' in Chinese means precisely one who waits till the fruit of victory is ripe, then snatches it for himself.

There is only one place in your book where — almost despite yourself — you do manage to see through the Red Revolutionaries. You suggest that their turning on Chang Ch'un-ch'iao must be connected with the attack made by Rebel leader K'uai Ta-fu on K'ang Sheng and Hsieh Fu-chih in Peking. [*Shanghai Journal*, pp. 230–1.]

That's a marvellous insight! In fact, the ones who were pulling the strings — this has been clear for a long time now — were Wang Li, Kuan Feng, and Ch'i Pen-yü. *They* were Liu Shao-ch'i's successors. The nation-wide Second Headquarters — which included Shanghai's Red Revolutionaries — was controlled by them. At the time, they still *seemed* revolutionaries, so some Red Revolutionary leaders were deceived by them, and followed their ultra-left line of creating chaos...

Round the time the Shanghai Commune was set up, there were several other problem groups. There were whole sections of the Workers Headquarters — the Second Regiment, for example — which carried out independent activities. But in the end they all came over to the side of the Workers Headquarters.

The Commune eventually changed its name to 'Revolutionary Committee'. 'Commune' was seen to be a clumsy and misleading term. One of the first tasks of the new Committee was to purify the class ranks. This was found necessary, because class enemies were impeding progress. Class enemies are not normally imprisoned, but handed over to the people for remoulding. The only people imprisoned here were some 'arch-villains', guilty of causing serious social disorder.

At this point, dinner was served in an adjoining room. Though we were scarcely half a dozen, a banquet was considered obligatory. One wonders, at the best of times, how this custom of the old élite has survived into New China. That night, the sumptuous food contrasted boldly with the unspiced puritan politics being expressed.

I'm glad I've had this chance to go through your book with you. My advice remains the same: if you looked at things from a class point of view, you'd be able to tell the wood from the tress, to distinguish the essential from the superficial. I don't expect you to write like a Party cadre. But some of your language — 'Mao Tse-tung's disciple', the 'Red Guard Bible', and so on — is surely inappropriate. It distorts important things.

I don't expect you to evaluate the Cultural Revolution as a good Marxist-Leninist would, either. Marxists believe, though, that the *motive* of a person's actions cannot be divorced from the *effect* of those actions. The two should be the same. In your case, the *motive* of the book — to present a more accurate picture of China — may not have been the same as the book's *effect*.

I can see what you *meant* to do. I can also see you are friendly to China and the Chinese people.

On Sunday, I met the American Youth Delegation, and William Hinton's mother. Some of the people there had read your book. They had a range of views.

Some said it did try and correct the bourgeois picture of China, even to defend the Cultural Revolution.

Others said it had good points and bad.

Still others said it had no good points whatever.

I feel, as a friend, I should try and evaluate the book properly, not simply negate it.

Of course, if old Wang here [gesturing at my interpreter, who blushed crimson] had written it, I'd have come down on it very hard indeed.

But the situation's different. You live in another country...

Introduction

This 'critique' — as a statement of the mentality of Chang Ch'un-ch'iao and his group — revives all the scorn I felt for them, when I watched them 'at work' in the Cultural Revolution. Their attitude — not just to literary criticism or politics, but to the whole spectrum of human behaviour — is far too negative and filled with hate. It is certainly the last mentality China needs at this stage of her revolution.

It is dangerously anachronistic.

In one way, it is half a century out of date. It would have been an appropriate attitude in the years *before* 1949, when there *was* a time for hate in China. I would not deny any oppressed people — French, American, Russian, or Chinese — the right to hate, as well as the right to resort to revolution.

In other ways, it is half a millenium out of date. For the kind of hate that my critic represents — the kind that has continued and become worse in China *since* 1949 — is so reminiscent of traditional Chinese patterns of hate that it suggests the old society is alive and well, and weaving its spell on the new.

Old China certainly had its share of hate. It had the normal load, built in to most societies by structural injustice: women 'inferior' to men; peasants open to landlord rapacity; all classes subject to the whim of the élite. But it also had types of hate that expressed themselves in peculiarly Chinese ways.

One was the peasant rebellion. The Chinese have had a record number of these. They always proceeded in alternating and worsening 'rounds' of revolt and reprisal. The final 'pacification' — as the Emperor called it — could leave tens of millions dead, and provinces barren for decades.

The other Chinese speciality was feuding. The most destructive kind was not that between peasant clans, but that between rival groups of high officials, competing for the ear of the Emperor. These feuds also went in 'rounds': two groups would succeed each other in power, the winners each time punishing — often exiling — the losers. This high-level feuding always weakened China. At the end of the Manchu dynasty, China's best generals and politicians, when needed to meet some foreign threat, were often in exile. It continued well into the twentieth century, the war-lord rivalries being merely another expression of it. Such a healthy tradition is likely to have survived, in some form, to the present. The logical place to look for it is in the new élite: the Communists themselves.

Seen in this light, the 'two-line struggle' — which has been waged in the Communist Party itself since the 1920s — is particularly suspect. Of course, it is a real political fight, between incompatible lines. But the tendency for it to proceed in 'rounds' — the winners each time proscribing or punishing a 'hit list' of the losers (thereby increasing their determination to win the next round) — smacks of the feud. The increasing bitterness of it also smacks of the feud.

It would be tragic if the Cultural Revolution were — even *partly* — one gigantic episode in such a feud. But that would explain a paradox about it: its *leaders* claimed to be breaking new ground, world-wide, in Marxist theory; but they were not dismayed when the *led* responded by parading victims in dunce caps, moronically chanting slogans, saluting at frenetic rallies 'the Red, Red Sun in our Hearts' — reliving, in other words, Chinese history at its most ancient and primitive.

When my critic in Shanghai could refer to his 'work' — in that modern metropolis — as hunting class enemies, this is also a reversion to the primitive. We are out of the realm of constructive politics, and back into demonology and the ducking-stool.

The worst future I could wish on China would be a continuation of this cycle of hate — even if it went on one more 'round', with a revitalized 'left', getting up and trying to unseat Teng. If that happened, I think it would mean the beginning of the end of communist ideology in its present form. The Chinese would ultimately see that the cause and focus of most of the country's negativity and hate was the Party itself. They would surely insist then that the leadership provide the positive ideology China needs today. Or they would look elsewhere for it.

In fact, the cycle of hate is not a political problem, but a *moral* one. The Communists have set up an ethical imbalance. They have over-developed and over-used the negative side of the theory (hate) without any corresponding growth of the positive side (love). They have not allowed any theory of love to exist.

Introduction

There are ironies here.

One is that the Chinese people — politics aside — treat each other much more gently than they did in the old society. It could even be said that, in their normal workaday lives, they express more love for their fellows than they did.

The other irony is that the Communists made this possible. They changed the old society from one where love was rare to one where it is at least possible. Yet these same Communists go round talking of hate, or of any subject under the sun except love.

Marxists are supposed to think in opposites. The Chinese Communists will talk *ad nauseam* about the proletariat and the bourgeoisie, progressive and reactionary forces. They believe in natural opposites like sweet and sour, even (secretly) in old ones like *yin* and *yang*. But you will never hear love and hate mentioned as a dialectical pair. Only hate. It is as though the very word 'love' were a taboo, or an embarrassment.

Yet, in 1919, when the Communist Party was being formed, the subject of love was high on the agenda of left-wing Chinese thinkers, openly discussed in the press, and an expected feature of any future society. Lu Hsun — recommended to me by my critic in Shanghai as a model of class hate, wrote in that year:

> the evil results of loveless marriages continue uninterrupted...
>
> But now the east is light...some light must shine through the fingers of the devil: he cannot shut it all out. The son of man is awake. He knows there should be love among mankind...
>
> We shall cry of the bitterness of life without love...
>
> (*Selected Works* [Peking, Foreign Languages Press, 1980], Vol. 2, pp. 36–8.)

The question of love has remained 'on the shelf' since then. One reason is that, starting in the 1920s, a whole generation of Chinese was picked up and swept along by the sheer pace of history — through Civil War, the War against Japan, the Second World War, the War for Liberation. And after Liberation the pace did not slacken, in some ways it accelerated.

Even during the most turbulent of these times, the ordinary

Chinese somehow found time to marry, raise children, and live at least vaguely normal lives.

The Communists did not. They married — everyone in China does — but they had no time to devote to their families, to be family people. There was always one more urgent task for the Party. These were heroes, who literally sacrificed their personal lives for the Chinese revolution. But this has made them the last people in China who can understand personal needs — including the need to love. They are very good at organizing, mobilizing, spotting class enemies. But they cannot handle even the *concept* of love.

Meanwhile, China's needs are changing. Every succeeding generation will be less like its revolutionary forebears, will expect more and more to lead a normal life, a life including love.

Even my students' generation showed a real reluctance to follow the Party into a new round of hate. Their children might refuse.

With their leaders at present providing no positive ethic, the Chinese might have to 'shop around', to get new ideas where they can. Since they are shopping in the West these days, they might be tempted to import from the West a concept, already packaged and gift-wrapped, and labelled 'love'. But it might be the opposite of what they need. It might include pornography, or the soap operas that choke our television sets, or the Grim Reaper of divorce.

Some 'self-reliance' might be wiser. They could develop a theory of 'class love', for instance, without even leaving their Marxist tradition.

The best future I could wish for China would be that she should have the word 'love' somewhere on her banner, as she heads into the next century — even if it's only in fine print, even if it's only a typically mean, typically myopic, Marxist moral concept, like 'class love'. 'Class love' would be infinitely more productive than the 'class hate' preached and practised by my critic in Shanghai.

Who knows? China may even run out of class enemies one of these days.

Her chances are better than ours.

NEALE HUNTER
1988

Glossary of Personal and Place Names

Wade-Giles	*Pinyin*
Canton	Guangzhou
Chang Ch'un-ch'iao	Zhang Chunqiao
Ch'en P'ei-hsien	Chen Peixian
Ch'i Pen-yü	Qi Benyu
Chiang Ch'ing	Jiang Qing
Futan (University)	Fudan
Hsieh Fu-chih	Xie Fuzhi
Hsü Ching-hsien	Xu Jingxian
K'ang Sheng	Kang Sheng
K'uai Ta-fu	Kuai Dafu
Kuan Feng	Guan Feng
Liu Shao-ch'i	Liu Shaoqi
Lu Hsun	Lu Xun
Mao Tse-tung	Mao Zedong
Peking	Beijing
Sinkiang	Xinjiang
Teng Hsiao-p'ing	Deng Xiaoping
Ts'ao Ti-ch'iu	Cao Diqiu
Wang Hung-wen	Wang Hongwen
Yao Wen-yuen	Yao Wenyuan

CONTENTS

Classes struggle; some classes triumph; others are eliminated. Such is history, such is the history of civilization for thousands of years.—MAO TSE-TUNG

Class struggle should not be overpopularized, for it can be destructive. It can get to the stage where you only have to mention class struggle and *everything* becomes class struggle. . . . The theories of class and class struggle are part of the science of Marxism. They must be applied with a strict sense of proportion. Used inappropriately, they will only lead us into error.
>   —CH'EN P'EI-HSIEN, *First Secretary,*
>   *East China Bureau, Chinese*
>   *Communist Party*

> Sticks whack tigers,
> Tigers eat chickens,
> Chickens eat insects,
> Insects eat sticks. . . .
>   —TU CH'IEN, *member, Shanghai*
>   *Municipal Party Committee*

Introduction

Whichever way you look at it, China's Cultural Revolution is one of the most momentous, most complex, and most intriguing developments in modern history.

It could be argued, of course, that almost anything China does is significant, for a quarter of the world's people live within its borders. In this sense, the Cultural Revolution certainly demands our attention, since it has had a profound effect not only on all the urban centers and most of the rural areas of China but also on the government itself and on the concepts of authority on which that government is based. The China that emerges from the Cultural Revolution will be a very different country from the one that plunged into it in 1966.

Nor will the world as a whole ever be quite the same. The governments of Hong Kong, Macao, Burma, Cambodia, Japan, Britain, France, and a dozen other countries have already learned at first hand the meaning of the phrase "armed with the thought of Mao Tse-tung." The Soviet Union has responded to the withering hail of Red Guard invective by launching a nationwide counterpropaganda campaign. Students in France, Germany, and the United States have to some extent been inspired by their Chinese counterparts, whose cry of "Rebellion Is Justified!" has added a dimension to what seems almost a global revolt against the establishment. Guerrilla movements in Asia, Africa, and the Americas see the Cultural Revolution as a proof of China's determination to preserve its revolutionary *élan* and to root out any capitalistic or bureaucratic tendencies. The superpowers, in particular, have watched the Chinese upheaval with considerable fascination—and more than a little apprehension—taking infinite pains to gather information about it. They have done this because they know that the way the world will look in the year 2000 will depend more than they would care to admit on the changes that have recently taken place in China.

With this in mind, it is a sobering experience to sample public opinion on the Cultural Revolution. One soon finds that no two people can agree on what it is about. "It was just another purge," one man says. "On the contrary," says another, "it was a great leap forward of the human consciousness!" "You're both wrong," says a third, "it was a struggle for succession." "No," says a fourth, "it was the triumph of a socialist culture." A fifth says, "It was civil war!" Then there are those who dismiss it as "mad Mao again" or "the irrational Chinese."

Some of the blame for this appalling confusion must be placed on the Chinese themselves. It so happened that the movement began in literary and artistic circles, though the men who started it—the disciples of Mao Tse-tung—had far bigger victories in mind. Their initial intention was to nag away at certain writers until the Party authorities responsible for tolerating the "seeds of revisionism" were forced into vulnerable positions. Their ultimate aim was nothing short of the complete overthrow of a powerful segment of the Communist Party itself and the recapture of control for Chairman Mao and his supporters.

In its narrowest sense, this was a struggle for power. More broadly, it was a fight to the death between conflicting visions of China's future. It was never purely "cultural," though, largely for tactical reasons, it grew out of a squabble over literature. The Maoists had to be careful in the early stages; they were not in a position to stand up and openly denounce the men they believed were leading China to perdition. They therefore began by probing the enemy's weakness in the artistic field. This roundabout but typically Chinese approach deceived not only their opponents but almost every foreign observer as well.

As a result, millions of people in the West think of the Cultural Revolution as primarily a movement to reform China's art and literature, a movement that then belied its name by becoming an all-out battle for political power. Former U.S. Under Secretary of State Nicholas Katzenbach summed up this attitude in a speech to the National Press Club on May 21, 1968, when he referred to "Mao Tse-tung's curiously misnamed 'Cultural Revolution.' "

This misunderstanding could have been avoided. Much of it stems from an inadequate translation of the Chinese term *wen-hua ke-ming*. *Wen-hua* means culture, certainly, and *ke-ming* means revolution. But the two words together do not mean Cultural Revolution. The full Chinese title for the movement is *wu-ch'an chieh-chi wen-hua ta ko-ming*, which could best be rendered as "a full-scale revolution to establish a working-class culture." This is a far cry from the usual "Great Proletarian Cultural Revolution," which is not only clumsy but meaningless.

The mistake was first made by Chinese translators, but Western scholars and journalists immediately repeated it, thus blurring their vision of the movement. Because they could not understand the events that followed, they tried to compensate by reporting sensational tidbits of violence, factionalism, and disruption, but they rarely made any attempt to see the Red Guards as part of a historical process.

Then, gradually, some began to go beyond the newsworthy aspects of the movement—the slashing of tight trouser cuffs, the destruction of old art works, the clashes between student groups —and belatedly discovered the political origins of the Cultural Revolution—its links with the partial failure of the Great Leap Forward, the feud between professionals and amateurs in the Chinese army, the Sino-Soviet split, and so on.

By this time, the damage had been done. The image of the Cultural Revolution in the eyes of the average newspaper-reader in the West was that of a chaotic and criminal mass movement, stirred up by Mao in a fit of cynical ambition, involving the manipulation of hundreds of thousands of young people, and causing untold suffering to the Chinese population as a whole.

This is a false picture. Not only is it factually untrue; its perspective is wrong, since it fails to view the Cultural Revolution against the background of Chinese history. It would be absurd to pass judgment on the black movement in the United States without taking into consideration the centuries when black people were slaves in a white society. In exactly the same way, the Cultural Revolution can be understood only when seen as a continuation of China's century-long struggle to absorb and survive the impact of Western culture. The Red Guards are but the latest installment in the explosive interaction of two proud, distinct, and coherent civilizations. The student wall posters that fulminated against "revisionist" and "bourgeois" tendencies in the Communist Party are direct descendants of earlier writings in which the Chinese sought desperately to evade the Christian-capitalist formula proposed by Europe, to find instead a solution that would allow China to digest the technology of the West while retaining its own cultural character. The final choice of Communism was not made lightly. It was essentially a commitment to the millions of impoverished peasants and a rejection of any system that would perpetuate their poverty by concentrating power and wealth in the hands of an elite. The Cultural Revolution has repeated this commitment; whatever political jiggery-pokery went on behind the scenes, it cannot be denied that the students rose up against a privileged class within the Communist Party itself, an almost tyrannical bureaucracy that had managed to gain control of the machinery of government.

The failure of the China-watchers and Sinologists to convey an intelligible explanation of the movement to their people is understandable. At bottom, it is a prolongation—dangerously anachronistic in this day and age—of nineteenth-century Western attitudes to China. The missionaries, who saw the Chinese as heathen, the businessmen, with their vision of hundreds of millions of "customers," the generals and diplomats, with their purely military or strategic assessments of China, all made the same mistake. They looked at China from the outside, instead of endeavoring to see with Chinese eyes.

The saddest part is that the Cultural Revolution offered a perfect chance to get the feel of China. It was one of the rare occasions when a whole culture drops its mask, when thousands of people come out and speak their minds. Red Guard wall posters and newspapers revealed more about China and the Chinese in that first year of debate than all the *lettres édifiantes* of the Jesuits, pompous scholarship of the old Sinologists, or jargoned doctoral theses of our day. It was a unique opportunity to listen and learn.

In the pages that follow, I have tried to let China speak. In particular, I have tried to present the authentic voice of one Chinese city—Shanghai—during the period from November, 1965, when the first murmur of an impending upheaval was heard, through Christmas, 1966, when the struggle reached its peak, to April, 1967, when I left the country.

The choice of Shanghai was dictated by circumstances. My wife and I were teaching English at the Foreign Languages Institute there when the movement began, and, apart from a 6-week traveling holiday in July and August, 1966, we remained in the city throughout. All formal classes were canceled at the Institute for the duration of the Cultural Revolution, which therefore rendered the foreign teachers virtually unemployed. The Chinese insisted on honoring their contracts, however, so that no pressure was put on us to leave nor were our salaries stopped. This left me free to wander the streets on foot or on a bicycle, by car or public transport, stopping to read the ubiquitous wall posters or jump for the leaflets that fluttered down on peak-hour crowds. My wife's students and mine visited us frequently, and we were often invited to meetings at the Institute. In this way, I was able to keep up with events as they occurred and to feel that I was participating in the drama being enacted in Shanghai.

The key to understanding this most populous and productive of China's cities is to remember that, for the Chinese, it remains the very type and symbol of imperialism. It was from Shanghai that foreign power expanded inland. From here, the missionaries and traders penetrated up the rivers. From here, opium spread. Here the first factories were built and a class of Chinese sprang up who knew that industry meant power. Here, too, the first meeting of the Communist Party took place—twelve men hiding in a girls' school in 1921.

The full-scale Japanese attack in 1937 was the last in a series of incursions by foreign powers, and it was the one that broke the camel's back. When the Japanese were finally driven out in

1945, the hope of sending the others packing with them was too strong to resist. The Communists, who had won extensive popular support during World War II, defeated the forces of Chiang K'ai-shek in a bitter civil war, and, in 1949, took control of the country. The army of Ch'en Yi, now Foreign Minister, entered Shanghai after 3 days of fighting in the western suburbs. In the countryside, one can still see the concentric rings of pillboxes built by Chiang K'ai-shek. Most of them look unscarred, as if the defenders were only too glad to abandon them. The peasants, who are used to plowing around the garbage of history, grow lush crops of rice and vegetables that almost submerge the irrelevant tumuli.

The rebirth of Shanghai after 1949 was something of a miracle. The city had known degradation comparable to that of modern Calcutta, with intolerable extremes of wealth and poverty, rampant disease, honeycombs of opium dens and brothels, sinister alliances between big business and gangsters. This mess was cleaned up by a mixture of ruthlessness and tact. Prostitutes and dope fiends were shipped out to work on farms. People who had worked for foreign firms or been heavily influenced by the capitalist ethic were subjected to more gradual pressure from colleagues and neighbors, who tried to persuade them to throw in their lot with socialism. Capitalists who had fled abroad were invited back, their factories and houses were returned to them, and they were paid interest on all their investments. This was enlightened government, and the city responded quickly. Its economy was soon prospering, and a spirit of optimism replaced the despair of the past.

From the Marxist point of view, it should have been the easiest part of China to socialize. Here the contradictions between capital and labor had reached their most acute stage, with blatant exploitation the order of the day. Yet it proved the most difficult of cities to reform and one of the most persistent sources of political reaction. This was due to the existence of a large middle class, a product of foreign imperialism. There were thousands of people in Shanghai who were congenitally obsessed with the business of making money and amassing possessions. These preoccupations, normal in Western societies, were anathema to the

Communists, who saw in them a threat to the even development of the whole population. The Party therefore took on the unenviable job of persuading a city the size of Paris to live by the principles of altruism and frugality.

For a time, while the contagious excitement of the Revolution lasted, considerable progress was made. It was not class struggle in the usual Marxist sense, for there were few property-owners, employers, or big investors to attack. It was more a fight against selfishness, personal ambition, and greed, which is far more difficult to win than a war on capitalism. The Party soon found itself wrestling with shadows rather than tangible enemies, trying to change stubborn features of human nature rather than simply to "liquidate" an exploitative class.

Nor was the Party very well equipped for the task, since many of its own members had bourgeois backgrounds. Immediately after 1949, Shanghai needed every administrator and organizer it could get, and the Party bothered little with the screening of applicants. Some of the most capable men in the city had been educated in mission schools or had worked with foreigners or traveled abroad. Many joined the Party and even rose to positions of power. The Cultural Revolution was a massive reaction against this type of person and an attempt to eradicate the "poison of revisionism" that they were said to have injected into the society.

When I arrived in Shanghai in April, 1965, I noticed nothing of this supposed decline in spiritual and ideological standards. I found the city refreshingly unsophisticated, more like a big country town than a great metropolis. I visited factories and communes, hospitals and temples, universities and shipyards. Everywhere I went I was impressed with the simplicity of the people—their obvious pride in Shanghai's achievements, their naive confidence in the future, the easy affection that characterized relations between friends and workmates. It was almost a two-dimensional society—too good to be true, perhaps, but good nonetheless. Its problems seemed problems of growth, which would be solved in time. History, said the feeling in the air, was on Shanghai's side.

When the Cultural Revolution began, therefore, I was skeptical. All the talk of dark plots and class enemies seemed exaggerated, and my first fear was that Mao's men, in their zeal, might undo 16 years of patient work and considerable success. As the movement unfolded, and as more and more facts about post-1949 Shanghai were revealed, I had to admit that my first impressions of the city had been superficial. Its people were not as united or enthusiastic as I had imagined. There were deep undercurrents of discontent, wide rifts between factions of the Party, bitter personal feuds in the administration, and many doubts about the program for the future.

I also realized that the Mao group's aims were as much moral as political. They were determined not only to oust the revisionists from the Party but also to galvanize Chinese society from top to bottom. In this sense, they were waging not class struggle but a veritable "moral war"—a war against the policies of compromise as well as against the men who had carried them out. This became clearer as the tactics of the movement took shape. Even before the Red Guards appeared, the Central Committee stated categorically that violence would not be tolerated. "Fight nonviolently" was the watchword, and there was hardly a student in China who did not know the adage "You can change a person's skin by hitting him, but you can't change his soul that way."

This unconditional rejection of violence as a way of waging the Cultural Revolution was practically ignored in Western press reports, while the occurrence of violence received special attention. As a result, it seemed that China had been overwhelmed by a "red terror," with slaughter and destruction rampant throughout the country. In contradicting this impression, I am not denying that there was violence. There were frequent outbreaks of fighting from the very beginning of the Cultural Revolution, and they tended to increase in scope and intensity as the months went by. But they occurred in particular places at particular times and were always accompanied by reams of outraged protest from the groups concerned. They were never accepted as legitimate means of combat but were always deplored as sinister attempts to resolve complex problems at one stroke. They were not the remarkable part of the movement, and the journalists who over-emphasized their importance revealed more of their own morbid interest in violence than of the true situation in China. The truly astonishing thing about the Cultural Revolution was that it was conceived and executed as essentially a *non*violent, almost Gandhian strategy for social reform.

In Shanghai, the casualties were minimal. The Red Guards themselves, who probably deserve a prize as the world's most outrageous exaggerators, complained of no more than a dozen deaths through violence—and only two of these were admitted by all factions. Had there been more, they would have been mentioned, for the rival groups were eager to discredit each other on the slightest pretext.

Nor was Shanghai as spectacular as the Red Guard posters suggested. Most of the fighting took place inside colleges and factories, leaving the city a mask of "business as usual." There was an early spate of name-changing, and many streets and shops were "revolutionized." The houses of the "bourgeoisie" were also entered and searched during this initial period. Later, however, there was a visible lull. The best gauge as to the progress of the movement was the fluctuating tempo of the wall posters, the processions of Red Guard groups, and the presence of the little three-wheeled vans that roamed the city, broadcasting Red Guard opinions.

It depended partly on where you lived. I knew an old German woman—admittedly not quite right in the head—whose house was next to People's Square in the heart of the downtown area. She saw so many flag-waving, drum-beating columns of demonstrators pass her window that she exclaimed: "Ah, in China it is always like this. Always war. I remember when the Japanese were here . . ."

But it was not war and rarely even looked like it. I spent months in the streets without ever seeing what Americans would call a riot. I watched plenty of heated quarrels, which sometimes ended with individuals punching each other, and I witnessed people being subjected to public humiliation and forced to wear dunce caps. But I never in all that time saw a pitched battle.

The clashes featured in so much Red Guard literature were often rather petty in themselves. Casualty lists mentioned not only the noses bloodied and the eyes blackened but also the glasses broken and the clothing torn. Far more interesting than the actual violence was the tremendous indignation it inevitably aroused. Here the Red Guards were in their element. They were much better writers than pugilists, and they took more pleasure in verbally demolishing an opponent than in cracking his skull with an ax handle.

This is where the wall posters came into their own. These angry and amateurish tirades so set the tone of the movement that the Chinese word ta-tzu pao (literally "big-character newspaper") became a commonplace in European languages. This gives some indication of the extent to which the Cultural Revolution was a paper war, waged and decided on the walls of China's cities.

Wall posters varied enormously in length, content, and importance. Most of them made no claim to objectivity but set out explicitly to praise friends and condemn enemies. Anyone could write one, and most people seem to have tried their hand. They began with a quote from the writings of Mao, went on to set the time and place of an incident, and then launched into an utterly black or utterly white interpretation of the facts. They were not meant to be so one-sided, and Mao probably had something else in mind when he called them "a new and most effective weapon." But weapon they certainly were, and no one pretended to look for the whole truth in them. One overwritten piece would be followed by an equally overwritten reply, and the truth was supposed to emerge from this "dialectic" of opposites.

My account of the Cultural Revolution is based as much on Red Guard writings as anything else, and the question of reliability naturally arises. Paradoxically, the exaggeration of the wall posters often helped more than it hindered. By setting two opposite accounts side by side, it was possible to draw a line down the middle and arrive at a kind of truth. "Objective" reporting by both sides might only have confused the issue. The story that follows is the result of this method, checked wherever possible by reference to my personal experience in Shanghai during this time. It is, I hope, a coherent story, woven from wall posters and leaflets, articles from Red Guard newspapers and the official press, student meetings and rallies, discussions and conversations with individuals. It does not attempt to cover the whole of China but simply gathers the passions of one city during a year of its life and presents them as they appeared to the participants themselves—the students and workers, the clerks and Party cadres, the shopkeepers, farmers, schoolteachers, housewives, and children of Shanghai.

1. The Initial Thrust

On November 10, 1965, a Shanghai newspaper called *Wen Hui Pao* published a seemingly trifling piece of literary criticism. In retrospect, this article was seen to have blown the lid off a veritable Pandora's box of strife and led directly to China's Cultural Revolution. The writer, a young Shanghai journalist by the name of Yao Wen-yuan, had already established a reputation as a strict ideologue and a fervent disciple of Mao Tse-tung. His article was a devastating analysis of a historical play entitled *The Dismissal of Hai Jui,* written 4 years earlier by a Peking writer, Wu Han. Perhaps only in China could a fight over a play about a man who lived 400 years ago have provoked such an extraordinary social and political upheaval.

Hai Jui was a Ming-dynasty official, famous for his sympathy with the poor and his enlightened sense of justice. Wu Han followed the history-book interpretation, laying particular stress on Hai Jui's courage in confiscating land from powerful landlords and distributing it among the people. Yao Wen-yuan argued strongly that the real Hai Jui was totally devoted to the imperial power structure and that the effect of his "righteousness" and "justice" was to make the peasants satisfied with the system. His land reform, too, was designed to strengthen, not weaken, feudalism and could not by any stretch of the imagination be called a revolutionary act.

This raised questions as to why Wu Han had presented the character of Hai Jui in such a favorable light and why he had

written about Hai Jui in the first place. Referring to 1961, the
year of the play's appearance, Yao wrote,

> China, as everyone knows, ran into temporary economic difficulties,
> caused by 3 successive years of natural calamities. The imperialists,
> the reactionaries of various countries, and the modern revisionists
> launched wave after wave of attacks on us, and it was at this time
> that evil people in China started clamoring for "individual farming."
> . . . They played up the "superiority" of "individual farming" and
> called for the restoration of a private economy and the "return of the
> land." In other words, they wanted to demolish the people's com-
> munes. . . .[1]

This took the article well beyond literary criticism. Yao accused
the playwright of speaking for those who opposed the communes.
And that was only the beginning, for Wu Han was no struggling
writer trying to make a living from historical dramas. He was,
in fact, a vice-mayor of Peking.

To understand what Yao Wen-yuan was driving at, we will
have to assume that there was widespread opposition within the
Communist Party itself to some of Mao Tse-tung's ideas. The
formation of the people's communes in 1958 was one bone of contention; the Great Leap Forward was another. Many high Party
members considered that these abrupt social somersaults had
broken the back of the economy.

The split in the Party became apparent in 1959, when Defense
Minister P'eng Te-huai and several other high Party officials were
dismissed. Those who had dared to oppose Mao and his followers
were called "right-wing opportunists." The three bad seasons
from 1959 to 1962 caused near starvation in parts of China. The
resulting disillusionment of a whole segment of the Party, not to
mention the people, cannot be overemphasized. It had been
widely assumed that China, once it had been "liberated" from
the past by revolution, would automatically progress toward
prosperity. The disaster of the 3 bad years convinced many
officials otherwise. It was not that they rejected the theories and

---

[1] "On the New Historical Drama, *The Dismissal of Hai Jui*," *Wen Hui Pao*
(Shanghai), November 10, 1965.

aims of socialism, but they considered that the Maoists were pushing too hard and that there were better, if slower, ways of building China's future.

From 1962 on, these pragmatists, as they have sometimes been called, seem to have won control of the Central Committee. Steps were taken to decentralize the administration of the communes, give the peasants back some private land and allow them to sell certain produce on a free market, and introduce money incentives to spur industrial production. These and similar moves probably helped get the economy back on its feet, but there is no doubt that they were semi-capitalist techniques—at least, in comparison with the ideals of the Mao group. This is what led to the charge, repeated *ad nauseam* during the Cultural Revolution, that some people wanted to "lead the country back to capitalism."

The Cultural Revolution was in part an attempt to reverse this trend and re-establish the predominance of the Mao group. It did not happen suddenly. There were several other fields in which the Maoists had been patiently at work for a long time. In the army, Marshal Lin Piao, a Mao appointee, was building an exemplary spirit of altruism, frugality, and democracy among the soldiers (and, at the same time, instilling into them an unprecedented dedication to the ideas of the Chairman). In the whole field of cultural reform, there was also a strong thrust from the Maoists, particularly from Mao's own wife, Chiang Ch'ing, who had been given the job of cultural watchdog for the nation. The Socialist Education Movement, starting in 1963, had represented yet another attempt by those loyal to Mao to oust the opposition from responsible posts in industry, education, and the rural and urban bureaucracies.

If we assume that a struggle of this magnitude had been going on for several years before 1965, then Yao Wen-yuan's article can be seen in its proper perspective. Yet few of those who read it that day in November can have had any idea that they were witnessing the first salvo of a coup d'état, launched by the Mao group from a power base in Shanghai, in an attempt to dislodge their enemies from entrenched positions in the capital.

It was almost 12 months before the identity of the protagonists was revealed. The enemies of the Mao group were then declared to be under the leadership of President Liu Shao-ch'i and Party Secretary-General Teng Hsiao-p'ing. They had apparently managed to get their men into China's highest government and Party posts. From the provincial committees to the grass roots, it was the pragmatists who had power.

In Peking, Mayor P'eng Chen seemed to have gone further than anyone in resisting Mao's theories and keeping the Chairman's disciples out of power. The Mao group later produced reams of material to prove that he had made Peking his satrapy and that *his* ideas, not Mao's, reigned supreme in the capital. Here is a sample of those ideas, as reported in an anonymous leaflet that circulated in Shanghai at the beginning of 1967:

On Class Struggle

P'eng made a speech in 1958 in which he said that all the landlords and rich peasants had become ordinary commune members and that counterrevolutionaries were extremely scarce. Therefore, he concluded, class struggle was just about dead in China and should be put in the museum!

On another occasion, he said that 75 per cent of China's capitalists had been successfully absorbed into state enterprises. Only a quarter still lived for the interest they received from their investments. So, he said, one could no longer speak of class antagonism between capitalists and workers. Some individual capitalists might be antagonistic, but not the whole class.

In 1961, he declared that the capitalists were behaving very well during the temporary economic difficulties. Chinese capitalists, in his opinion, were more progressive than the American working class! And the Chinese bourgeois political parties were further to the left than the Communist parties of Europe!

He visited the homes of a lot of capitalists and found their lives Spartan. "A Soviet worker lives better than most of our capitalists!" he said.

As long ago as 1957, he said that China's main contradiction was no longer between workers and capitalists but rather between man and nature. "The great challenge now," he declared, "is to change China from a backward country to an advanced socialist one."

In 1963, he opposed the idea of putting politics first. "Politics alone does not work," he said. "It must be combined with material incentives. Men are like leeches; where there is blood, they flock to it."

On the People's Communes

In 1961, he ordered an investigation into the commune system around Peking, hinting that the Peking Committee should criticize it if it were found to have been unsuccessful. "We must give the masses more liberty," he said. "Why, even Marx and Engels were different from each other. How could we think of organizing our 500 million peasants into one vast monotonous movement?"

On the Great Leap Forward

The Great Leap Forward, he said, was "not in accordance with objective laws." It was "beautiful, empty talk," a "romantic" vision. He also accused the leaders of the Central Committee of "standover tactics" and "authoritarianism" in their attitude to the masses.

On Culture

He opposed Chairman Mao's theories on art. In 1964, Chairman Mao said the stage was still "dominated by dead men and foreigners." P'eng's reply: "What about Marx and Lenin? Aren't they dead and foreign?"

In 1963, Chiang Ch'ing [Mme. Mao] was put in charge of reforming Peking opera. She recommended a modern work and the Peking company started rehearsals. The tickets were sold out in 2 days, but P'eng said the opera was no good and got the theater to refund all the money. . . .

In 1964, a festival of modern opera was organized in Peking. P'eng insisted that some ancient operas should be included. As a result of this mixture of old and new, the festival failed to impress.

In 1965, P'eng ordered reproductions from a tape recording of ten ancient operas. He also had eight tapes made from American and Japanese recordings from the 1930's. . . . His reasons: "Modern opera is tiring; the old kind is restful."

On His Own Importance

Even back in 1946, he had his own quotations on the wall of his office!

As mayor of Peking, he took credit for every success. So much so, that one of his cronies remarked: "To understand Chairman Mao's ideas, you first have to understand those of P'eng Chen!"

In 1965, he spent 2 months organizing a banquet for Li Tsung-jen.[2] He got all the famous cooks, even a man who had worked for the emperor! As a result, the banquet was far more lavish than the one offered to Li Tsung-jen by Chairman Mao and Premier Chou En-lai!

When he was invited to join the Politburo, he became even more arrogant. Whenever Chou En-lai and the other leaders were absent from Peking, P'eng gave the orders, though he was way out of his depth. . . . He even asked for access to military secrets, instructing the chief of the general staff to pass all new information on to him. . . .

It was at this man and the ideas he represented that Yao Wen-yuan's article was ultimately directed. By criticizing the Vice-Mayor of Peking for his revisionist play, Yao was indirectly attacking P'eng Chen himself.

P'eng was vulnerable for a variety of reasons. For one thing, he had been more outspoken than others in his opposition. For another, he had run up against people like Mao's wife, who hated him for blocking her cultural reforms. Another major reason for his weakness at this time was the part he had played in the Indonesian debacle. He had personally visited that country in May, 1965, and made important speeches on tactics and strategy. Aidit, the leader of the Indonesian Party, came to Peking on August 1, 1965. I was on the same plane and watched him run down the gangway into the embrace of P'eng Chen. Whatever the facts of the Indonesian coup of September 30–October 1, 1965, the massacre that followed left P'eng in an awkward position. He was the obvious scapegoat for recrimination, and it is interesting that Yao Wen-yuan's article appeared just 40 days after the coup.

The question then arises: If the Mao group's opponents had control of the Party, how was Yao Wen-yuan able to get his article into a Shanghai newspaper? Shanghai was one of the few places in China with a strong Maoist pressure group on the Party Committee. This was largely due to the efforts of former Mayor and First Secretary of the city K'e Ch'ing-shih. Until his

2 Acting President of China after Chiang K'ai-shek's flight to Taiwan in 1949. Li resided in the United States after the Communist victory, but he returned to China in 1965 and died in 1969.

death in May, 1965, he had resisted the encroachments of the pragmatists. With the support of the very able Director of Propaganda, Chang Ch'un-ch'iao—a man later to achieve great power in the Cultural Revolution—he had worked to make Shanghai what the Mao group wanted it to be. Politically and economically, he seems to have failed, for the nationwide trends were too strong. Culturally, however, he and Chang Ch'un-ch'iao had managed to provide Mao's wife with the cooperation she could not get in Peking, and Shanghai became the model for the rest of the country in the development of truly proletarian and revolutionary opera, ballet, cinema, music, and other art forms.

In this sense, Shanghai was the capital of the Mao group. It was therefore the obvious springboard for an attack on P'eng Chen. The plot involved powerful people; I was told by a Red Guard group that Mao's wife was in Shanghai at the time and gave Yao "concrete assistance" with his article. Subsequent reports in Red Guard papers revealed that Shanghai authorities were powerless to stop publication of the article but were extremely anxious about its possible effects. The question was: How would P'eng Chen react to this damning indictment of his vice-mayor?

The Party leaders in Shanghai at this time—successors to the late Mayor K'e Ch'ing-shih—were appointees of the opposition group and quite out of sympathy with the Maoists. They certainly did everything in their power to block the publication of Yao Wen-yuan's article.

A Red Guard newspaper later quoted the mayor of Shanghai, Ts'ao Ti-ch'iu, as saying: "What was mostly on our minds at that time was our relationship with Peking, with P'eng Chen in fact. Should we alert him? If we did not, he would be caught unawares. If we did, it would be against the wishes of Chairman Mao. What were we to do? Our Secretariat puzzled over the problem again and again" (RG 8:3.1).[3]

According to this source, the Committee eventually decided to get word to P'eng Chen so that he would at least be prepared to meet the challenge.

[3] See the key to the Red Guard newspapers in the Appendix, pp. 302-7.

After the appearance of Yao Wen-yuan's article . . . P'eng Chen and his gang refused to reprint it in the Peking papers. A few Shanghai Municipal Committee secretaries, led by the head of the East China Bureau, Ch'en P'ei-hsien, and the Mayor of Shanghai, Ts'ao Ti-ch'iu, were deathly afraid of P'eng Chen and even more afraid of Liu Shao-ch'i. So, as soon as the article was published, they warned P'eng Chen . . . of his danger.

Our question to these gentlemen is this: Why were you afraid of P'eng Chen? Was it not the fear that you would be caught in the trap set for him? When you alerted him, what did you expect him to do? Did you not want him to initiate open resistance to the plans of the Central Committee and Chairman Mao? Did you not hope he would lead a movement to restore capitalism in China? (RG 8:2.2)

The Red Guards also mentioned that "P'eng Chen made two trips to Shanghai during this period" (RG 8:3.1). If this is true, it shows he did not underestimate the threat.

Months later, after P'eng Chen had fallen, the Shanghai Municipal Committee seems to have claimed the credit for the whole affair. The radicals produced this refutation:

The Shanghai Municipal Committee boasted that it had organized the writing of the article. . . . The fact is, it was written under the guidance of Chairman Mao himself. The operation was personally directed by Chiang Ch'ing, and the ones who did the work were Chang Ch'un-ch'iao and Yao Wen-yuan.

When the article was still in its sixth draft, the members of the Shanghai Municipal Committee found out about it. Loyal to their alliance with the Liu "dynasty" and the old Peking Committee, they not only opposed its publication but actually plotted to strangle it at its birth. (RG 8:1.2)

This passage shows the secrecy and care that accompanied the setting of the trap. P'eng Chen, despite the efforts of the Shanghai Committee, was caught. For a time, it seemed he would suppress the article in Peking, but too much interest had been aroused, opinions about Wu Han's play were flying back and forth, and he finally had little choice but to capitulate. On November 30, after what must have been a torrid 3 weeks, the Peking *People's Daily* reprinted the article.

This triggered several months of debate. At first, it was carried on mostly by students and intellectuals; the bulk of the population, if they noticed it at all, probably considered it rather remote and abstract. Even in the universities, if the Shanghai Foreign Languages Institute was typical, the argument remained on an intellectual level until March, 1966. Some students complained of this later:

> At ·the instigation of the Propaganda Department of the Institute's Party Committee, a Marxist-Leninist study group organized discussions to criticize the play *The Dismissal of Hai Jui*.
>
> On March 25, 1966, a member of this study group "summed up" the results of the debate in a half-hearted speech, which in fact succeeded in diverting an acute class struggle into a purely academic issue.

The top Party men in China, both those who identified themselves with the Mao group's policies and those who opposed them, must have been engaged in all kinds of maneuvers during the early months of 1966. We can assume that the conservative majority knew that nothing but trouble would follow should the debate get out of hand and used all their power and influence to keep the affair within academic circles.

In April and May, however, their worst fears were realized. The attack on Wu Han spread ominously to include two other Peking writers—Teng T'o, a magazine editor, and Liao Mo-sha, a well-known journalist. All three men, who came to be known collectively as "the three-family village," held important jobs in Peking's political and cultural hierarchies. The implication was that they, along with other as yet unnamed collaborators, had plotted to take control of Peking's ideological machinery and use it as a weapon against Mao Tse-tung's policies and followers. This escalation brought the struggle much closer to P'eng Chen. It began to look as if he and his Committee had allowed, if not encouraged, Peking to become a stronghold of anti-Mao sentiments and policies.

All through April, however, the establishment kept the lid on. Some students at our Institute described how this was done: "A special study group produced a poisonous document entitled 'Let's All Take Part in the Debate on *Hai Jui*.' This was supposed to 'unite' us, but in fact it openly defended Teng T'o and Wu Han and completely obliterated the basic question of class struggle."

Even at this early stage, there were nuclei of outspoken teachers and students in major universities all over the country. The driving force behind these radical groups often came from cadres who had at some stage suffered persecution—during the Socialist Education Movement, for example, when the pragmatists had put men into university posts formerly held by Maoists. These malcontents were evidently worrying the administration, for, in April, the President of Peking's Tsinghua University called a "conference on political work." Representatives of no less than thirty colleges, including the Shanghai Foreign Languages Institute, were invited. It is interesting that the man who went from our Institute was one of the first to be criticized when the movement entered the wall-poster stage in May.

During April and May, the Mao group concentrated on "the three-family village," attempting to show that the revisionism of such men extended throughout the whole field of education. Later documents included selections from speeches made by prominent academic administrators. The following remarks, attributed to Chiang Nan-hsiang, President of Tsinghua University, were probably typical:

Some people say that Chuang Tse-tung's excellence at table tennis and his winning of the world championship are great victories for the ideas of Chairman Mao. . . . Now, as long as Chuang Tse-tung keeps winning, this is fine. But what do we say when he loses? If we attribute every success to the ideas of Chairman Mao, then our failures must logically bring disrespect to those ideas. In the past, Chiang K'ai-shek took the memory of Sun Yat-sen to similar extremes. We had streets, buildings, even lavatories named after him! [From a speech made in 1960]

In the international world, we should be modest. We should speak of "Marxism" and of "Chairman Mao's works"; but we should avoid the phrase "Chairman Mao's thought." [1960]

When you go abroad, don't boast. Don't say things like "China is the world's greatest country because it has Chairman Mao's thought." The more you go around saying "China is marvelous!" the more you turn people off.

Some people say that to be "red," to be a good Communist, one must study Chairman Mao's works. This is only partly true. Studying Chairman Mao's works can *help* a person be "red," but it will not *ensure* that he is "red." John Foster Dulles, after all, studied Mao. Was he "red"? Just because cats have four legs doesn't mean everything with four legs is a cat. Dogs have four legs too. [From a speech of farewell to foreign language students going abroad; July 23, 1965]

The idea of an athlete running around the track reciting Chairman Mao's works is quite ridiculous. That can hardly be called "studying Chairman Mao's works."

It is not enough for intellectuals to study only Chairman Mao's works. It is essential reading, of course, but it is not enough. They must also have a knowledge of basic Marxist theory. They must at least read *Capital* and *Communist Manifesto*. [From a speech of welcome to new students. August 31, 1965][4]

Such sentiments were certainly shared by a large segment of Party members, particularly those in positions of authority. May, 1966, however, was not the time to air them, for the Mao group was out for the political scalp of anyone who had shown the slightest disrespect for the Chairman's ideas.

There was no stopping the thrust from Shanghai. On May 10, Yao Wen-yuan struck again, this time with an even longer and more devastating article against the "black line" emanating from Peking. It was perhaps indicative of an increase in the Mao group's strength that this second article was published in both *Wen Hui Pao* and *Liberation Daily*, Shanghai's two most influential newspapers, and quickly reprinted all over the country.

The radicals in the universities took their cue from Yao Wen-yuan and intensified the campaign against revisionism. Even before May 10, Peking University teachers and students had written more than 100 articles against "the three-family village." Now the pressure mounted so much that the Deputy Director of

---

[4] Notes taken from an anonymous undated leaflet entitled "The Reactionary Utterances of Chiang Nan-hsiang."

Peking's University Affairs Department had to call for a strengthening of Party leadership on the campuses.

On May 16, the Central Committee reacted to this by warning that "the most dangerous enemies" of China were "the Khrushchevs sleeping in our midst." This set off a series of emotional rallies in colleges all over the country. In our Institute, the first mass meeting took place on May 18, with speeches and slogans shouted through bull-horns and classes neglected for the politics of mass indignation. Nothing remotely like this had happened during my stay there. The Institute had in fact been an easy-going place, with no visible trace of active "class struggle." From the middle of May, 1966, until I left China almost a year later, the Cultural Revolution was the sole activity of the 3,000 people whose lives revolved around that college.

Also in May, the Peking radicals began writing wall posters in earnest. Braving the wrath of the Party establishment, they came out with stinging attacks on high officials. One of these posters, written on May 25 by seven members of the philosophy department at Peking University, became the instrument of the Mao group's first major breakthrough. It was said that Mao himself ordered the text broadcast over Radio Peking on June 1. Be that as it may, the Peking press carried it on June 2, and it was soon famous nationwide.

The poster, which quickly became identified with the name of Miss Nieh Yuan-tzu, was directed at three top men in Peking's political and academic power structure. This time, the publicity led to their disgrace, and the Peking Committee looked very shaky indeed. On June 3 came news that rocked the country: The Committee had been "reorganized." In other words, P'eng Chen had fallen.

This was a tremendous success for the Mao group, crowning 6 months of cultural and political guerrilla activity. With consummate patience and organizational skill, they had probed and nagged at the weaknesses in their opponents' armor, striking only when sure of victory. Whether Mao himself conceived the strategy or not, the group that waved his banner certainly applied the old man's theories.

The question now was whether this radical minority, having broken the opposition in Peking, could go on to take power all over the country. On their side were the factors that had helped them win so far: the claim to be acting on the orders of Mao himself, with the prestige that surrounded the person of the Chairman; the support of a significant part of the army under Marshal Lin Piao, without which it is doubtful whether they could have taken Peking; the weakness of P'eng Chen and the proven revisionism of his followers; and the temporary alliance with powerful members of the Central Committee, who, seeing that P'eng could no longer be saved, had therefore shifted their support to the Mao group for the time being. On the other hand, they controlled little besides beachheads in Shanghai and Peking, and their popular support was limited to a few thousand highly indignant students, who were vulnerable to repression by the Party authorities.

But if they could only prove to the rest of the students that the rule of men like P'eng Chen had resulted in a loss of ideological purity, a lulling of revolutionary fervor, the compromise of socialist economic principles, and the repression of popular initiative in every field, then their potential strength was incalculable.

Ironically, one of the greatest obstacles was loyalty. Most of the students had profound faith in the Party, seeing it as a single authority stretching unbroken from the lowliest cadre up to the Central Committee. When a minor Party official spoke, his voice was magnified a thousandfold and his instructions were almost as sacred as the words of Mao. The establishment, therefore, did not find it hard to command the allegiance of the majority.

This was to change dramatically. For the Maoists to win the sympathy even of the students, not to mention that of the workers and peasants, they were going to have to smash the concept of blind obedience. In practice, this would mean the destruction of the whole Party monolith.

That process is the story of the Cultural Revolution in Shanghai, and we shall follow its course from the fall of P'eng Chen, through a period of "phony revolution," to the formation of Red Guards and the explosion of the struggle into a movement that "touched the soul" of every man, woman, and child in this city of 10 million.

2. The Phony Revolution

The fall of P'eng Chen and his Peking Committee was the signal for an uprising against opponents of the Mao group all over the country. In most urban and provincial centers, small but relatively well informed groups of radicals launched paper wars against Party authorities suspected of revisionism. The Central Committee, apparently afraid this would get out of hand, took the advice of President Liu Shao-ch'i and Party Secretary-General Teng Hsiao-p'ing and sent out "Work Teams" to "keep an eye on the movement" in the universities. Each of Shanghai's six major campuses got one. The Teams consisted of about thirty members, and each was headed by a senior Party official. They functioned throughout most of June and July.

The behavior of these Work Teams, and of the Shanghai hierarchy in general, was extremely deceptive. On the surface, the whole Party was a paragon of revolutionary fervor, repeating the Mao group's call for all-out war on the forces of revisionism. Behind the scenes, however, energetic efforts were made to keep the movement within manageable bounds.

With or without Work Teams, the Shanghai Party wielded great power. Although there was a democratically elected People's Committee, which theoretically controlled its own bureaucracy, in practice the Party held all the key posts. This was hardly surprising, and most Shanghai people had no illusions about it. Before the Cultural Revolution, however, few were aware of the exact composition of their government. By the end of 1966, even the children knew the names and precise positions of every top Party official in the city.

They knew, for example, that the highest organ of power in the area was the East China Bureau. This was one of six regional bureaus, which were direct appendages of the central government led by members or alternates of the Central Committee. Since each bureau controlled several provinces, its power was far greater than that of any local authority.

The head of the East China Bureau when the Cultural Revolution began was a man named Ch'en P'ei-hsien. At 55, he had had 30 years of Party experience in political and military capacities. Most of that time had been spent in East China, particularly Shanghai and Kiangsu, so he was well qualified for his position. He was a tall, good-looking man, somewhat overweight as a result of his years in office. His manner was witty and assured, with more than a touch of conceit and a definite coarseness. Perhaps his trip to Leningrad in 1961 had impressed him too much, for there was something of the Soviet bureaucrat in his attitudes and methods.

He kept in the background for the first 6 months of the movement. In December, 1966, when circumstances forced him to emerge from obscurity and play a leading role, he was quoted as saying: "I have been sick for a long time. I don't know too much about what's been going on" (RG 9:3.1). The radicals then produced evidence to show that he had in fact been pulling strings from the beginning and that he had done more than any other man to thwart the will of the Mao group in East China.

Though Ch'en P'ei-hsien eventually became the most notorious name in Shangai, the man who bore the brunt of the radical onslaught for the first 6 months was Ts'ao Ti-ch'iu, First Secretary of the Shanghai Municipal Committee and Mayor of the city. The Municipal Committee, as distinct from the People's Committee, was a Party organization. Within it were departments of education and public health, transport and communications, propaganda, agriculture, trade, sports, and so on. The highest officials in these departments often held corresponding posts in the People's Committee, thus weaving the Party and state bureaucracies into one seamless organization. For practical purposes, the Municipal Committee was the governing body of the city.

Mayor Ts'ao, as he was affectionately known before the movement, was a chubby little Szechuanese with sparse white hair. He had worked his way up to mayor of Chungking before being transferred to Shanghai in 1955. He was in many ways the opposite of Ch'en P'ei-hsien. Where Ch'en was quick and caustic, Ts'ao gave the impression of a plodder; he had an orthodox, almost retiring personality, a quiet and careful voice. He looked the part he played—a professional administrator of a complex industrial city, a man better versed in Marxist economics than in the utopian vision of a Lenin or a Mao Tse-tung. He was unfortunate in that his position in Shanghai corresponded exactly to that of P'eng Chen in Peking. He was therefore a logical target for the radicals, whether he did anything to deserve it or not.

Conscious of his vulnerability, he took the initiative from the beginning. In his speeches, he called for an all-out effort to rid Shanghai of revisionism and establish the ideas of Mao as the basis for future policy. On June 4, for example, just one day after the fall of P'eng Chen, he was said to have made the following statement on behalf of the Municipal Committee:

> The clearest definition of our policy is this: The main targets, the people who will be most severely criticized in this movement, are those who hang up lamb but sell dog's meat. . . . If it should turn into an inner-Party struggle, the target will remain the same: namely hypocrites who wave red flags as a cover for an attack on the red flag. . . . (RG 5:4.2)

Remarks like these persuaded most people that the Mayor was determined to lead the fight against influential revisionists in culture and education.

The radicals in the universities were far from convinced. They saw the Cultural Revolution as a movement against types like P'eng Chen—people who had risen to the top posts in the Party but who were mortally opposed to the policies of the Mao group. For them, it was a movement to bring down not just a handful of academics or Party bureaucrats in the cultural field but men in the highest echelons of government—including Ts'ao Ti-ch'iu himself! They therefore responded to the Mayor's call with undisguised scorn. As one of their newspapers put it:

> The Municipal Committee said the main target would be those who "hang up lamb but sell dog's meat" and those who "use the red flag to attack the red flag." This was an attempt to confuse the issue. They were already planning to deceive the people. Terrified that the movement might turn against the Party, they did their best to protect reactionary authorities by denouncing a few selected academics, who were actually "dead tigers," with no power at all. (RG 5:4.2)

Despite this discontent, most Shanghai students were prepared to go along with the Mayor. Ts'ao Ti-ch'iu knew this, but he did not underestimate the opposition. He therefore came out with a statement so strong that even his detractors could find no fault with it. He told a mass rally on June 10:

> The great Cultural Revolution that is now under way will be an exacting test for the Party spirit and the revolutionary spirit of every Party organization, every individual Party member, every revolutionary cadre. The way you approach the crucial questions raised by this great movement will reveal whether you really believe in socialism or only pretend to believe in it or are actually opposed to it, whether you really support Mao Tse-tung's ideas or only pretend to support them or are actually opposed to them.[1]

This speech seemed to give the lie to those who saw the Mayor as another P'eng Chen. Even the radicals accepted it as a clarion call. In the Foreign Languages Institute, for example, the reaction from the left was enthusiastic:

> On June 10, the Municipal Committee held a rally of 10,000 people, at which Mayor Ts'ao made a speech that carried the mobilization for the great Cultural Revolution a step further. He advised all Party committees that they would have to "pass through an ordeal by fire," and he stressed three times that the movement was principally directed against Party authorities who were leading China back toward capitalism. . . .

[1] From "An Anthology of Wall Posters," published by the Field Army Red Guards of the Shanghai Foreign Languages Institute.

Encouraged by his words, the revolutionary teachers and students of the whole Institute resolved to put daring above all else, to speak out boldly in the fearless revolutionary spirit of the working class, the spirit of being "willing to suffer death by a thousand cuts, in order to unhorse the emperor."[2]

The Party Secretary of our Institute went along with the Mayor's bravado. In a poster of his own, he declared:

I take this opportunity to repeat to the revolutionary teachers, students, and staff that it is the intention of this Party Committee to mobilize the masses and submit to an "ordeal by fire." I want everyone to put up more posters, to bring out faults in the work of the Committee and in that of individual leaders. Monsters must be rooted out. Please help us pass this test of our socialism. We want to be real revolutionaries; we want to stand side by side with the teachers and students and hold high the great red banner of Mao Tse-tung's ideas. With these ideas as our compass-bearing, we will sincerely carry out every instruction from the Central Committee and the Shanghai Municipal Committee. We will sweep all monsters from our midst, root them out, expose them to the light, denounce them, overthrow them, make their names stink to high heaven![3]

The irony in statements like this is that it was often the very men who uttered them whose names stank in the end!

There seems little doubt that the Mayor was playing a double game—publicly exhorting the masses to make revolution and warning the Party that it must submit to scrutiny while privately advising his Municipal Committee to pursue a quite different policy.

His two most powerful lieutenants were the heads of education and propaganda. The Education Department was the power behind the college authorities; the Propaganda Department controlled the mass media. The radical students soon realized that the repression they were suffering stemmed precisely from these two sources. The campus Party committees tried to keep them quiet, and the press ignored them completely, praising

2 *Ibid.*
3 *Ibid.*

instead the loyal student majority. The first campaigns by the left wing were therefore against the heads of education and propaganda and, for a time, the Mayor slipped out of the limelight.

Ch'ang Hsi-p'ing, the head of education, was susceptible to attack. He had previously spent 10 years as Party Secretary of Shanghai's main teacher-training institute, the East China Normal College, which meant that the students and teachers who wanted evidence against him did not have to go far to find it. In trying to discover his role in the Cultural Revolution, we have only subsequent radical accounts to go on. One of these described his reaction to the events of early June:

> On June 2, Ch'ang hurriedly called a meeting of all Party secretaries in higher education and issued these sinister instructions: "There is a possibility that some wall posters may attack us. Don't worry about these. As they come up, their true nature can be exposed, and we will be able to counter them systematically. . . ."
>
> On June 5, he had this to add: "Some vicious posters have definitely appeared. We must be more careful. We must renew our resolve to root out evil wherever we find it. We should not be afraid of it; instead, we should expose and destroy it systematically."
>
> As a result of these instructions, many Party committees in higher education deliberately organized people to make a furious onslaught on any of the revolutionary masses who dared to put up posters against the Party authorities. The writers of such posters were branded "counterrevolutionary," "anti-Party," or "antisocialist." They were forced to write self-criticisms; evidence against them was collected, and their names were recorded for future punishment. In this way, the fire of the revolutionary mass movement was almost put out. (RG 1:4.1)

The charge of persecuting outspoken students was only one of the accusations brought against Ch'ang Hsi-p'ing, but it was the most serious one. The whole mood of the Cultural Revolution was antibureaucratic; it was, as Mayor Ts'ao had said, a challenge to every Party member—those who encouraged "the masses" to criticize them were revolutionaries; those who secretly tried to suppress dissent were bureaucrats, revisionists, and opponents of Mao Tse-tung's ideas.

Once the radicals got their teeth into Ch'ang Hsi-p'ing, they never let go:

> At the start of the movement, Ch'ang Hsi-p'ing came out with remarks such as: "The main thrust of this Cultural Revolution is directed against bourgeois reactionary intellectuals."
>
> This prompted the Party Committee in every Shanghai college to start the movement by stripping a few reactionary academics of their "authority." These were flattered by being called "prime targets," and the students and teachers were told to write "high-quality articles" denouncing them. . . . This was done to shift the spearhead of the struggle and ultimately to save the skins of the Party officials. (RG 1:4.1)

They also accused Ch'ang of having tried to ban or limit the use of wall posters:

> Chairman Mao called the wall poster "a new and most effective weapon," but at the beginning of the movement Ch'ang Hsi-p'ing sent out an order: "Do not put up wall posters."
>
> When he saw there was no stopping them, he resorted to the feeble argument that "a distinction must be made between Party affairs and non-Party affairs. The Party has its own discipline," he said, "just as the state has its own laws and the Youth League its own rules. . . . The Party's internal affairs should be handled within the Party."
>
> His aim in making such statements was to intimidate the revolutionary teachers and students and stop them finding out too much about the Party. (RG 1:4.1)

He was also accused of having insisted on obedience to the Shanghai Municipal authorities:

> Ch'ang Hsi-p'ing popularized ideas like "the Shanghai Municipal Committee carries out the orders of the Central Committee in Peking," "the Shanghai Municipal Committee is free from error," and so on. He also praised certain college Party committees, saying that they "follow all the instructions of the Shanghai Municipal Committee." "We must have faith in our local Party Committee," he said, "in exactly the same way that we have faith in our Municipal Committee and in the Central Committee itself." By equating all

Party committees with the Central Committee, he made the masses
very reluctant to speak out against local authorities. (RG 1:4.1)

The radicals also charged that he had instructed Party authorities not to put up wall posters themselves but to sit tight and
watch what came out. When the students in one college complained of this lack of leadership, Ch'ang was quoted as having
said: "The Party Committees in other colleges have not put up
wall posters. *I* have not put up any. Chairman Mao himself has
not put up any. Can you conclude that we are therefore not revolutionary?" (RG 1:4.1)

This little piece of conceit drew an indignant retort from the
students concerned: "What a perfect example of a dog baying at
the moon! The treacherous Ch'ang Hsi-p'ing must not be allowed
to profane our great leader in this way!" (RG 1:4.1)

Because Ch'ang used all his power to protect the college authorities, said the radicals, they praised him loudly in their speeches
to the students. It was apparently common to hear such compli-
ments as "The head of the Education Department has set very
high standards" or "Comrade Ch'ang Hsi-p'ing is a fine man!"
(RG 1:4.1). Before the year had ended, he was to need all the
praise he could get.

The other man to fall foul of the radicals at an early date was
acting propaganda chief Yang Hsi-kuang. He had a Party record
remarkably similar to that of Ch'ang Hsi-p'ing, having put in
more than 10 years as Party Secretary of Shanghai's Futan University. Since Futan was the strongest single source of radical
opinion in Shanghai, it was not long before the students had
compiled a dossier on him.

His rise to a position of power had been somewhat unorthodox.
From a top job in the Education Department, he had been
appointed Alternate Secretary of the Municipal Committee in
1965. When the Cultural Revolution broke, Chang Ch'un-ch'iao,
whose power had allowed the movement to take root in Shanghai,
joined the Mao group in Peking. This left open his job as head
of Shanghai propaganda. Yang Hsi-kuang, though never officially
appointed to the vacant post, quietly took over the running of
the department.

Radical newspapers later claimed that he had exercised great power over the press. As we have seen in the case of Chang Ch'un-ch'iao and his protégé Yao Wen-yuan, control of Shanghai's newspapers was a crucial factor in the Cultural Revolution. Yang Hsi-kuang, according to his detractors, persuaded the press to criticize only academics and intellectuals and to leave high Party officials well alone. Not only that, said the radicals, but he even decided which intellectuals were to be denounced:

> At the beginning of June, the counterrevolutionary revisionist Yang Hsi-kuang issued instructions about who was to be censured during the movement. He listed three separate categories:
>
> 1. *Prime targets.* By these he meant eight prominent academics already singled out by the Municipal Committee. These eight men were "dead tigers" and had no real power.
>
> 2. *Targets of moderate importance.* Here he was referring to bourgeois intellectuals in general and run-of-the-mill college professors.
>
> 3. *Cases calling for a mild degree of self-criticism.* These were in fact the real targets of the movement—the Party authorities leading the country back to capitalism. Yang Hsi-kuang said: "If there are faults among the leaders, they too must make self-criticisms." This sounded good, but in fact he practically told them what to say: "The leaders can simply declare that they have been a little conservative, tended somewhat toward the right wing . . . their statements should not go into too many details." (RG 5:4.2)

Later, the radicals began to attack the press for ignoring or criticizing their activities. Yang Hsi-kuang was said to have told the newspaper editors: "The press must not waver for an instant, for its influence is enormous. It is not a bad thing for the masses to have their doubts, but if they go to extremes the press can gently put them right and prevent them from getting too excited" (RG 5:4.2).

When the radicals demanded that certain papers examine their editorial policies and publish self-criticisms, Yang Hsi-kuang reportedly said: "The press must carry on regardless. No Shanghai papers will engage in any self-criticism" (RG 5:4.2).

Around the middle of June, said the radicals, Yang was still telling the press what to write:

Many ordinary people are not too clear about how the Cultural Revolution should be carried out. We must give them some guidance in the press. We must publish a few model cases. There is the head of the Conservatorium of Music, for example. We could write that story up, showing how and why he has been criticized. (RG 6:4.1)

The radicals were infuriated by these attempts to "set the tune":

The suggestion that the President of the Conservatorium should be denounced was a perfect example of the phony revolution! The man in question was an old Party member, to be sure, and titular head of the Conservatorium, but he had no power; he was merely a bourgeois reactionary academic who had sneaked into the Party. The question to ask was whether there were any Party officials at the Conservatorium who were actively taking the road back to capitalism. But that never even arose. (RG 6:4.1)

As acting head of propaganda, Yang was also in charge of Radio Shanghai. The radicals claimed that on June 4 he issued the following statement to all radio employees:

The Shanghai Municipal Committee scrupulously follows the instructions of Chairman Mao. It is nothing like the Peking Municipal Committee. We must have faith in our Committee; the leadership must be strong. If not, our power will be smashed. We must be on the alert. We cannot work on the principle of anarchy. We cannot tolerate the idea that "everyone is open to suspicion." (RG 5:2.3)

Remarks like these made the radicals really angry. To them, Yang Hsi-kuang was saying "Hands off the Party leaders! Criticize anyone you like, but the Municipal Committee is sacrosanct." This was precisely the attitude they were out to destroy, the feudal concept of "rule by divine right." They were determined to break the bureaucratic grip of the Party hierarchy and put men in power who would be responsive to the people. The haughty stance of officials like Yang Hsi-kuang was crudely caricatured by the radicals as an attitude of "You don't slap a tiger on the backside with impunity!" Well, they said, we are going to do more than *slap* the tiger. We are going to drive him from the stage of history!

Yang Hsi-kuang and Ch'ang Hsi-p'ing paid for their delaying tactics by becoming the principal objects of the left wing's wrath. Yet, Mayor Ts'ao Ti-ch'iu, as First Secretary of the Municipal Committee, was ultimately responsible for their actions. And Ch'en P'ei-hsien, as head of the East China Bureau, was to blame for decisions made by the mayor. Tracing this line back further still, the Central Committee in Peking, or a powerful segment of it, was the original source of all policies implemented in East China. But it was 6 months before the students fully understood this chain of causality.

It was the role of the East China Bureau that confused everyone. By lying low, Ch'en P'ei-hsien managed to avoid criticism for many months. Yet it seems from leaflets written later by employees in the East China Bureau that Ch'en's organization was the key to the suppression of radical dissent:

> On June 2, *People's Daily* published the nation's first wall poster. . . . and there was immediately a great upsurge of the Cultural Revolution all over China. But we employees of the East China Bureau administration were told to keep quiet. It was 10 days before we were permitted to put up wall posters, and even then we were hemmed around with all sorts of restrictions. First we were told that our posters had to be "approved" by the Party branch concerned. When some revolutionary cadres disobeyed this rule, it was revoked, only to be replaced by another: that we were not to reveal any "secrets" in our posters. Any criticisms of top officials still had to be submitted to the leadership for approval. . . .
>
> At the beginning of the movement, we exposed two revisionists. . . . one of whom had opposed Chiang Ch'ing in her efforts to reform Peking opera. We were informed that this was not to be made public "for security reasons."[4]

The East China Bureau was also accused of having protected the right wing. A Shanghai journalist named Lin Fang, for example, was heavily criticized by the radicals; they alleged that he was Shanghai's equivalent of Teng T'o in Peking and that he had written many articles against the Party during the 3 bad

[4] From a leaflet entitled "Open Fire on the East China Bureau!" dated December 22, 1966.

years 1959–62. They claimed that a representative of the East
China Bureau had defended Lin Fang as follows: "It is one
thing to recognize that he has made mistakes. If, however, it was
simply a temporary lapse during the 3 bad years, that does not
warrant denouncing him by name in the press" (RG 5:4.2).

The paper that had published Lin Fang's writings, *Shanghai
Evening News,* then defended him: "From 1959 to 1962, Lin Fang
wrote 472 articles. Ninety per cent of these were good or comparatively good" (RG 5:4.2). Because of this intervention, the
case of Lin Fang, which could have led to an embarrassing situation for the Shanghai Party leaders, was not pursued.

It would seem that the repressive activities of the East China
Bureau also extended into industry and that every effort was
made to crush dissent in the factories. A radical account described
a personal intervention by Ch'en P'ei-hsien himself:

During the Socialist Education Movement, Ch'en P'ei-hsien lived
and worked for a time in a Shanghai instruments factory. At the
beginning of June, 1966, the workers at this factory, responding
to the great call of Chairman Mao, rose up and started to expose
certain Party authorities who were leading them back to capitalism.
When Ch'en P'ei-hsien heard that the factory where he himself had
worked was getting out of hand, he immediately sent the vice-director
of the Shanghai branch of the New China News Agency to calm the
situation. This man had no sooner arrived than he began to manipulate people, initiate reactionary trends, and incite the workers to
fight among themselves.

When Ch'en P'ei-hsien found that this did no good, he sent
several more men, one after the other. . . . These men kept trying
to suppress the workers by insisting that they concentrate their
attacks on people who had already been denounced during the
Socialist Education Movement. . . .

When Ch'en P'ei-hsien had been there, he had personally endorsed
the appointment of a certain man as manager. Now he went so far
as to reaffirm his approval of the choice. . . . As a result, the movement at the factory was seriously retarded, and a dozen or more
people became the victims of a wall-poster campaign and had the
worst kind of political labels applied to them. A reign of white terror
engulfed the whole factory.

Ch'en P'ei-hsien called this "a successful experiment" and sent top
men from the East China Bureau and the departments of Industry

and Propaganda to collect material for an article about the factory.
. . . When published, this article was called "a breakthrough, the first
of its kind in the country." (RG 9:3.1)

This passage gives us a glimpse into the background of the Cultural Revolution. It implies that men like Ch'en P'ei-hsien had
used the Socialist Education Movement to get their own people
into office and that the Cultural Revolution was an attempt to
replace them with appointees of the Mao group. It also suggests
that the Mao group might have succeeded, if not for personal
intervention at the highest level by the pragmatists.

In the administration, too, there was repression. We have seen
that Work Teams were sent to the major universities with the
express purpose of keeping the movement in check. At some previous stage, Work Teams had also been sent into the administration. The radicals later published a detailed account of the
Cultural Revolution in Shanghai's Second Bureau of Mechanical
and Electrical Industry, where no less important a person than
the Security Police Chief Huang Ch'ih-po led the Team! When
the Cultural Revolution began, the radicals in the Bureau formed
a "combat group," which caused the authorities considerable embarrassment. Here is a description of the police chief's reaction:

Huang said: "You people in the 'East Wind' combat group are a
terrible lot! . . . You seem to think the Work Team is . . . just a joke,
some kind of traveling theater!"

On July 5, three comrades were talking to Huang. One of them
said: "You say we have rejected the leadership of the Party. I disagree. On June 22, the day after we started our activities, we invited
the head of the Political Department to attend a meeting. . . . On
June 23, we invited you . . ."

Huang, without letting him finish, sprang off the couch so fast
that he left his shoes behind. Arrogantly placing his hands on his
hips, he said: "Do you still want to argue the point, you stupid young
punk? You've forgotten all about Party leadership! You don't give
a damn about the Work Team! You say you want the Party to lead,
but you really think we're not revolutionary enough. You're the only
revolutionaries around here, I suppose. Do you think that just because
you've fooled the workers you can pull the wool over our eyes too?"

On the afternoon of July 16, he told the radicals: "You're not
supporting Chairman Mao; you're supporting Chairman Chiang

[K'ai-shek]! Sure, you wave the red flag—we call that 'using the red flag to attack the red flag.' . . . You have opposed the Party and the Youth League. You haven't listened to advice from anyone—even from your own wives! . . . You've tried to create chaos. You've made things so difficult for the Party cadres that their work has been paralyzed. What kind of people are you? If you thought about your position, you'd break out in a cold sweat!"

At a rally on July 18, ostensibly called to hear "self-criticisms" from six people, Huang said: "These six men have refused to be led by the Party. They have styled themselves 'revolutionaries' and looked on the broad masses as 'arch-conservatives.' . . ."

Later, he said: "I've tried to talk to you. If I were frightened of you, I wouldn't have bothered talking. Now I'm *telling* you: If you don't obey my orders, I have the police, I have the Security Bureau, I have the dictatorship of the proletariat. You youngsters had better smarten up!"

And on another occasion: "Don't you realize that we are the Municipal Committee's Work Team? . . . If you don't do as we say, then we have other methods, not such nice ones. If you're devious with us, we'll be devious with you!"

And again: "You *still* insist on disobeying the Party! Chiang K'ai-shek had 8 million men in his army, and he could not defeat us. He could send that many agents again, and they would fail again. What chance have you got? . . . The Work Team *is* the Party. If you try to take power here, we will see that you lose that power. . . . Exactly how far do you intend to go? . . . Has the Communist Party become an object of hatred in your eyes? If so, you are in grave danger. . . ." (RG 11:4.1)

If these random remarks are in any way reliable, they show that the radicals were not in the least deterred by Huang's bluster. They knew, as he did, that his threat to use the police was an idle one, for that kind of open repression was exactly what they were hoping for. The Cultural Revolution, in these early stages, was certainly not a time for the use of force. It called for the tact and guile of a politician.

Meanwhile, the Municipal Committee tried to provide cover for the hierarchy by preaching the need to raise production. Mayor Ts'ao Ti-ch'iu was quoted as having said in July: "The Work Teams must see that production keeps rising. . . . There must be no interruption in the manufacture and testing of new products. A slackening-off now would set us back years" (RG 6:4.1).

And the head of the Shanghai Party's Industry Department was said to have commented: "Production in Shanghai for the first half of the year has been good. Now we must really roll up our sleeves, and if people accuse us of 'giving priority to industry,' we must not be intimidated" (RG 6:4.1).

This conflict between the Cultural Revolution and production was later to become one of the main issues in the movement. In July, however, most workers agreed with the Shanghai Party's line that production was their first responsibility. As a result, the left wing of the working class stayed small and was constantly open to persecution by the authorities. But these radical groups survived and provided the impetus for the great workers' movement that erupted in November and December.

All in all, the power structure in Shanghai handled the first wave of the Cultural Revolution rather competently. In the colleges, in industry, and in the bureaucracy, dissenters were discouraged and Party authority prevailed. This smothering of left-wing sentiment explains the angry tone of those who kept speaking out. For the radicals, the formation of Red Guard groups, when it came, meant salvation. They were truly brought out, like Jonah, from the jaws of death, and their gratitude to "the great leader, Chairman Mao" was not feigned.

July was their most trying month, for this was the time when the Shanghai authorities achieved almost total independence from the power of the Mao group. According to subsequent newspaper reports, the Central Cultural Revolution Group, the cutting edge of the Maoists' strength, sent representatives to Shanghai to see how the movement was progressing.

In June and July, the Central Committee sent some comrades to see the Shanghai Municipal Committee secretaries. They were met with the reply: "We have no time for social visits." But they persisted. . . .

Ch'en P'ei-hsien and Ts'ao Ti-ch'iu were in Peking at the time, but the top Party officials in Shanghai rang them long distance and together they worked out a plan to deceive the visitors. First, the wall posters that had been kept under lock and key were brought out and put on the walls. Second, the Municipal Committee's own reports on the Cultural Revolution were hidden, and only the ones that would have been sent to the Central Committee anyway were produced for inspection. Third, a request to attend a Municipal Committee meeting was refused point-blank.

The worst of it was that when the representatives went to examine the written materials, the people who worked in the building were ordered to lock their doors, shut the windows, and speak in whispers. The atmosphere was as if an enemy were coming. It was in fact the silence that accompanies a theft. (RG 8:3.1)

On the heels of this official delegation, which presumably went away empty handed, President Liu Shao-ch'i was said to have dropped in. The radicals explained his satisfaction as follows:

Mayor Ts'ao was fond of saying that the Cultural Revolution was far less chaotic in Shanghai than Peking. It was a model for the rest of the country, he boasted. Why was he so brazen? Because a certain person named Liu Shao-ch'i had given him the green light. . . . On his way through Shanghai in July, Liu had told Ts'ao: "Shanghai is very orderly. There is no disruption. This shows that your Municipal Committee enjoys high prestige and commands the obedience of the masses."

Emboldened by this flattery, Ts'ao Ti-ch'iu opposed Chairman Mao even more blatantly and worked even more energetically against the mass movement. (RG 8:3.1)

This, of course, is only half the story. The radicals could not bear the thought that perhaps the prestige of the Municipal Committee arose from a genuine respect on the part of the people for a government that had visibly improved their lot. Everyone remembered the 3 bad years; everyone knew that Shanghai had come a long way since 1962. Perhaps it had all been done with the trick mirrors of revisionism, but it had been done.

This was anathema to the radicals. For them, the course that Shanghai was following could lead only to disaster. It was their job to wrench the leadership back onto the straight and narrow path of Maoism. Let us see how they survived the dark days of June and July and emerged as Red Guards in the triumphal month of August.

3. Student Unrest

To understand the Red Guards, it is important to know what happened in the colleges during the 2 months prior to their appearance. Let us concentrate, then, on one particular campus—the Shanghai Foreign Languages Institute—and study the suppression of student dissent in detail. Although the Institute was not considered important enough to warrant a Work Team, it nevertheless went through essentially the same experience as Shanghai's larger colleges and can therefore serve as a fairly typical model.

First, a word about the way the Institute was structured. The administration was headed by a president and four vice-presidents. This line of authority extended down through the deans and vice-deans of each faculty, or language department (English, German-French, Arabic-Japanese, Spanish, and Russian), and on to the night school, the attached middle school, the library, the language laboratory, and the trade union.

Parallel with these office-holders was a hierarchy of Communist Party committees. The two lines, though distinct in theory, interwove at various points, through people who "wore two hats"—that is, who fulfilled a dual function as Party members and educators. The highest executive body was the Party Committee, headed by a Party secretary. This was where the real power lay, and nobody—especially after the Cultural Revolution began—pretended anything else. Below the Party Committee was a whole network of administrative departments—bureaus of general affairs, educational affairs, propaganda, personnel, publishing, liaison, research, and so on—and below these were the Party committees of the various faculties.

The link between the Party and the student body was provided by "political instructors," who taught each class some 3 or 4 hours a week. The aim of these teachers was not only to raise the general level of political understanding in the class but also to get students to join the Youth League and, eventually, the Communist Party itself. In this sense, their role was not unlike that of the clergy in a Catholic school.

The Institute when my wife and I taught there had more than 2,000 students and roughly 300 Chinese teachers. Many of the teachers were old and semiretired, so that, in practice, the average class had about fifteen students. There were 200 Party members altogether, very few of them students. Four or five students in each class were Youth League members, but probably less than one per class was even a probationary member of the Party. There were also 100 "workers"—cooks, gardeners, groundsmen, carpenters, electricians, and so on. Finally, there were the foreign teachers, who numbered about 40 at the maximum.

Oddly enough, it was the foreign teachers who provided the authorities with their initial pretext for restraining the students. The first wall poster to criticize the Party Committee appeared on June 3, 1966, just when the Cultural Revolution was starting to blow holes in Peking. Entitled "A Few Questions for Our Party Secretary," it ran as follows:

Why doesn't the Party Committee get this Cultural Revolution really moving? The whole country has been howling for months about these writers who have been attacking the Party, yet we didn't have a mass rally until yesterday—and that was only after the Peking University wall posters were publicized. We feel our Party Committee has been lagging behind.

We've spent a lot of time examining our curricula for faults, and that's been necessary. But this is a struggle that will affect the fate of our nation and the world revolution! It's a struggle to defend the Central Committee and Chairman Mao's ideas and the dictatorship of the proletariat! Since it's a matter of life and death, we should hurl ourselves headlong into it! What we want to know is: Can we or can we not commit ourselves totally to this fight?

The Party Secretary says we can't put up posters in the corridors, because the foreign teachers might read them. He says we can't put them up on the campus, because the foreign teachers might go for a walk and see them. He says the dining room is no good either, because the foreign teachers might go in there. Would he mind telling us just where we *can* put them? To say we can write posters, and then to add that the foreigners must not see them, is equivalent to saying we cannot write posters.

If the Party Secretary cares to wander around, he will see that posters have gone up anyway. Does he now want us to take these down?

We invite everybody to comment on these questions.[1]

The Party Secretary's response was quick. The very same day, a poster signed by him went up in the Institute. It did not reply directly to the challenge but turned the attack aside by calling for all-out war on an old scapegoat, the "bourgeois academic." His appeal is worth quoting, as a perfect example of how the Mao group's *political* intentions were sidetracked into less dangerous fields:

A great socialist cultural revolution is blasting through our country, sweeping away all antisocial elements. . . .

For thousands of years, the culture of the exploiting classes has produced "scholars," "authorities," and "academics." Among the present crop are leaders of groups that have contacts abroad, loyal ministers to the throne of foreign interests. Our country has been liberated for 16 years, yet these bourgeois "gentlemen" refuse to surrender to the people. They go on dreaming that the old world will come back.

Some have put on masks and slipped into the Party. Some have even risen to leading positions. They have dug themselves bunkers in the field of culture and posed as "professors" and "experts." But their real purpose has been to attack the Party and to poison the minds of the people. They have maintained relations with imperialists, revisionists, and reactionaries overseas. In 1957, they joined with

[1] From "An Anthology of Wall Posters," published by the Field Army Red Guards of the Shanghai Foreign Languages Institute.

these external forces to launch a furious assault on the Party and the people. In 1959, when our own revisionists were attacking the Central Committee and Chairman Mao, these people again joined in.

Students and comrades, think about this! We cannot coexist with these people. Until they are rooted out, we will not have a moment's peace, nor will we be able to establish socialism. Our country's destiny and the whole world revolution hang in the balance.

These evil people are everywhere. Our Institute is no "Kingdom of Heaven"! We must put on the armor of Mao Tse-tung's ideas and root them out to the last man! We must take over the fields of culture and education and see that Chairman Mao's banner flies proudly over them.[2]

As a direct result of this poster, many of the older teachers in the Institute were criticized. There was no shortage of scholarly types on the staff—people who had at one time studied abroad or attended missionary colleges in China or engaged in research of a purely academic nature.

At no stage did the Party Secretary blatantly order the criticism of this or that teacher. Such tactlessness would only have alienated the students, particularly the radicals, who were very conscious of their right to lead the movement. Nor was there any need for him to play the dictator; he knew from experience that the students were an enthusiastic and excitable lot, with a highly developed sense of moral and political purity. The slightest suggestion that anyone was working against the common good or the teachings of Chairman Mao would provoke a flurry of indignant posters.

He was also aware that student action had to be restricted to harmless targets. If they started investigating the Institute too zealously, they might begin to want to know why any reactionaries had been tolerated on the staff in the first place. This could lead to an attack on the Party Committee, which was ultimately responsible for the educational and administrative policies of the Institute.

He therefore "played it cool" and avoided anything that might provoke a scandal. He used the Youth League as much as pos-

2 Ibid.

sible, keeping himself and his Party Committee out of the lime-light. It was the Youth League, for example, that started a campaign against the Dean of English. A few hints here and there were enough to get young teachers writing posters against this man, who was, after all, very easy to criticize. He came to the Institute once in a blue moon, spending most of his time buried in English literature. He was said to have translated the complete works of Chaucer into Chinese. It would have been hard to find a more typical example of a "bourgeois academic," an antisocial individualist with no concern for the real needs of his people.

The Youth League Secretary also organized a paper war against the five young teachers in the Russian Department who had written the June 3 poster. This was a warning that even such mild criticism of the Party authorities would not be tolerated.

For a while, it seemed that these tactics might work. Most of the students responded energetically to the Party's leadership. They had, after all, been brought up to believe that the Communist Party of China was a "great, glorious, and correct" institution that had saved their country from humiliation and chaos and given the people a dignity and vision they had not possessed for a century. In their growing years, they had seen little or nothing to challenge this interpretation, so they naturally tended to obey the Party.

There were some students in the Institute, however, who were far from being yes men. These were the ones who had seen that the Cultural Revolution was unlike any previous movement. Although the Mao group in Peking had been unable, for tactical reasons, to come out and state unequivocally that this was to be a campaign against Party officials, quite a number of students and teachers in various parts of China had come independently to this conclusion. This nascent left wing was not prepared to obey anyone but a proven Maoist—and the touchstone of Maoism for them was whether a person listened to the people's will and trusted the people's wisdom or whether he acted like a *noli me tangere* bureaucrat.

In our Institute, therefore, the Youth League's campaign against the Dean of English and the five Russian teachers was suddenly interrupted by the appearance on June 7 of a poster attacking the Vice-Secretary of the Youth League himself. He was accused of being a degenerate, the son of a landlord, and a totally irresponsible person who had no right to exercise leadership over the young. (There may have been some truth to this charge, for even the foreign teachers had noticed this man's habit of racing a motorcycle around the campus running track.)

This was a dangerous trend for the Party authorities. The Youth League was a sensitive organization; it was not only an integral part of the power structure but also the level at which students and Party members had most contact with each other. The June 7 poster therefore caused quite a stir, and it was followed by hints from the Party hierarchy that perhaps there were "antisocial elements" among the students.

This sparring became far more serious on June 13, when eight students from fourth-year French put up the following poster:

Something fishy has been going on in the auditorium. Most of the posters on the walls are in good condition, but some that are critical of certain Youth League officials are tattered and torn. In one case, an important heading has been covered by another poster. We would like to know who did this, and for what purpose.

At this stage of the movement, it is still not clear which people in our Institute should be criticized and which should not. But the more we debate, the clearer the issues become. A true Communist is not afraid of criticism. . . . Sticking up a poster so that it partly masks a criticism of the Youth League is an act that betrays some ulterior motive. . . .

On the whole, the progress of the Revolution in our Institute has been excellent. Several thousand wall posters have been put up by revolutionary young teachers and students. But the curious thing is the lack of leadership shown by the administration officials and the top Party political cadres in the various departments—particularly those who know most about the Institute. How many posters have they written? Can they be less well informed than the students? What kind of attitude does this reticence reveal?

Everyone knows it is right for the students to express their opinions. The cadres should encourage them in this. If the students' posters contain factual errors, the cadres should correct them in posters of their own. What they should *not* do is stay on the sidelines. They *must* commit themselves one way or the other.

Mayor Ts'ao Ti-ch'iu said on June 10 that the Cultural Revolution would be a great test for all Party organizations and for every individual Party member. . . .

This is a life-or-death struggle, from which everyone will emerge either a revolutionary or a counterrevolutionary. There is no middle way. We call on our administration officials and top Party political cadres to learn from the fearless spirit of the Institute's masses. Let them be "willing to suffer death by a thousand cuts, in order to unhorse the emperor"! Let them stand up and speak out![3]

This was precisely the kind of challenge the Party Committee wanted to avoid. Although there is no way of proving that the authorities instigated a "spontaneous" reaction to the offensive poster, there was certainly a hail of critical rejoinders from the students and teachers. The radicals later alleged that the Party leaders had been so upset by the threat that they dashed straight off to the Shanghai Municipal Committee for advice. The Education Department was supposed to have told them: "Don't try to answer the charges. Let the Party's critics stick their necks out."

This story could be apocryphal, for the charges were certainly answered. Here, for example, is a poster written by members of the Youth League in the same fourth-year French class of the June 13 attack:

Comrades, we fully support your censure of this poster. You have acted correctly. You have done well.

The poster is a venomous piece of warmongering, which only serves to expose the true intentions of its writers. Some of those who signed it may be merely overzealous, but others are guilty of all kinds of wrong thinking. Because they do not identify themselves with the working class, they have taken this opportunity to vent their spite on the Party and the administration. We sincerely hope that these misguided people will be helped by the Cultural Revolution to rein in before they reach the precipice!

Let us always listen to the voice of the Party and do as it says. Let us raise the great red banner of Mao Tse-tung's thought on high,

[3] *Ibid.*

stand shoulder to shoulder with all the revolutionary teachers and students of the Institute, and open a withering fire on representatives of the bourgeoisie who have sneaked into the Party, and on "scholars" and "authorities" who are against the Party and socialism![4]

This kind of argument was hard for the left wing to refute without seeming disloyal or even subversive. The fourth-year French students evidently decided to let it go at that for the time being, for the next 10 days were relatively calm. But the radicals were undaunted by this opposition and went ahead with plans for more drastic action.

The Party officials seem to have been busy, too. The radicals later claimed that the Municipal Committee ordered all college committees to select a representative list of "bourgeois academics" for future criticism. The names were to be chosen from those most frequently attacked in student wall posters, so "the masses" would feel that it was they who were running the movement. Actually, said the radicals, this was simply a plot to distract attention from the authorities.

Perhaps the Party Secretary at our Institute felt he should include a high official, to show how "ruthlessly" he was carrying out the Cultural Revolution, or perhaps he was settling a personal score. Whatever the reason, he came out on June 22 with a long poster attacking one of the Institute's vice-presidents. The man in question was a great favorite around the campus, a burly, jolly old fellow, with crew-cut gray hair and a passion for tennis and swimming. It was common knowledge that he had been with Mao in Yenan, and he was treated as a kind of retired revolutionary. The general attitude toward him was that he had served his country well in its time of trouble, and that if he now chain-smoked or took a lot of holidays or avoided manual labor like the plague—well, he was old, he should take it easy now.

There were many men like this in pre–Cultural Revolution China. Perhaps this was one meaning of the word "revisionism." Anyway, Vice-President Chou got a hair-raising blast from the Party Secretary:

4 *Ibid.*

Everyone knows that the years 1959–62 were very difficult for our country. On the home front, besides three bad harvests due to natural calamities, there was an attack on the Party by right-wing opportunists. Throughout the society, there were four retrograde tendencies —toward regional independence, toward liberalization, toward the rehabilitation of people labeled "rightists" in 1957, and toward pessimism. On the international front, the imperialists, the reactionaries, and the revisionists joined in a chorus against us. Soviet revisionism, in particular, put intolerable pressure on our Party, trying to intimidate us.

At that time, many good comrades, members and nonmembers of the Party, rolled up their sleeves and battled against adversity.

Comrade Chou, on the other hand, took this opportunity to attack the Party. In 1960, when I had not been long at this Institute, I happened to be in his office one day and saw him putting on a terrible act, baring his teeth and holding his head, snarling and pounding the table and saying: "That Shanghai Municipal Committee is a bunch of damn bureaucrats! You ask for an interview and you don't hear from them for 6 months! I've never experienced such leadership! What have I done wrong that they treat me like this? Can't they tell a man from a beast? I'm not some second-rate hack. I want to see the Mayor. I want to make a report to the Central Committee. After all, I was sent here by the Central Committee Secretariat!" And he repeatedly demanded an apology from the Municipal Committee.

Everyone think a minute. At that time, who was cursing the Party? Landlords, rich peasants, counterrevolutionaries, antisocial elements, rightists, and Khrushchev types—*they* were cursing the Party! Now why did Chou want an apology from the Municipal Committee?

In 1960–62, people were really suffering. But Chou spent all his time complaining about a "skin disease" and insisting he had to convalesce. He went to various lakes and mountain resorts and then he simply had to take the waters at Tsingtao. The Municipal Committee told him the Shantung situation was serious and he could not go. He was furious and pointed out that a certain member of the Municipal Committee [probably Mayor K'e Ch'ing-shih, who had a chronic kidney ailment] had gone north for the sake of his health, so why couldn't he?

Was he sick? No. And I can prove it.

On November 3, 1960, the Institute invited a German expert to dinner. Chou said he was not feeling too well, so we sent him to the East China Hospital for a check-up. The doctor examined him and said: "It's nothing. He needn't stay in the hospital. If he goes home and rests for a couple of days, he'll be fine."

But Chou refused to leave! When the doctor tried to persuade him, he shouted: "So, a man doesn't even have the right to be hospitalized!" After trying for some time to make him see reason, the doctor gave in. Chou stayed in the hospital for quite a few days, though there was nothing whatever the matter with him. He did this for two reasons: to have a good loaf and to embarrass the Party.

Later, when the Socialist Education Movement started, he refused to do manual labor or live with the workers. "I simply couldn't stomach it," he said. At the Institute, he consistently avoided Thursday-afternoon manual labor; he just took a holiday on Thursdays and didn't even come to the office. He also refused to live with the students for a while, though Chairman Liu Shao-ch'i said that top cadres who were unwilling to share the same conditions as the students would not be permitted to hold high office. Chou's reaction was: "*You* go and make small-talk with them!"

There is no need to describe his opposition to the Party Committee, his insulting and disruptive behavior. Enough has been said to show the kind of person he is.[5]

This malicious attack put Vice-President Chou under the blackest of clouds for the next 9 months. The students had no way of proving or disproving the charges against him; most of them simply believed the Party Secretary.

This tactic kept the Institute nicely under the control of the Party Committee until the end of June. The students and teachers concentrated their energy on the handful of scapegoats that had been "rooted out," spending a full 2 weeks on an intensive criticism of the Vice-Secretary of the Youth League. The Party Committee had decided to sacrifice this official but used his disgrace to stall for time. While everyone was busy denouncing him, the movement lapsed.

This situation was radically changed by an open letter that arrived at the Institute at the beginning of July. It was sent by some graduates of our Institute who had gone to Peking No. 2 Foreign Languages Institute for further studies. They had writ-

[5] *Ibid.*

ten, they said, because they had heard that the Cultural Revolution in their former college was meeting with resistance.

The letter could not be hushed up, for it had also been pasted on the walls of the Peking Institute, where it had received a lot of publicity. Our Institute was soon talking of nothing else. The Party Committee must have watched anxiously, for the gist of the letter was that the revolutionary masses of the Shanghai Institute should not waste their time on small fry but should strike at the heart of the trouble—the Party Committee itself!

The importance of this threat was acknowledged by the Party Secretary, who immediately wrote a brief wall poster. The text could be summed up in the one word *touché:* "After reading the poster by some former students of ours, now studying and working in Peking No. 2 Foreign Languages Institute, I consider it a revolutionary document. It shows that our comrades are deeply concerned for the Cultural Revolution in their alma mater. . . ."[6]

If he thought that that would do the trick, he was in for a disappointment. On the same day, July 5, five students from the Spanish Department produced the strongest criticism to date of the Party authorities. In a long and detailed poster, they listed seven grievances against the hierarchy:

1. Neither the Party Committee nor the faculty branches of the Party have given any person-to-person leadership in the campaign against anti-Party writers. Why is this?

2. We were going to criticize our Vice-Dean, but both the Party Secretary and our branch Secretary came out and said he was a good comrade. As a result, we never got to put up our posters, and some students even apologized to the Vice-Dean. Is this not repressing student initiative?

3. Quite a few people have been denounced in the course of the movement, but precious few have been fully exposed. The only person we have investigated thoroughly is the Youth League Vice-Secretary, and he was a rather obvious case anyway. While we have been busy exposing him, more dangerous enemies still have power, and they are using this time to learn how to avoid our attacks. What we want to know is: Where do we go from here?

6 *Ibid.*

4. Some of the people who have criticized the Party Committee have been accused by their fellow comrades of "having an antisocial outlook," "spreading poisonous ideas," "diverting the main thrust," and "acting from ulterior motives." Now, if the Party Committee is free from error, it should not be afraid of criticism. On the contrary, it should protect and encourage its critics. And if a few counter-revolutionary posters appear, what harm is there in that? They can be dealt with at a later date.

5. The cadres who know the facts about this Institute have not revealed them. Some say they don't want to put words in people's mouths. But if they criticize someone, and he's proved guilty, they've done the right thing. If he's innocent, surely no amount of posters could make him guilty. So what are they waiting for? Do they want to be accused of "defending the emperor"?

6. We've been criticized for refusing to do manual labor. We have profound respect for manual labor, but at a time like this, when the fate of the Party and nation is at stake, how can we afford to relax and do odd jobs? Three hours a week for more than 2,000 teachers and students is 6,000 man-hours! We can't waste that kind of energy. In 6,000 hours, we could dig up evidence that would make the Party's enemies shake in their boots!

7. Not all the students have been mobilized. Some say there's no use mobilizing everyone, because they won't find anything anyway. We say they will! They must be free to criticize the Party and examine the available evidence. The Party must trust the masses. Party members should not be able to eat or sleep until everyone is fully mobilized! We will certainly not eat or sleep until all the questions in this Institute have been answered! And it won't be done in a day. . . .[7]

This poster led to a switch in tactics by the radicals. Instead of merely sniping at the administration, they began to produce facts. Wall posters many pages long appeared, full of name lists, statistical tables, and analyses of the class backgrounds of office-holders, teachers, and students.

The source of this information is something of a mystery. Part of it could have come from the graduates in Peking, but the material is so thorough that it might have been provided by Party members in the Institute. If so, the "defectors'" were running a

[7] *Ibid.*

risk, for at this point most people on the campus suspected the radicals of engaging in a deliberate, cynical, and ultimately subversive attempt to embarrass the Party leaders. The walls reflected this pro-Party sentiment in no uncertain manner.

The radical posters, however, made up in quality what they lacked in numbers. Their allegations simply could not be ignored, and the more conservative students, in the very act of trying to refute the material, found themselves forced to confront some startling possibilities. In comparison with their own often juvenile and stereotyped work, that of the radicals was outrageous in scope and vicious in execution.

As an example, here are some extracts from a poster signed by seventeen "sons and daughters of revolutionary cadres." This was put up on July 7 and became famous as one of the most timely and hard-hitting exposés of the movement. Entitled "Who Has the Real Power in the Shanghai Foreign Languages Institute?" it began with a preamble about the Institute's working class:

> Workers, peasants, and soldiers are the main force in this Cultural Revolution. They are the best at studying Chairman Mao's works; they are the strongest opponents of antisocial elements; they are a dependable and invincible army.
>
> Some of the workers at our Institute have been here a long time and know better than anyone what goes on. We must mobilize and organize them, encourage them to tell what they know. There are more than 100 workers here, yet not one has been asked to join the Cultural Revolution Office. Why is this? We are going to see that the workers play their part in the movement![8]

After the preamble came a criticism of people who tried to bog down the movement in petty details. This was an obvious reference to the Party Secretary's attack on the Vice-President:

> Some Party cadres avoid the main issues. They bring up little things like "Vice-President Chou used a car to go to the hospital," "Vice-President Yao has a filthy temper," "President Wang takes her children to the beach." We are involved in a grave political

8 *Ibid.*

struggle between the bourgeoisie and the proletariat. The issue is ultimately whether or not there will be a restoration of capitalism in this country. Yet some Party cadres are more interested in the details of other people's lives than in whether they are working against socialism. One woman cadre in the Russian Department has written a poster against her husband. Fine, but she's never come out with a word against a *real* enemy. And it's not as if there were nothing to criticize! For a long time now, this Institute has been peddling stuff that is foreign, feudal, revisionist, or just plain irrelevant! There are plenty of skeletons in the cupboard, and we mean to expose every one![9]

This was followed by an elaboration of the charge that the Institute had pursued a reactionary education policy:

This university belongs to the people. Its job is to train linguists urgently needed by our country. It should be the kind of institution where the children of the working class can study. In the past few years, however, it has served the sons and daughters of the bourgeoisie. Although it was built with the sweat and blood of the people, it has become a bourgeois salon and a citadel of counterrevolution. . . . Comrades, does this not make you seethe with indignation? How can we allow such a state of affairs to continue?

In 1964, so the story goes, the Institute "opened its gates" to children of the working class. But let's have a look at what happened to those who enrolled. In the English Department, for example, there were four classes for students starting from scratch. With one exception, all these youngsters came from villages. At the Institute, no attention whatever was given to their political training. The faculty Party branch practically ignored them. Their teachers were infected with a bourgeois outlook and were too busy demanding respect from their students to bother about their class backgrounds. The teaching methods were downright fascist! If a student couldn't answer a question, he was ordered out of the classroom. If he made mistakes in pronunciation, he was teased mercilessly. "Go to the clinic and get some medical attention!" one boy was told. And some teachers said: "Your brain seems to be different. When *I* hear a thing, I master it immediately. You can't." Students were reduced to tears by this kind of treatment. Some were so upset they couldn't eat for days. Many were so terrified of their teachers that they spent

9 *Ibid.*

their whole time trying not to make them angry. As a result, their morale was abysmally low. . . .

On the other hand, there were "special" classes for "advanced" students. Here, the accent was on professional rather than ideological ability. So much so, that the students began to look on their intellect as an investment! One girl who graduated from this sort of class was assigned to work in a military foreign languages institute. She wept and made a great fuss and absolutely refused to go. She even got her mother to come to the Institute and plead her cause. . . .[10]

The poster then went on to even more serious charges, alleging that the Party authorities had not only discriminated against the children of the working class but had also deliberately prevented them from getting any kind of political foothold in the Institute. And here, for the first time, statistics began to play a part:

Let us now turn to the Russian Department and see what kind of students were enrolled between 1962 and 1964 and what kind of students were appointed to responsible positions in the Youth League:

In 1962, there were 114 new students of Russian. Of these, 15 (13 per cent) were from working-class families. Of the 6 who became cadres in the Youth League, 3 were working-class children.

In 1963, 93 students enrolled. Thirteen (13 per cent) were from working-class families. Of 6 who became cadres in the Youth League, only one was from the working class.

In 1964, after the Institute had supposedly "opened its gates" to working-class children, not a single boy or girl of working-class origin was appointed as a cadre in the Youth League!

The reason for this is not hard to find. When we look at the class backgrounds of people in authority in the Russian Department's Youth League Party branch in 1964, we see that 2 were from rich or reactionary families, 1 was from a small-industrialist's family, and 1 was from a petty-bourgeois family!

No wonder the morale of the Russian Department was so bad![11]

In a final burst, the writers appealed to all students to make a thorough investigation of their own departments and not to

10 *Ibid.*
11 *Ibid.*

tolerate an instant longer the presence of notorious reactionaries
in important Party and administrative posts. Note that we have
come a long way from the cautiously probing criticisms of a
month earlier. It was unthinkable in June that a student poster
would end with questions like these:

> How is it that roughly 20 of the departmental officials come from
> big-landlord and big-capitalist backgrounds? How is it that only 3
> out of more than 100 workers on the campus have got as far as
> joining the Party? How is it that the name of this Institute stinks
> across the length and breadth of the land? And how is it that Tung
> Chi-p'ing, who graduated from this Institute in 1963, brought shame
> to the whole country by his defection to the United States?[12]

The Party Committee was shaken by the severity of this attack.
Nor could it very easily strike back. In the atmosphere of the
moment, which my own students described to me as "unprecedented freedom of speech," it would have been foolish for the
Party authorities to make any overt move against the left wing.
Instead, they applied as much political and ideological pressure
as they dared. In every department, meetings of student leaders
were held, in an effort to "unify their thinking." At the same
time, the routine discussion groups were asked to consider the
question: "Is the Party Committee 'Yenan' or is it 'Sian'?" This
drastic oversimplification shows the extent to which the Party
had been forced onto the defensive. They were asking the students and teachers to say, in effect, whether the Party Committee
was revolutionary or reactionary.

Faced by this dichotomy, most people agreed that the Party
leaders were still a good deal closer to "Yenan" and Chairman
Mao than to "Sian" and Chiang K'ai-shek. The Youth League
helped the waverers make up their minds by formally declaring
the Party Committee "Yenan" and putting up a lot of posters to
prove it. Before long, the radicals again found themselves the
target of a "spontaneous" propaganda campaign.

They persisted, nevertheless. They seemed in fact to thrive on
attempts to silence them, and it was not long before even more

[12] *Ibid.*

detailed and virulent analyses of the Institute's shortcomings were appearing on the walls. On July 14, for instance, some third-year French students produced revelations that must have shocked even the most skeptical:

In 1963, 16 students graduated from the French Department. (There should have been 20, but 1 was sent abroad to study, 2 had to repeat a year, and one was so appalled by the 3 bad years that he ran away to Hong Kong.)

Of the 16 graduates, no less than 6 got into serious trouble later: One (Tung Chi-p'ing) defected to the U.S. Embassy in Burundi in 1964.

One got mixed up with a counterrevolutionary clique in a certain university and was arrested in 1965 and sentenced to 3 years in prison.

One was tainted by revisionist ideas and had connections with counterrevolutionaries. After his graduation, he was sent to work in Peking. Overburdened with guilt, he tried to commit suicide in the river at Tientsin. This attempt failed, and he was taken back to the capital in custody.

One had a bourgeois outlook. He was appointed to a post in Peking but refused to go, saying it was too far from home. The following year, he was given a job in the Shanghai Academy of Sciences but again refused. To this day, he still lives at home, enjoying a purely parasitic existence.

One was quite a playboy while he was at the Institute. After graduation, he, too, was sent to Peking, but he adopted a very poor attitude and proved incapable of doing his job.

One showed signs of mental illness even before graduation. He was assigned a job in Peking but simply could not do the work.

You may not know this, comrades, but it costs the state 1,300 yuan to put a student through a year of college. (In our Institute, it costs more, because we have foreign teachers.) In 4 years, then, the state shells out 5,200 yuan per student. In other words, 8 peasants toiling for a year could just produce the cost of a year's schooling for a student! These 6 graduates from the French Department cost the state 31,000 yuan, or the equivalent of 192 peasants slaving for a year! And these 6 turned out traitors, counterrevolutionaries, and lunatics!

Then consider the political effects: A defector like Tung Chi-p'ing brought untold shame on the Party and the country. By praising

U.S. imperialism, by insulting our socialist system, our Party, and our great leader Chairman Mao, he did immeasurable harm to China's international prestige.[13]

On July 19, the same French students came out with a long supplement to their poster. They were particularly angry about the training of "specialists" and the tendency of the Institute to neglect the students' political development:

> Students in these "special" classes had better teachers, better equipment, and better conditions. They had access to textbooks that other classes could not read. They had the best tape recorders. They were "teacher's pets"; they were often told of things before anyone else, and, when visitors came to the Institute, it was they who showed them around. They were even given nice sunny dormitories facing south!
>
> As for their class background, their political and ideological level, this was not considered important. All they had to do was be technically proficient.[14]

And more statistics were adduced to make their point. Although the students lacked figures on the size of two English classes, here is a table[15] of which that any sociologist would be proud:

Faculty	Year	Class	Number of Students	Per Cent Not from Proletariat
French	4	1	9	86
French	3	1	14	36
German	4	1	12	75
German	3	1	14	72
English	4	2	—	57
English	3	4	—	70
French	1	4	15	60
English	1	15	10	60

The last two lines of the table, said the students, proved that even after 1964—when the Institute was said to have begun favoring children of working-class background—more than half

13 *Ibid.*
14 *Ibid.*
15 *Ibid.*

of the students enrolled were from nonproletarian backgrounds.

The aim of the authorities, the poster went on, was "to ensure that the successors to the Revolution would be bourgeois; they planned to stuff the students with the literary heritage of eighteenth- and nineteenth-century Europe, so that after graduation they would go out with their minds thoroughly poisoned and preach the values of the bourgeoisie."[16]

Material like this was dynamite to the Institute's Party Committee, and steps were taken in July to strengthen the power of the administration. One of these moves was to transfer the Party Secretary of the English Department, a tough and experienced organizer, to head the Cultural Revolution Office, the body responsible for running the movement in the Institute.

Another step, apparently carried out on orders from the Municipal Committee, was to classify all teachers and students into one of three categories: left wing, middle of the road, or right wing. This was an extension of the principle applied to older teachers in the month of June, whereby their names were noted down for future criticism. Now the whole Institute was to get a similar rating, and the findings would be inserted in the personnel files and student records.

This was a departure from previous policy. The Institute had always kept a record of each student's academic progress, and this had almost certainly included comments on his general sociability, political attitudes, level of ideological understanding, and so on. But there had never before been a sudden-death classification of students into "good" or "bad," "for" the Party or "against" it, "revolutionary" or "reactionary."

It was done not only in our Institute but in every college in Shanghai. Later, the practice spread to schools, factories, and offices. Wherever it occurred, it was surrounded by great secrecy, as if the authorities knew they were doing something wrong. When the radical students found out about it, they immediately assumed that their names had been put in the right-wing column, and that "goody-goody" students and Party toadies had been classified as left wing.

16 *Ibid.*

They were probably right to suspect the worst. There is evidence that the classification of students and teachers was a nationwide phenomenon and that it emanated from the Work Teams sent out by Liu Shao-ch'i and Teng Hsiao-p'ing to police the movement in all the major colleges. Premier Chou En-lai, in a statement made on July 22, referred specifically to the Work Teams. They had all, he said, to a greater or lesser degree, compiled material that could be described as "intimidating the students." He listed seven ways of collecting such information:

1. Reports from the Work Teams to higher levels, listing the students in two groups, with those who had found fault with the Work Team put in the category "counterrevolutionary."
2. Illegal lists, classifying people as left wing, middle of the road, and right wing.
3. Confessions made under pressure.
4. Evidence contributed by supporters of the Work Teams.
5. Memos labeling people "good" or "bad," depending on whether or not they approved of the Work Teams.
6. Diaries kept by Work Team members, with notes of conversations.
7. Minutes of Work Team meetings.[17]

By the time Chou En-lai made this statement, significant changes had taken place in the capital. There were signs that the Mao group, having lost the initiative for the greater part of June and July, was now once again winning the upper hand. For one thing, there was Chairman Mao's famous swim in the Yangtze on July 16 and the wide publicity given to it. For another, there was mounting criticism of the Work Teams, culminating in their removal from the colleges by order of the Central Committee on or around July 18.

This should have meant a great boost for the radical students, but the power of the establishment was still very strong. In the colleges, despite the erosion of confidence caused by the relentless attacks from the left, the Party Committees still retained the allegiance of most students and teachers. Few people realized

17 *Ibid.*

what the withdrawal of the Work Teams meant, and only a minority believed the Party had repressed the radicals.

Because of this power, the Shanghai Municipal Committee kept control of the movement. At this stage, it seems to have been anxious to slow the pace, for, according to a later radical newspaper, it got the head of the Education Department, Ch'ang Hsi-p'ing, to apply the brakes:

At the end of July, just when the teachers and students were on the point of finding out what had really been going on inside the Party, up popped an anxious Ch'ang Hsi-p'ing with an announcement that every college was to pass into the "summing-up stage" of the movement. And he was careful to allot plenty of time for this premature conclusion: "If 3 weeks are not enough," he said, "take 4." (RG 1:4.1)

This was an interesting remark in the light of what followed. As we shall see, Ch'ang Hsi-p'ing's "3 or 4 weeks" just happened to overlap a crucial Party meeting in Peking, from which the Mao group was to emerge with unprecedented strength.

Small wonder, then, that the Shanghai authorities—and, presumably, their counterparts all over the country—wanted to bring the movement to an early end.

4. The Eleventh Plenum

The bitter power struggle of June and July culminated on August 1, with the convening of a Party Plenum (the Eleventh Plenary Session of the Eighth Central Committee of the Chinese Communist Party). There were rumors that the Mao group had forced the Plenum by moving units of the People's Liberation Army into positions around the capital. Be that as it may, the 13-day conference was a victory for the Maoists.

The subject of the Red Guards was not broached at the Plenum but was kept as a trump card should the Mao group's plans go awry. Nuclei of subsequent Red Guard organizations were present at the conference table, however. *Peking Review* Number 34 for 1966 listed "representatives of revolutionary teachers and students from institutions of higher learning in Peking" among the participants. This was a novelty, and it must have given the old Party professionals plenty of food for thought.

The Plenum had a profound effect on the Cultural Revolution. Even before the formal sessions were over, reports reaching the provinces spurred the radical students to renew their attacks on the Party authorities. And there was another burst of activity when the delegates returned from Peking.

The Mao group anticipated large-scale resistance. Mao himself is reported to have said as the Plenum ended: "They agree now, but what about when they get home?" We shall see from our study of Shanghai that this doubt was well founded and that the Party authorities, far from obeying the decision of the Plenum

64

and letting the students have their head, actually intensified their efforts to control the movement. The creation of the Red Guards, less than a week after the end of the conference, was a drastic attempt by the Mao group to circumvent this opposition.

Shanghai's resistance took several forms. One was the suppression of material. The radicals claimed that Mayor Ts'ao Ti-ch'iu, while attending the Plenum, had been given a copy of a wall poster written by Miss Nieh Yuan-tzu, the Peking University philosophy teacher whose poster of May 25 had led to the fall of P'eng Chen. Miss Nieh, it appears, had produced a second poster, revealing the "crimes" of Ch'ang Hsi-p'ing, the head of Shanghai's Education Department. This was designed to have the same effect on Shanghai that her first had had on Peking. Mayor Ts'ao, according to the radicals, took the poster straight to Party Secretary-General Teng Hsiao-p'ing, who advised him not to mention it in Shanghai.

Ts'ao denied this later, claiming that neither he nor any of the other Shanghai delegates had exchanged so much as a word with Teng Hsiao-p'ing throughout the Plenum. The radicals were scornful: How could the leaders of China's largest city not have had dealings with the Secretary-General of the Party during a conference lasting almost a fortnight—especially with the country embarking on a great new movement? (RG 8:3.1)

Another form of resistance to the Mao group involved the interpretation of the decision of the Plenum. This document—the famous Sixteen Points—represented a reluctant compromise between highly antagonistic forces and was therefore vague and semicontradictory in places. It gave the students carte blanche to combat "bourgeois reactionary authorities," yet it barely mentioned that Party members were to be the principal targets. It restricted the students' power by forbidding violence. It exempted scientists, technicians, and white-collar workers altogether and left the army to its own devices. It also gave local Party committees the right to decide which of the people criticized would be featured by name in the press.

The Sixteen Points caused much of the subsequent strife among student groups. It was for a long time the Bible of the young revolutionaries, the only clue they had as to what was expected of them. It was easy for unscrupulous Party authorities to sway large numbers of students by using the Sixteen Points as a weapon against extremism and a shield for the Party. This happened in cities as far apart as Canton and Harbin, and it is clear that the moderate delegates to the Plenum had agreed on a coordinated exploitation of the loopholes in the text of the document.

The radicals saw no contradictions; for them, the Sixteen Points was a broadside against the Party bureaucrats. Did not point seven state unequivocally: "In certain schools, units, and Work Teams of the Cultural Revolution, some of the authorities have organized counterattacks against the people who put up posters against them. . . . This . . . is absolutely impermissible"? There were groups of students all over the country who felt they had been victimized in this way; the Sixteen Points made them sure of themselves, and their actions against the authorities grew bolder.

The problem was that the left wing had no way of *proving* that the Party had deliberately repressed it, and the Sixteen Points offered no advice on this score. The Mao group had predicted this and tried to resolve it by appealing directly to the students. Wide publicity was given to two dramatic actions by Mao himself. The first was his writing of a wall poster on August 5, in which he called on the students to "bombard the headquarters!" The second was his appearance on August 10 with a large group of "Peking revolutionary students," when he said: "Concern yourselves with affairs of state; carry this Great Proletarian Cultural Revolution through to the end!" For those who had ears to hear, Mao was calling for an all-out assault on his opponents within the Party.

News of these events reached the provinces hot on the heels of the text of the Sixteen Points, which was made public on August 8. The reaction in the colleges was immediate. To get an idea of what happened, let us look again at the Shanghai Foreign Languages Institute.

Until August 11, only one person in the Institute had been publicly humiliated. That was in June, when the Vice-Secretary of the Youth League had been paraded around the campus.

Then, on August 11, a group of students in the Spanish Department responded to events in Peking by organizing what they called an exorcism—literally "a meeting to combat evil spirits." This was a distinct escalation of the Cultural Revolution. Staff, students, workers, and Party members attended the spectacle, at which no less than eighty-one people, mostly teachers who had been severely criticized in wall posters, were held up to ridicule. They were all led around the grounds wearing dunce caps, and some were pushed or hit as they went. "No one was seriously injured," said one of my students, "nothing a few sticking plasters couldn't fix." The Party authorities did nothing to curb the students. In fact, they probably encouraged them. As long as the teachers were being attacked, the Party itself was unlikely to come under fire.

Most of those who got hats on August 11 were people with obvious faults. Here is a list of the English teachers involved:

1. The Dean, an old man said to have translated the works of Chaucer into Chinese.

2. The Vice-Dean, a former member of the Democratic League, now very old.

3. A grammar teacher, declared a rightist in 1957, when he had joined with several others to attack the Party.

4. An old woman who had been educated in the United States. Her son was a rightist.

5. A phonetics teacher, whose case is described below.

6 and 7. Two contracted teachers, who had not worked for years but had been drawing salaries. Later, they were both dismissed.

8. A fourth-year teacher whose father had been Premier of China under Chiang K'ai-shek. He was accused of slandering the Party and spreading poison in his teaching. Later, pistols and rifles were found in his house. He had been labeled a rightist in 1957, and this classification had never been revoked.

9 and 10. Two young teachers. The statement of one of them appears below. The students later decided that these two had been hatted by mistake, and they received official apologies.

11. A graduate of St. John's University, Shanghai. She was accused of retaining a bourgeois mentality.

12. A nun who had worked in the church before 1949, when, it was claimed, she had collaborated with the imperialists for counterrevolutionary purposes.[1]

Such people made perfect victims. With or without high hats, they were no threat to anyone, and the Party authorities knew this very well. There is even evidence to suggest that the Party itself decided who was to be hatted that day. Here is a statement made by the phonetics teacher (5 in the above list), in which he describes how he came to be selected for punishment.

During the early phase of the movement, I attended teachers' study groups, but, whenever I tried to speak, I was refuted with such force that I became afraid to open my mouth.

A while ago, after reading some wall posters against the Party authorities, I did speak out at a meeting. I said that, if we were to expose the faults of the Party Committee, then those who knew the facts should make them public.

After the meeting, I was surrounded threateningly by many young teachers and students, who demanded to know why I had said this. They shouted slogans at me and accused me of wanting to dispense with the Party's leadership.

I went out to read posters, but my heart was so full of pain that I could not concentrate. Just then, a young teacher came up and asked me to go with him to the reference library. There I found some twenty teachers waiting. Before I could even sit down they shouted at me: "You got up at that meeting and threatened to write an attack on the Party. What's the difference between you and the 1957 rightists?"

This is the treatment I got, and I hadn't even written a thing! All I did was make a suggestion.

That evening I went to see the Secretary of the English Department. I told him: "Since liberation I have always supported the Party and the socialist system."

He replied: "You had better write out all the things you have said and done against the Party."

I protested my innocence, but he insisted. I now realize that it was then that he put my name on the list of teachers to be hatted. I had previously seen a list of the teachers who had been most severely criticized in student wall posters. My name was not on it; yet, I was

[1] From notes taken during meetings at the Institute.

dragged out and hatted on August 11. It is clear that I was added at the last minute.

Since then, even my children have been reviled.[2]

Another teacher hatted that day (9 above) had similar criticism to make of the English Department Party Secretary:

He put me on the black list as a rightist. He said his criterion was the behavior of teachers during the 3 bad years [1959–62]. And what did *he* do during the 3 bad years? He raised sheep! Two or three of them, right in front of his house! I also happen to know that he once bought a watch for 12 yuan, which he repaired and sold again for 60 yuan. [The Secretary denies this vigorously but is told to be silent.]

I have faults, certainly. But he never helped me overcome them. In the 4 years since my graduation, he has only spoken to me twice. To my face he called me "a responsible teacher"; behind my back, he said I was "a complicated case."

When the Cultural Revolution began, I had many wall posters written against me. The Secretary said: "Don't worry. You won't be punished for that." The truth was, he read all the posters before they were put up! He even told one young teacher: "Write anything you like, but it should be harsher." This was as much as to say: "Don't be afraid to exaggerate." Under his direction, that young teacher wrote things about me that were neither true nor relevant.[3]

The Secretary of young teachers in the English Department then added his evidence:

The English Department Party Secretary told me this young teacher had serious faults. He also jeered at me and said I was not daring enough in my criticisms of others. I asked him to talk to the teacher, but he said he had no time. (Actually, he spent most of his time repairing transistors and motorcycles!)

He first got us to write posters against old and middle-aged teachers, then extended it to include young teachers also. "Just base your criticisms on impressions," he said. "If you insist on investigating the details, you'll never get around to writing anything."

In July, one of this teacher's own students wrote a poster against

2 *Ibid.*
3 *Ibid.*

him. The Secretary was delighted. Other students followed suit, but some of them suggested that the root cause of their teacher's faults was the lack of guidance from the Party authorities. The Secretary was upset at this and told me to write a poster saying the Party had done all it could but the teacher had not listened.[4]

These testimonies are not entirely reliable, because the witnesses were trying to clear themselves, but they represent a widespread belief among the students and teachers that the Party itself had selected the victims of August 11.

Among the eighty-one people hatted that day, however, were ten who must be considered separately. They too were scapegoats, and they too may have been chosen by the Party. The important thing is that they themselves were *members* of the Party.

The ten were described in a radical poster as follows:

    1. Head of the Institute Party Committee's Propaganda Bureau, member of the Party Committee, head of the Marxist-Leninist Study Group. Family background: merchant. Has made serious mistakes. His wife is a counterrevolutionary.

    2. Head of the Institute Party Committee's Education Affairs Bureau, in charge of the President's office, member of the Party Committee. Has made serious mistakes. He had control of educational and administrative affairs, as well as the United Front.

    3. Dean of the Russian Department, member of the Party Committee. Class background: big landlord. Has made serious mistakes.

    4. Vice-Dean of English. Big-landlord background.

    5. Vice-Dean of English. Father was a highly placed office-worker.

    6. Second in Command of Party members in the German-French Department. Comes from a worker's family. Former member of the Kuomintang. Has made serious mistakes.

    7. Dean of the Japanese-Arabic Department. Former member of the Party Committee. Bourgeois background. Father a rightist. Has made serious mistakes.

    8. Second in Command of Institute Party members in the Preparedness Bureau [possibly a civil defense office]. Bourgeois background. Has made serious mistakes.

[4] *Ibid.*

9 and 10. Two vice-chairmen of the trade union in the Institute. Both from big-landlord families.[5]

This is a scrappy list. At the time it was drawn up, the students did not even know all their victims by name, much less the exact nature of their "crimes." Yet they had managed to root out ten Party members, three of whom were on the Party Committee. From the authorities' point of view, however, this was not a great price to pay. There were more than 200 Party members at the Institute. They had sacrificed 10, in a movement that was, in theory, aimed specifically at Party authorities taking the road back to capitalism. They had every reason to congratulate themselves—as long as the students were content to stop there and not raise the next question: Whose fault was it that 10 Party members with bad class backgrounds had been permitted to hold important administrative posts? This question was to be avoided like the plague, for it pointed directly at the Party Secretary himself, and through him to the Shanghai Education Department and the Municipal Committee. If too many students started this sort of probing, where would it stop?

But on August 11, the Party at the Institute was still safe. Most of the students agreed in principle with the exorcism. Only a handful of radicals were dissatisfied and wanted to continue the process to its logical conclusion. Unfortunately for the hierarchy, this radical group had a dynamism and a determination that were almost irrepressible. Even before the end of the August 11 incident, they were already preparing for a bigger and better exorcism the following day. Their stated aim was "merely to rectify some of the errors of the first rally." They would take six or eight of the people already humiliated and do the job again but more thoroughly.

This is what they said, but the Party had reason to suspect more ambitious plans. One fourth-year student reported having seen them prepare at least fifteen hats; another student said more than seventy were ready and waiting.

Somehow, the word got around that these hats were destined

5 From "An Anthology of Wall Posters," published by the Field Army Red Guards of the Shanghai Foreign Languages Institute.

for the heads of the political teachers; another rumor said they were for the Party Committee; yet another predicted that the Party Secretary himself was to be hatted. The group denied these stories vehemently at the time and continued to deny them for months afterward, claiming that they were fabricated by the Party leaders to provide them with an excuse for suppressing the radicals.

Whatever the truth of the matter, the Party acted as if the threat were real. That evening, said the radicals, student representatives were told by their departmental secretaries:

> Some people are planning to put high hats or the political instructors. This is against Party policy. Such people can in no way be called true leftists. . . .
>
> The Party Committee has decided that tomorrow will be devoted to the study of documents and editorials about the Cultural Revolution. If anyone wants to attend the exorcism, he may, but he will do so at his own risk. . . .
>
> Should anything occur that is against Party policy, I trust the broad masses of teachers and students can cope with it.[6]

It was a busy night for the Party leaders. At 1:00 A.M. the English Department Party Secretary (who had been put in charge of the Cultural Revolution in the Institute) called the young teachers and Youth League members together and gave them special instructions. At 2:30 A.M., he sent a message to the children of revolutionary cadres. "Tomorrow is your big test," he was quoted as saying. "You must promise to take no part in any attempt to hat the political instructors." At 3:00 A.M., a meeting of all Party members was held, to which a certain number of students were also invited.

At this stage, it becomes hard to separate fact from fiction. The accounts of what happened that night were mostly written after the event by the radicals, who were bent on discrediting the role of the Party leaders. Some of their accusations were a bit far-fetched. They claimed, for instance, that the authorities prepared a detailed plan to counter the exorcism meeting, that they ar-

6 *Ibid.*

ranged for alternative chairmen, organized cheerleaders to inter-
rupt proceedings, and even formed an "inspection team" to act
as police. This team was issued badges of identification but told
not to put them on until a signal was given. The students were
advised to wear long-sleeved clothes, and the girls were warned
against coming in skirts, in case fighting should break out. People were sent to other universities to foil any attempt at liaison
with like-minded groups. And, finally, the 100 workers attached
to the Institute were enlisted as a kind of bodyguard for the Party
officials. All this should be taken with a grain of salt. The Party
could hardly have predicted everything with such accuracy. As
in most incidents during the Cultural Revolution, part of what
happened was planned and part was spontaneous.

By 4:30 A.M., we are back on firmer ground. All factions agreed
that five of the top Party members then left the Institute and
went to see Ch'ang Hsi-p'ing, the head of the Education Department. The five were: President Wang Chi-yü, the Party Secretary,
the head of the Cultural Revolution Office, the Acting Secretary
of the English Department, and the head of the Institute Party
Committee's Propaganda Bureau.

They went first to the Municipal Buildings. Ch'ang Hsi-p'ing
was not there—hardly surprising at that hour of the morning.
They found him asleep at his home. He got up to receive them,
listened to their story, and made the following comments:

In Peking University, more than fifty people got hats. Now, if the
students want to put hats on young teachers or political cadres, a
stand must be made. You must insist that the issues be settled through
debate. Hold a meeting; get everyone to attend and to bring a copy
of the Sixteen Points and the relevant articles of Chairman Mao.

It all boils down to this: If you are a monster, then submit to
having a hat put on you; if you are not a monster, don't submit.[7]

This last remark, innocent enough in appearance, later caused
bitter controversy among the students. The radicals claimed it
betrayed a reactionary attitude, for it implied that Party mem-

7 *Ibid.*

bers did not have to trust the judgment of the masses but could decide for themselves whether they were good men or not.

On that August morning, however, Ch'ang Hsi-p'ing's words must have sounded comforting to the five weary cadres, who went straight back to the Institute and called a meeting of all the political instructors, who in turn got the Party members of each department together and told them that if the students tried to put hats on them they should resist.

The exorcism started at 7:00 A.M. At precisely the same time, the main body of the students gathered for a "study meeting" led by the Party. The rival groups were within sight of each other, on opposite sides of the playing field.

The Vice-Secretary of English stood up to announce that the Party Secretary was going to speak to the majority. But first he put a question to the students, a very simple question, but one that contained the essence of the Cultural Revolution. "Do you or do you not," he asked them, "want the leadership of the Party?"

The question was loaded. It sounded as if he were asking "Do you want the leadership of the Communist Party of China?" In fact, he was saying "Do you believe that we, the Party Committee of this Institute, are worthy of obedience as *representatives* of the Chinese Communist Party, and, more especially, of its leader, Chairman Mao?" Most of the students, brought up to think of the Party as a monolith, all parts of which were always equally reliable, were in no position to distinguish between the Party as a whole and the particular section of it that controlled their Institute. For them, the Party Committee was still "Yenan" rather than "Sian," still the incarnation of the Central Committee's authority. So they answered in one voice: "We want the leadership of the Party!" The implication was clear enough: If the Party Committee merited allegiance, then the students on the far side of the campus were "outlaws."

The Party Secretary then rose to speak. Both meetings were using public address systems, and by this time the exorcists were making such a racket that no one could hear what the Secretary said. A few minutes later, the small group's amplifiers went dead, and the voice of the Party prevailed. The exorcists swore they had been sabotaged. Judging by a statement from the Institute's chief electrician, they might have been right:

> On the morning of August 12, two meetings were going on at once on the campus. It was bedlam. Then someone came into the sound room and said: "Switch off the power to the exorcists' meeting." One of the electricians asked: "On whose orders?" "The Party Secretary's," was the reply. "If there are any questions, I will personally be responsible."
>
> I ordered the electrician to cut off the power. This was not easy, for the power supply to the exorcists was in the barber shop, and the door was locked. We had no choice but to cut the wires.[8]

The Party Secretary's speech was brief and emotional, ending with the line he had learned from Ch'ang Hsi-p'ing: "I hear that some people have prepared a high hat for me. Well, I want to say this loud and clear: If I am a monster, I will wear it; if I am not a monster, I most certainly will *not!*"[9]

The audience was shocked, and there were shouts of "We will defend the Party Secretary!" and "We will defend the Party Committee!" Some even called out "Long live the Party Secretary!"—a formula usually reserved for Mao himself.

The majority group then crossed the campus and crashed the exorcists' meeting, which was just in the process of nominating its chairmen. They completely took over the proceedings, shouting that they were the majority and did not agree with the choice of chairmen.

Pandemonium broke out. The Party Secretary was pushed on stage by some and off again by others. A group of workers settled the issue by bodily carrying away those whom the exorcists had selected as chairmen. After something of a brawl, a new list of chairmen was read out by the Vice-Secretary of the English Department, and from then on the meeting was entirely in the hands of the majority. Needless to add, no Party members got high hats that morning.

In the afternoon, and again in the evening, full-scale debates were held in the auditorium. At the evening session, a vice-

8 *Ibid.*
9 *Ibid.*

secretary of the Municipal Committee came and spoke. It seems he was making the rounds of all the Shanghai colleges, preaching the nonviolent resolution of student disputes. Clearly, our Institute was not the only place where there was trouble.

The debates were no easy victory for the majority. The radicals denied having "rejected the Party's leadership" and "cut themselves off from the masses." They defended their autonomy by quoting from the newly published Sixteen Points: "Any method of forcing a minority holding different views to submit is impermissible. The minority should be protected, because sometimes the truth is with the minority. Even if the minority is wrong, they should still be allowed to argue their case and reserve their views."

On the question of whether they had "cut themselves off from the masses," they argued as follows:

It is true that we made one small mistake: We did not do enough preparatory work among the teachers and students before holding our exorcism meeting. But we certainly relied on the help of the masses. We asked the opinion of people in every year of every faculty. We made contact with Futan and Tungchi universities. Everyone knew about our meeting. The masses supported us. Before the Party Committee interfered, no one had suggested changing the list of chairmen.

What is more, our group was a spontaneous one. We had a difference of opinion with certain people, but the Sixteen Points says this is quite natural. We respected their opinion, but we did not have to accept it. They certainly had no right to force it on us. We were under no obligation to accept people with different ideas on our panel of chairmen.

Our theory is that we should fight first and unite later. A lot of reactionaries say we should first unite 95 per cent of the people on our side, then fight. We do not agree.

We admit, however, that the August 12 affair was a setback to us. Many of our supporters turned against us.[10]

The Party authorities were given little time to enjoy their victory. The very next day, August 13, some students at the Institute received a letter from Heilungkiang University, contain-

[10] *Ibid.*

ing serious charges against President Wang Chi-yü. It appeared that Mrs. Wang had served 18 years as President and Party Committee member of Heilungkiang University, before being transferred to the same posts at our Institute. The letter accused her of having led a reactionary clique there and also charged that, in 1964, she had ruthlessly suppressed the students of Peking University, to which she was assigned as part of the Socialist Education Movement.

The radicals quickly had this letter made into wall posters, adding such barbed questions as "If our Party Committee knew all along what type of person the President was, why have they defended her so carefully?"

The Party decided to nip this threat in the bud. A poster appeared almost immediately, signed by the six top men in the Institute's hierarchy. It was short and to the point:

> The time has come for Wang Chi-yü to make a clean breast of everything to the people. She worked for a very long time in Heilungkiang University, and we are told she made mistakes of a serious nature. We have therefore asked the Municipal Committee to relieve her of her job on the Institute's Cultural Revolution Group. She will be transferred back to Heilungkiang, where she will have to make a confession to the revolutionary teachers, students, and staff. We acclaim the success of our own revolutionary teachers, students, and staff in exposing the errors of Wang Chi-yü.[11]

This sounded fine, but it turned out that the Heilungkiang students had sent a similar letter exactly one month earlier. Some English Department students who had received it had passed it on to the Party Committee. For obvious reasons, the matter had been hushed up.

The situation deteriorated further when the radicals finally heard about Miss Nieh Yuan-tzu's poster attacking Ch'ang Hsi-p'ing and Mayor Ts'ao's efforts to suppress it. This revived the whole campaign against Ch'ang, who had successfully weathered the June–July period and was still in charge of the Cultural Revolution in Shanghai. The news of Miss Nieh's poster against

[11] *Ibid.*

him convinced the leftists that they had been right all along, and
the Mayor's protective role in the affair seemed to prove the
existence of a conspiracy.

At our Institute, the radicals assumed that the Party Secretary
had known about the attack on Ch'ang Hsi-p'ing when he went
to see him at dawn on August 12. To have sought advice from
such a man, and to have applied his suggestions so faithfully,
implied that the Institute's Party Secretary was in on the plot.
What is more, he had taken along President Wang, although he
knew she was under fire from Heilungkiang. The case against the
authorities was taking shape.

August 16 was a bad day for the Institute Party Committee.
For the first time, it was attacked from within, by one of its
trusted members. A poster went up, signed by the new Vice-
Secretary of the Youth League. Entitled "The August 12 Incident
Was the Result of Scheming by the Institute Party Committee,"
it caused a furor among the students. Until then, only the radicals
had made allegations about what happened on the night of
August 11, and the majority of the students had seen no reason
to believe them. Now a Party official gave credence to the story;
he confirmed that the authorities had been up all night planning
ways to stop the exorcists, and he described in detail their clan-
destine visit to Ch'ang Hsi-p'ing's house.[12]

The result of this poster was another big debate, which started
at midnight on August 16 and lasted until dawn. The Acting
Secretary of the English Department, who had the unenviable
job of spokesman for the Party Committee, defended the authorities strongly, calling the Youth League official "a traitor" and
declaring that his poster was "not in accordance with the facts."

But attack was always easier than defense, and the radicals
made the most of their position. Here is a short statement of
support for the poster, written by a third-year English student.
It is probably much milder than the speeches of the younger
students:

> I believe this poster is a revolutionary one and I support it with all
> my heart.

12 *Ibid.*

The Youth League Vice-Secretary's orientation is correct. His poster is in the spirit of the Sixteen Points and shows great courage. He is the first Party political cadre to stand up and point out the errors of principle made by the Party Committee. This is a change from the previous attitude of the Party, which was more along the lines of "One does not slap a tiger on the backside with impunity!"

He has shown true proletarian fearlessness in his attack, knowing the handful of conservatives in the Party will be out for his skin. His poster is not perfect, but we should give it our full support. If we do not, who will dare write another like it?[13]

At some stage during the debate, Shanghai Municipal Committee "observers" arrived. It seems they had been invited by the left wing but backed the moderates and the Party Committee. Their unexpected stand reinforced the bitterness of the minority and deepened the split between the radicals and the rest of the student body. This split was important, for it carried over into the formation of Red Guard groups a few days later.

The net result of the affair was not a defeat for the radicals, however. The Party Committee had definitely lost some face. For one thing, a minority had been suppressed; for another, fighting had broken out among the students, and hatred had been generated in the process. It is one of China's legacies from Confucianism that disorder reflects adversely on the authorities. Whether or not the Institute's hierarchy had planned the August 12 incident, they were nonetheless somehow to blame for letting it happen.

More important in the long run was the suggestion of a conspiracy of authority, extending from the colleges, through the head of the Education Department, Ch'ang Hsi-p'ing, and the mayor of Shanghai, Ts'ao Ti-ch'iu, to the Central Committee itself. This idea was to mature with time, and Shanghai's January Revolution of 1967 was the fruit of these seeds sown in August, 1966.

Ch'ang Hsi-p'ing was the weak link, and Nieh Yuan-tzu's attack on him, coming at the height of her fame, was extremely danger-

13 *Ibid.*

ous for the Shanghai Municipal Committee. Ch'ang himself, if
we can trust this radical account, tried to bluff his way out:

> When Nieh Yuan-tzu and others exposed the towering crimes
> committed by Ch'ang Hsi-p'ing at Peking University during the
> Socialist Education Movement, Ch'ang not only refused to acknowl-
> edge his guilt, but actually launched a furious counterattack against
> the revolutionary teachers and students of Peking University.
>
> He cynically remarked that the whole movement there was nothing
> more than "one group of rightists criticizing another group of right-
> ists." It was "dog eat dog," he said. And this great traitor described
> himself as "heroically countering first one group of rightists, then
> the other." He even had the audacity to offer to debate the matter
> with the revolutionary teachers and students of Peking University.
> (RG 1:4.1)

It is in connection with the case of Ch'ang Hsi-p'ing that we
must now turn from what happened at the Foreign Languages
Institute to study the over-all effect of the Eleventh Plenum on
Shanghai.

Mayor Ts'ao Ti-ch'iu got back from Peking on August 16. The
first thing he did, according to subsequent newspaper accounts,
was make a speech at East China Normal College, where Ch'ang
Hsi-p'ing had worked for 10 years as Party Secretary and where
an attack on him would be most likely to succeed:

> As soon as Ts'ao Ti-ch'iu got back from the Eleventh Plenum, he
> shot around to East China Normal College. Why? To put out a
> fire! At that time, Nieh Yuan-tzu's wall poster exposing Ch'ang
> Hsi-p'ing had kindled a blaze of revolution in that college, and row
> after row of revolutionary posters had appeared, all aimed at the
> traitor Ch'ang. Ts'ao Ti-ch'iu was hardly out of his car when he
> started spouting stuff like "Ch'ang Hsi-p'ing is a good comrade."
> [Another account had "not a bad comrade."] He also said: "The
> Municipal Committee has faith in Ch'ang Hsi-p'ing."
>
> This is how he countered Nieh's wall poster. Within a few days,
> the situation had changed; the campus was bedecked with posters
> reading "Ch'ang Hsi-p'ing is a good student of Chairman Mao,"
> "Ch'ang Hsi-p'ing is a cadre after the style of Chiao Yü-lu [a model of
> unselfish leadership]." The raging fire at East China Normal College

was extinguished. This was Ts'ao's first act on his return to Shanghai, and it was an act against the Sixteen Points. (RG 1:3.1)

This single initiative by Ts'ao Ti-ch'iu must be multiplied many times if we are to have an idea of the nationwide resistance to the decisions of the Eleventh Plenum.

On August 18, after waiting a week to gauge the extent of the opposition, the Mao group launched the Red Guards. At a rally in Peking, Mao gave his blessing to a million students; the following day, the Shanghai Municipal Committee organized a big parade to welcome this new stage of the Cultural Revolution. There is evidence, however, that the Shanghai authorities were most reluctant to follow Peking's lead and let Red Guards be formed. Here, for instance, is an account of what happened during the speeches at the August 19 parade. It was written some months later, by journalists in the Shanghai branch of the New China News Agency (NCNA):

> During the meeting, some young revolutionaries from the middle school attached to Shanghai Teachers College got up on the rostrum, despite the efforts of people like Li Chia-ch'i, Assistant Secretary-General of the Municipal Committee, to stop them. They called for the immediate creation of Red Guards in Shanghai.
> . . . When we wrote up this story and handed it to Yang Hsi-kuang [in charge of propaganda in Shanghai] for his inspection, he got very angry and said: "I don't care about the rest of it, but you've got to rewrite this bit about forming Red Guards." He was also heard to bellow at Ma Ta [editor of *Liberation Daily*] and Yang Ying [Vice-Director of NCNA's Shanghai branch]: "Why does Shanghai have to form Red Guards too?" (RG 5:3.1)

Some *Liberation Daily* Red Guards had this version of the story:

> At the meeting, some Futan University students wanted to read a telegram they had received from a Futan group called the "Red Guard Combat Team." This group had been in Peking and had seen our beloved leader, Chairman Mao. The telegram had been written when their emotions were still at fever pitch, and it described the revolutionary atmosphere of the occasion.
> Some other students, from Shanghai Teachers College Middle

School, wanted to suggest forming Red Guard organizations. They tried to speak but were prevented by Assistant Secretary-General Li Chia-ch'i. They protested vigorously and were finally permitted to say their piece.

In the *Liberation Daily* report of the rally, these events were glossed over. Editor Ma Ta said: "It has not yet been decided whether Shanghai will have Red Guards."

Someone on the editorial board noticed that the coverage was inadequate and suggested some changes. Ma Ta said: "When Yang Hsi-kuang has approved something, not one word can be altered."

He rang Yang Hsi-kuang nonetheless, and the passage was slightly revised. . . . (RG 6:4.1)

The Municipal Committee bowed to the inevitable. The very next day, August 20, a rally to prepare for the creation of Red Guards was held. Mayor Ts'ao, perhaps with tongue in cheek, gave a speech of encouragement.

It was on this same day that the radicals formed the first Red Guard group at our Institute. The title they chose for themselves was, to say the least, revealing: Red Guards, Peking Head-quarters, Shanghai Foreign Languages Institute Branch (later changed to Field Army Red Guards). It is doubtful whether this group, or many of the other Shanghai left-wing groups formed at this time, had anything but loose and spasmodic relations with Peking, but the names they chose for themselves showed where their hearts were and also rebuked the Shanghai Municipal Committee, which, in the eyes of the students, clearly did not constitute a source of correct leadership.

On August 22, there was another rally, this time of "revolutionary teachers and students from the whole of Shanghai." The Mayor spoke again, ostensibly "to explain the Sixteen Points." A Futan Red Guard later remarked: "He made no attempt to explain the important parts. From start to finish, his speech was about the 'special circumstances' of Shanghai and how careful we had to be to act according to them" (RG 1:3.1).

The radicals were particularly annoyed by the Mayor's patronizing attitude toward them. This came out, for example, in a reference he made to the Cultural Revolution committees in the colleges. These were supposed to be democratically elected bodies, composed of students, teachers, and workers. In practice, they had been appendages of the Party committees, which had used them against the radicals. Aware of this, the Mayor was probably trying to help when he pointed out that the committees should reflect "the concern of the majority for the minority." He went on to say:

> Some students who have played a most enthusiastic role in the Cultural Revolution find they have not been elected to these committees. . . .
> They should not let their emotions get the better of them. . . . Making revolution is not a question of "If I am elected I will join in; if not I will not.". . .
> In extreme cases, comrades should ask themselves: "Have I let myself drift away from the masses?" (RG 1:3.1)

Red Guard invective was at its best in tearing apart this kind of paternalism:

> We tell you straight, Ts'ao Ti-ch'iu: If "some students who have played a most enthusiastic role in the Cultural Revolution" find they "have not been elected to these committees," then you can bet your life they're going to "let their emotions get the better of them"!
> Chairman Mao teaches us that we fight for the power of the people and the Party, not for ourselves. If power is not in the hands of the revolutionary left wing, we are going to make one hell of a fuss!
> As for your stuff about our "drifting away from the masses," that won't work any more. What we are doing is cutting ourselves off from . . . committees that carry out a bourgeois reactionary line. That kind of committee must be rejected, denounced, and smashed! (RG 1:3.1)

Mayor Ts'ao knew he was on a collision course with the radicals, but he also knew he could count on the loyalty of the majority. With this in mind, the Municipal Committee organized a city-wide federation of Red Guard groups. This later came to be known as First Headquarters, to distinguish it from subsequent organizations, but its original title was General Headquarters of Red Guards from Shanghai Schools and Colleges.

From the beginning, it supported the Party authorities. Some of its best organizers were the sons and daughters of high officials —a pattern that seems to have been repeated all over the country.

The Mayor did not underestimate the danger from the left. He reportedly told a meeting of his Secretariat:

> Some students are directing their attacks at the Municipal Committee. . . . Their numbers are small, but their influence is considerable. We should keep a careful eye on their activities. . . . If such people flourish, they might win over the middle-of-the-road, in which case their ranks would swell. We must not discount the potential of this section. (RG 9:4.1)

As if to prove his point, he went to Futan University on August 24. This was dangerous because Futan had closer contacts with the Peking Red Guards than any other Shanghai college. But Ts'ao had no choice, for one of the weak links in his Municipal Committee—acting propaganda chief Yang Hsi-kuang— was under severe attack. Ts'ao went to bolster him, just as he had gone to East China Normal College to defend Ch'ang Hsi-p'ing. Whatever he said that day, he certainly riled the radicals:

> He glorified the conservatives and called them "models at implementing Party policy"; of the left wing he said: "They find one fault in a person and slap a big label on him." . . . "Without enough evidence . . . they have called a lot of people 'anti-Party' and 'antisocialist.' " . . . "This is not right." And so on—remarks that were about as helpful to the cause as a crack on the head or a bucketful of cold water. (RG 1:3.1)

They also quoted him as having arrogantly compared himself with the Central Committee: "Some say my speech of August 22 was too mild. I do not agree. Put my speech alongside the Sixteen Points. Is it mild in comparison?" (RG 1:3.1) The indignation of the Futan radicals may have been a measure of the Mayor's success. The more support Ts'ao received from the student majority, the fiercer the reaction from the left became.

The following evening, a joint force of radicals from Futan

and other campuses invaded Shanghai Drama Academy. It is not clear why they chose this particular place. They themselves said it was "to make liaison," but it was probably an act of defiance as much as anything. Upward of 1,000 students took part, making this far and away the largest intercollegiate link-up ever attempted by the left wing.

They met strong resistance from the Drama Academy students. Ironically, their most outspoken opponents were Tibetans, newly emancipated serfs who were studying opera in Shanghai. This group believed it was defending the honor of the Party and looked on the radicals as counterrevolutionary troublemakers. In the debate that began about midnight, as well as in the brawl later, the Tibetans seem to have acquitted themselves nobly.

The Futan moderates arranged a big meeting for the following evening. Once again, the stated purpose was "to study the Sixteen Points," but the left wing now saw this as a cover for repression. Mayor Ts'ao announced that he would come and make another speech, only 2 days after his first. But before going to Futan, said the radicals, he called a meeting of District Committee secretaries from all over Shanghai and warned that Peking Red Guards were infiltrating the city:

> Their activities must be controlled. They must not be allowed to develop into a real force. . . .
>   By all means denounce them, but do not go too far. It is the masses who should rise up and write wall posters against them. At the same time, their backgrounds should be examined. . . .
>   If we find that they are antisocial elements, we will notify the Peking Municipal Committee . . . these people must be restrained. . . .
>   We must not merely defend ourselves, for that only makes them more fanatical. When they attack, we must counterattack. The struggle is now very complex, and all sorts of creatures have come out into the light. . . . (RG 9:4.1)

That night, at Futan, the Mayor left little doubt about which side he was on. Speaking to the moderates, who had already condemned the "adventurism" of the left wing in the Drama Academy scandal, he suggested that certain people had "confused two types of contradiction." "And why," he asked "would anyone

want to make liaison at night? Night activities are most unusual." In this way, he imputed a sinister twist to the whole
escapade.

Such a speech had to be fairly tactful, for the Mayor knew
the radicals would ransack it for evidence against him. He therefore made full use of his talent for innuendo: "If you write wall
posters against these people, make sure you have the facts. If you
find that they have really said or done things against the Party
or against socialism, they will be classified accordingly" (RG
1:3.1).

What he meant, said the radicals, was "Get the facts and write
those wall posters!" As a result, they claimed, within a matter of
hours, the campus was full of posters condemning the part the
leftists played in the Drama Academy incident.

So, Ts'ao Ti-ch'iu had done it again! By a repetition of his
East China Normal College technique—though admittedly the
going was tougher this time—he had succeeded in temporarily
pacifying another trouble spot.

The Futan radicals did not call it pacification; they charged
that a "reign of white terror" had overwhelmed their university,
and they planned a rally in Culture Square (the former French
dog-racing track) to denounce the Municipal Committee.

The Party press was brought in to counter this move. On
August 27, the editor of Liberation Daily reportedly told a meeting of Party cadres that the Futan experience of August 26 was
a model of how to handle student disputes. Liberation Daily
then ran an article praising the Futan moderates for their excellent grasp of the Sixteen Points. The press was also used to
settle the aftermath of the Drama Academy incident. Some
Drama students were dissatisfied with the treatment of the left
wing and demanded to see the Mayor. Ts'ao sent an assistant
secretary-general to see how strong the group was. Finding they
were few in number, he agreed to speak to them. Again, his tact
and eloquence won the day; he spoke of his "concern" and "support" for the left wing: "I regard the majority and the minority
with equal benevolence" (RG 9:4.1). The radicals complained
that this speech fooled everyone.

The role of the press was to reinforce such victories. In this case, Yang Hsi-kuang used his control of propaganda to get the NCNA to do a story on the Tibetan students at the Drama Academy. They were described as "good students of the People's Liberation Army," the implication being that they were obedient and loyal citizens. This was little more than a way of saying thank you to the Tibetans for their part in repulsing the Futan probe.

These articles further alienated the radicals. They even challenged the reporters to a debate and called on them to confess that they were wrong. Yang Hsi-kuang is said to have told his staff: "You will not 'confess' anything. If they want a debate, fine. But for such a debate to be fair, the opposing points of view should be represented according to their numbers" (RG 5:3.1).

This was the weakness of the radicals. They were so few that the local authorities could easily swing public opinion against them. A speech by the mayor or some other high officials, a hint from a Party Committee, a turn of the propaganda machine—these were the methods used by the hierarchy to keep dissidents in check.

The only way around this bland and experienced power structure was to introduce from Peking a breed of Red Guards "straight from Chairman Mao," who, by virtue of a unique and unanswerable authority, would "dare to smash through and strike down." Shanghai was even then being bedeviled by the first wave of these little avengers with their relentless thirst for justice. They came to undo all the Party's careful work, to rip off the benevolent mask of officialdom and make the Mayor and his corporation pay dearly for their suppression of the local left wing.

5. The Peking Red Guards

My wife and I happened to be in Peking on August 25 and 26, 1966, at the very end of our summer holidays. The Red Guards, in the week since their appearance, had turned the place upside down. What had been one of the world's most relaxed cities was now alive with columns of flag-waving students, parading through the streets to the rhythm of drums and gongs. People stood arguing in groups beside walls and shop fronts bedecked with posters and slogans, and cars with their brand names changed to "Oppose Revisionism" honked their way slowly through the crowds.

Fortunately, there was an air of carnival about the whole thing that lessened the tension. There was no feeling that people would be killed; it was more like a huge Chinese opera, with students acting out the triumph of the revolution. The slogan on everyone's lips was "Smash the old; build the new!" Yet the oldest things of all—the palaces and temples of dynastic society—were not destroyed. The smashing was selective and symbolic: We saw stone lions broken with sledge hammers, wooden motifs chiseled off old house walls, statues of the Buddha carted away in trucks, Christian emblems replaced by red flags.

People suffered too, but mostly for the way they dressed. Conventionally attired, Chiang K'ai-shek could probably have walked through the city. Typical of the Red Guards' passion for symbolism was the lopping of girls' braids; short hair was a sign of female emancipation. We watched young coeds crying quietly as they submitted to the amateurish barbering efforts of their classmates.

It was a shock to see Peking so changed, and we were as bewildered as the man in the street. Only the Red Guards seemed to know what was happening, and they went about their business with scarcely disguised elation.

The train we took on August 27 was full of Red Guards, students from Peking's major universities. They spent the whole 30-hour journey to Shanghai reading, studying, and discussing sheaves of documents. A train trip in China is usually a gay occasion, but these boys and girls were utterly absorbed in their work, as if cramming for a tough exam. Their assignment turned out to be nothing so academic; they intended, in fact, to subvert a whole city. Their papers were prototypes of material soon to appear on Shanghai's walls, material that would threaten the very existence of the Party and government of China's greatest metropolis.

When the train pulled in on August 28, the station forecourt was crowded with youngsters waiting to welcome the Peking revolutionaries. We were met by a member of the Institute staff, who on the way home rather coyly asked what we had seen in Peking. When we had finished telling her, she replied: "Shanghai will not be like that. The movement here will be better controlled by the Municipal Committee. We are going to avoid the excesses of Peking."

At first sight, Shanghai did seem quieter. The girls still wore their hair long, and we saw styles in trousers and footwear that would not have survived in the capital. But the street names and titles of businesses had been changed, and everywhere there were knots of people reading wall posters. There were also many Red Guard detachments, traveling on foot, on bicycle carts, or in trucks, always to the accompaniment of drums and cymbals and streaming red silk flags. We were to get very used to their presence.

We lived in what had once been a bourgeois suburb. From our fifth-floor windows we could watch as the two-story foreign-style mansions around us were systematically searched by Red Guards. No attempt was made to hide things from us, and victims of the raids were often paraded past our house wearing tall white dunce caps or forced to stand on a makeshift dais in front of angry crowds. No one ever got hurt in these performances, though the student leaders were always stern and sometimes gave prisoners a shove.

We had only the vaguest idea of what was going on; all we knew was that we did not like it. The students did not share our scruples. They saw themselves as the vanguard of a new era, entrusted with the task of cleansing away every vestige of Shanghai's humiliating past. If their work involved some violence, forcing people to submit to indignities, they felt this was unavoidable. Revolution, they quoted from Mao, is not a dinner party.

In retrospect, it is clear that the energy expended by the Shanghai Red Guards late in August was not directly relevant to the movement. It was not wrong to attack the bourgeoisie, just as it had not been wrong to criticize teachers and academics. But this was not the ultimate aim of the Cultural Revolution. It took the average Red Guard months to realize that the target of the movement was the Communist Party itself.

This is where the Peking Red Guards came in. They knew what the movement was about, and they knew that local Party authorities would do their best to divert it. They had come to make sure that the Shanghai students did not lose direction in the excitement of flushing out less important victims.

The Shanghai Municipal Party Committee had every reason to resent the interference from Peking. It was quite content to let the local students go on "tilting at dead tigers" for as long as they pleased. It had therefore given the Shanghai Red Guards every assistance in their fight against the bourgeoisie; each group had the right to paper, ink, brushes, glue, mimeograph machines, loudspeakers, bull-horns, transport facilities, and finances.

The Peking Red Guards, however, got a very cold shoulder. Here is a typical complaint about the treatment they received:

Around the end of August, the first lot of Peking Red Guards arrived in Shanghai to make revolutionary contacts. They planned to set up a liaison center, so as to carry out their activities in a more

Children in People's Square (formerly the racecourse), where many rallies were held.

Itinerant tinsmith (perhaps a manifestation of "capitalist" policies before the Cultural Revolution).

Members of the second-year English class taught by the author's wife. Most of them were from worker or peasant families.

The author's students.

Former Nationalist pillbox in the midst of crops.

Pairs of women hauling loads metal.

A Shanghai church.

Pedicabs.

A shop front.

Fishing junks on Whangpoo River. Note eyes painted on junks to frighten evil spirits and ensure good catch.

A girl welder in dockyards.

One of an army of street-cleaners.

Dating in a park on a Sunday.

Village children on a commune near Shanghai come out to see foreign visitors.

Downtown Shanghai, looking south across Soochow
Creek toward the former British Embassy compound.

Downtown Shanghai, looking north. This was the Japanese quarter.

Scene in the dockyards.

Garden Bridge over Soochow Creek, with Whangpoo River in the background. Park in middle distance once carried sign reading, "No Chinese, No Dogs."

Logging on Soochow Creek, looking toward Shanghai Mansions (formerly Broadway Mansions), where author lived for nine months.

coordinated way. They applied to Ma T'ien-shui, Secretary [for industry and communications] of the Shanghai Municipal Party Committee Secretariat for permission to have a seal of office cut as well as for broadcasting, press, and propaganda equipment. The Municipal Committee turned down this revolutionary request. Why?

Ma Ta, a member of the Municipal Committee's Cultural Revolution Group [and editor of the Shanghai newspaper *Liberation Daily*], gave the following reasons:

1. The leaders of the proposed liaison center were "very doubtful characters."
2. They went about things in a most unorthodox way.
3. They "upset the normal relations between the sexes."
4. They were politically unsound.

None of these reasons was true, yet the Municipal Committee would not allow the liaison center to be set up. Ma Ta also got people to examine the class background of one of the liaison center leaders. When he found that the boy's father had joined the Revolution in 1945 but was now only an ordinary worker, he jumped to the conclusion that this was because of political faults and reported the matter to the Municipal Committee.

Under this kind of pressure, the Peking Red Guards' liaison center in Shanghai could not get started, and this first revolutionary contact was killed stone dead. . . . (RG 5:2.2)

In the face of this opposition, the Peking Red Guards demonstrated outside the Municipal Committee headquarters, demanding that the Mayor receive them and hear their complaints. According to students from Shanghai's Chiaotung University, the Committee maneuvered skillfully to relieve the situation, inveigling local people to resist the young "invaders" from the North:

After dinner on August 28, our leader Chai asked a certain Ch'en, a probationary Party member, to go with him to the Municipal Committee offices. On the way he said: "Things have been pretty tense down there lately. The Peking students have been standing around the door all day, shouting that the Shanghai Municipal Committee is corrupt and revisionist. They've even tried to break into the building. The officials all have splitting headaches and can't get on with their work, so they rang our university's propaganda bureau and asked us to organize some students to give them support. Our group got the job, so you and I are going down to see what we can do."

At the Municipal Committee building, they were met by an official, who told them: "These Peking students don't understand Shanghai. They are no sooner off the train than they start howling that the Municipal Committee is riddled with revisionism. For the last few days they've been besieging the building, calling for Mayor Ts'ao Ti-ch'iu, Secretary Yang Hsi-kuang, and other Committee members to come out and talk to them. They've even tried to break in, and they're still causing quite a disturbance. . . . I hope you'll organize some students to take part in a debate. The East China Normal College students came as a propaganda team, but that's no good. It looks too contrived. You'd better come as individuals, or in groups of two's and three's, and mingle with the people. Then you can participate in a spontaneous debate. . . . You'd better be prepared for a rough time, even for fighting, but under no circumstances are you to strike back; otherwise, the Municipal Committee will be in real trouble. . . . Take it in rotation with East China Normal College: You come on Mondays, Wednesdays, and Fridays; they can come on Tuesdays, Thursdays, and Saturdays."

. . . On August 29 in the afternoon, we went along to "debate." When we got there we found the Peking Red Guards still asking to see the Municipal Committee leaders and still being kept out. A lot of workers, cadres, and students were pressing around them, and some were even trying to drag them away, punching and kicking them.

We felt this was wrong and said as much to some Committee officials who were standing near us. They smiled sarcastically and said: *"They're* the violent ones. They tried to break into the building."

Some officials had even removed their badges and merged with the crowd and were egging the people on, saying: "These Peking Red Guards are setting a bad example. Shouldn't we stop them? . . . They say the Municipal Committee is rotten to the core. . . . Are we going to let them get away with that?"

This turned the crowd against the Peking Red Guards. They sat in a ring around them so they couldn't escape; some people even abused them as "hooligans" and said they were trying to start a "Hungarian uprising." When the disguised officials saw that their plan had worked, they quietly slipped away. . . . (RG 1:2.3)

As long as the Peking students kept demonstrating, the Municipal Committee was in an awkward position. The rules of the Cultural Revolution forbade the suppression of any Red Guard group, so the Shanghai Party leaders had to proceed with caution. Since it was dangerous for them to manipulate local students and workers, they used more subtle methods. One of these was the mass media. They could not print or broadcast anything overtly critical of the Peking Red Guards, but there was nothing to stop them using, say, *People's Daily* editorials as propaganda. The radicals subsequently complained:

> If an editorial suited their purposes, they broadcast it over and over again; if it did not, they ran it only a few times. The August 28 *People's Daily* editorial entitled "Young Revolutionaries Should Learn from the Liberation Army" was broadcast continuously for 3 days, thirty-three times on the 28th alone. This was seven times more than the Sixteen Points was broadcast. They also put on songs that emphasized discipline, such as "The Three Rules of Discipline" and "The Eight Points for Attention."
>
> The next day, the *People's Daily* editorial was "We Congratulate Our Red Guards." The spirit of this piece ran completely counter to the Municipal Committee's instructions against confiscating property, so it was broadcast only seven times. (RG 5:2.3)

Another Red Guard newspaper claimed that Yang Yung-chih, nominal head of the Shanghai Party's Propaganda Department, had required *Liberation Daily* to print no less than 1.2 million copies of the editorial "Young Revolutionaries Should Learn from the Liberation Army" but that no extra copies had been ordered of such editorials as "Workers and Peasants Should Support the Actions of the Revolutionary Students" (RG 6:4.1).

The Peking Red Guards maintained that the Municipal Committee had also turned public opinion against them by enlisting the support of famous Shanghai workers. They accused Mayor Ts'ao Ti-ch'iu of making the following statement at an August 29 meeting of leading cadres from every branch of government: "Shanghai has many people who are well known as model students of Chairman Mao's works. These people must be mobilized. They are standard-bearers; they have great prestige among the masses; they are a force to be reckoned with. We must get them to speak out" (RG 9:4.1).

On August 30, the Peking Red Guards escalated matters by calling a rally in Culture Square. It was later described as "the opening salvo in the war against Ts'ao Ti-ch'iu." The rally seems to have worried the Municipal Committee; radical Shanghai Red Guards described the reaction of Ma Ta, editor of *Liberation Daily*:

> That very night, Ma Ta went to the Municipal Committee building and did not emerge until 3:00 A.M. At 6:00 A.M., he issued instructions to cadres of medium rank, and the word later spread to all cadres. Ma Ta was prepared to admit, in the abstract, that "the main orientation" of the Peking Red Guards was "correct," but he still made them out to be basically terrorists. Later, in a meeting, he lied about them, saying they had "made up reactionary slogans" and were out to "provoke incidents, bring down the Municipal Committee, and smash the whole Party structure." (RG 6:4.1)

Some handwritten notes that were said to have been found in the *Liberation Daily* offices during the occupation of the building by Red Guards in December suggest the Municipal Committee's dilemma. These pertinent questions of a Party branch secretary were plainly meant to serve as the basis for discussion:

1. Is the main orientation of these Peking Red Guards correct or not? Would it be possible to say that the bad effects of their actions far outweigh the good effects?

2. In assessing whether their main orientation is correct, is it enough to consider the slogans they shout, or should we first find out who they're after, who they want to "revolutionize"? If they are bent on bringing *everyone* down, can we say their main orientation is correct?

3. If they spread simplistic slogans like "Long Live the Red Terror!" or "If Your Father Was a Revolutionary, You Are Automatically a Good Fellow," does this affect their main orientation?

4. There have been a lot of incidents in the streets, and these have been described in different ways. Are the Red Guards at fault

or is the Municipal Committee? Comrade Lin Piao's remarks seem
to indicate that the latter is not the case. What are we to make of
this? Or should we not even think about it?

5. Among the students there may be a few counterrevolutionaries
who are out to attack the headquarters of the proletariat. Should
these people be singled out and subjected to severe criticism? Some
say if we did this now it would have a bad effect on the full mobilization of the masses. Others say it would make the ultimate mobilization all the better. Which is the correct answer?

6. What about the Red Guards' relations with cadres, workers,
peasants, and soldiers? Are the Red Guards at present monopolizing
the right to speak? Is this just?

7. This revolutionary liaison has not given the Red Guards any
experience. All they have learned is that the children of revolutionaries must automatically be good fellows.

8. There's far too much disorder at the moment. The Red Guards
are doing as they please and demanding total power. Is this right?.
We have the dictatorship of the proletariat. Couldn't it do a bit more
dictating and get some order around the place? (RG 6:3.1)

These notes show the anxiety of the Party at this time and the
careful arguments they worked out against the Peking Red
Guards. They had every reason to be worried, for subsequent
events proved that the Mao group in Peking fully supported
their emissaries to Shanghai and were quite prepared for a
certain amount of chaos, so long as it showed their opponents
up as conservatives. Mao himself was reported as saying at a
working conference of the Central Committee on August 29:

The important question is: This "disorder" that the whole country
is talking about—in what direction is it leading? My own opinion
is that it can go on for several months, for I firmly believe that the
great majority is good and only a minority bad. It does not matter
if we have no provincial committees; we still have the district and
county committees. . . .

I do not think the disorder in Peking is so terrible. . . . Peking is
too civilized if anything. The protesters are a minority. So are the
hooligans. We should not interfere at this stage. . . .[1]

[1] Copied from a wall poster.

These remarks were not made public until later, so it is not certain that the Peking Red Guards in Shanghai knew of Mao's opinion. But, on August 31, Mao received his second million Red Guards in Peking's Tien An Men Square, and the speeches made on that occasion were soon common knowledge. Lin Piao's words were the most significant: Though he warned the Red Guards not to hit people, he also stressed that they were to oppose any attempts to suppress them.

In Shanghai, the response was quick. On September 2, more than 1,000 Peking Red Guards, determined to bring things to a head, staged an American-style sit-in outside the main entrance to the Municipal Committee offices. They kept this up for 2 days, in the face of constant harassment from local students and workers.

There is no way of knowing how much of the opposition was spontaneous and how much was planned. The Peking students swore it was all arranged; the Municipal Committee maintained it was a popular reaction. Later, radical Red Guard newspapers published the "confessions" of Shanghai people who had participated. Here is a typical example, written by some workers in No. 17 State Cotton Mill, who swore that they "would not be deceived again":

About the beginning of September, we formed part of a so-called inspection brigade, which was set up to attack the Peking Red Guards. It was organized directly by the Work Team in our factory, on orders from the Municipal Committee. After studying Chairman Mao's works and the Sixteen Points, and after making a careful analysis of the events of that time, we have come to realize that the Municipal Committee deliberately stirred up strife between workers and students. We intend to expose this.

On September 1 and 2, the Municipal Committee's Work Team put up two wall posters all over our factory. One, written by fifty-one Municipal Committee officials, was entitled "A Statement about the August 31 Incident." The other was called "We Old Workers Want to Have Our Say" and was signed by some workers in No. 2 State Cotton Mill. The Work Team also organized denunciation meetings and generally manipulated public opinion toward the view that the

Peking Red Guards were against socialism, that they hit and insulted people, and that they should be treated as enemies.

On September 3, the Work Team suddenly chose 130 of us workers for a "special assignment." We exchanged our Red Guard arm bands for ones that bore no name of a group—only a number. Some of the people in our task force were not even Red Guards at all. The Municipal Committee had ordered those of us who were militia members not to take along our membership cards, so the only identification we had on us was our trade union tickets.

During the briefing, there was a lot of talk about how the Peking Red Guards had "no right to make this disturbance" and about how we workers were going along to "protect the Municipal Committee" and "maintain revolutionary order." We were also told: "No matter how many punches they throw, you are not under any circumstances to retaliate."

To make sure we all had our stories straight, we learned by heart: "We are an inspection brigade. If the Peking Red Guards ask us what group we belong to, we simply return the question. If they ask who got us to come, we say we came of our own accord. If they ask who our leaders are, we say the trade union. We do *not* say the Municipal Committee Work Team." We practiced these answers a few times, so there would be no slip-up.

At about 8:00 P.M., we went into action. Our first job was to form a human barricade in front of the main door. After 11:00 P.M., we were transferred to a position behind a wall, where our leaders told us: "The Peking Red Guards are on the other side of this wall and might try to get into the Municipal Committee building through here. You must defend this position."

Around 2:00 A.M., it started to rain. We had no protection, so our clothes got sopping wet. The Work Team ordered us to stay at our posts. We were on guard all that night, and we were wet through all that night. As for the Peking Red Guards, we didn't see hide or hair of them. But we certainly got wet. Very, very wet. A lot of the men were saying things like "So we stand here in the pouring rain. Next time they give us a job like this, I vote we tell them what to do!" (RG 1:2.1)

On September 4, the Peking Red Guards got sick of waiting for Mayor Ts'ao Ti-ch'iu and decided to try to force their way into the building. The melee that followed was described in the Western press as "a riot." I rode past the scene the next morning and found the building liberally papered with wall posters but unscarred except for two broken windows.

The Peking students who managed to get in were almost immediately expelled. This overt violence was presumably what the Mayor had been waiting for. He delivered a short speech from the door of the building on the evening of September 4. From isolated excerpts quoted in Red Guard newspapers, we can guess that he expressed displeasure. Yet he knew he had won a kind of victory. If the Peking Red Guards had forced his hand, he had also forced theirs, showing that, despite the Sixteen Points, they were willing to use violence to achieve their ends: "On August 31, the Peking students hit some employees of the Municipal Committee. . . . Everyone has seen today's episode with his own eyes, so I won't say much about it. . . . If the Peking students hit people, the Shanghai comrades are not to strike back" (RG 1:3.1).

The radicals complained that this speech, coupled with Vice-Mayor Sung Chi-wen's repeated defense of Municipal Committee policy, instituted a "reign of white terror" in Shanghai: "Ts'ao Ti-ch'iu has treated the Peking Red Guards as counterrevolutionary terrorists. This is intolerable! These youngsters are straight from Chairman Mao; they have the guts to strike down and smash through. Anyone who denies them denies the Revolution. Anyone who attacks them attacks the Revolution. Ts'ao Ti-ch'iu will not escape his guilt" (RG 1:3.1).

The September 4 incident, as the affair was soon being called, did not stop there. Both sides strained to wring from it the last ounce of propaganda.

The Municipal Committee had far more power. For one thing, it controlled the mass media. For another, its influence reached deep into the grass roots of Shanghai. A radical leaflet alleged that the Party had tried to turn the people against them:

After the Red Guards broke into the Municipal Committee building, the Work Team at No. 1 State Cotton Mill spread propaganda against them throughout the factory, at the same time praising the role of the Municipal Committee. Some shops even stopped work to circulate the message. This broke a long-standing tradition. As some workers remarked: "In 17 years, no one ever stopped the machines to pass on news."

The head of the Work Team then phoned Vice-Mayor Chang Ch'eng-tsung (who, as head of the Socialist Education Movement in the weaving industry, had once done a stint in this factory) and said: "We're going to get the old workers to send a telegram to Chairman Mao." The reply: "Fine!" . . .

Vice-Mayor Chang's private secretary (who was in charge of propaganda for the factory Work Team) then called a discussion meeting of only five or six men, at which he read out the draft of the telegram he had written. Having made some alterations and revisions, he typed a clean copy and had it sent off that very night.

The whole thing was his doing, though some misguided workers signed their names and others had their names added even though they were not present![2]

At this stage, the Red Guards included some dialogues in the leaflet to prove their point. One purported to be a conversation between some Red Guard investigators and a worker:

Question: Did you attend the meeting that preceded the sending of a telegram to Chairman Mao?
Answer: No.
Question: Did you discuss this telegram at all?
Answer: No.
Question: Then why is your signature on it?
Answer: I've no idea. I only heard about it after the telegram had been sent.
Question: Can you read and write?
Answer: No.

Another dialogue in the same leaflet contained a confession by the Vice-Mayor's private secretary:

2 From a leaflet entitled "The True Story of Yang Fu-chen's Urgent Telegram" dated December 20, 1966. Signed The Headquarters of Revolutionary Rebels from the Capital, The Red Field Army of Red Guards from Peking People's University, The Revolutionary Rebel Headquarters of Red Guards from Shanghai's First Medical College, and The Red Guard Combat Team from the Part-Work Part-Study School at No. 1 State Cotton Mill. None of these groups played an important role in the Cultural Revolution in Shanghai.

Question: Tell us how this urgent telegram, signed by Yang Fu-chen [a famous Shanghai worker] and others came to be sent to Chairman Mao.

Answer: I drafted the telegram. From the evening of September 3 to the morning of the 4th, some of the workers from this factory were down at the Municipal Committee offices helping to maintain order. When they came back, they told me what had happened. We all felt the Peking Red Guards had gone too far. We couldn't tolerate their saying our Municipal Committee was "rotten."

That afternoon I got hold of a few workers and organized a discussion, thinking that we could then write a wall poster, signed by old workers, protesting the actions of the Peking students. We had already written some, but people said they didn't ring true, they didn't sound as if workers had written them. So we planned to take down what the workers said in the discussion and make it into a poster.

At about 7:00 P.M., the head of the Work Team came to see me and said: "I hear the workers in some factories are sending telegrams to Chairman Mao. What about the old workers here?" He suggested I arrange a discussion with Yang Fu-chen and a few others. "First tell them the facts very briefly and see how they feel. Then put your heads together and draw up a telegram." I did as he said.

Question: Did the workers sign their own names?

Answer: All those present at the discussion did. Then we looked at it and it seemed to need more signatures. So everyone suggested other names, mostly of model workers, and we added them. They were supposed to tell these people after the meeting broke up. The telegram certainly looked better with more names.

Question: Is this the first time you've written things for workers?

Answer: I've helped Yang Fu-chen with several things. His speech at the one-million-strong procession in Shanghai for example. Also an article he published. I did the first draft of these. I've also corrected some stuff for him. I checked the manuscript of something he did for *Branch Life* [an inner-Party magazine put out by the Propaganda Department of the Municipal Committee] about No. 1 State Cotton Mill.

Question: You are Vice-Mayor Chang Ch'eng-tsung's private secretary. How did he feel about this telegram?

Answer: He agreed with the idea. He also thought it should be run off as a leaflet, which was later done on the Shanghai People's Committee press. . . .

This leaflet had a much greater effect than the telegram itself, for the aim of the Party authorities was not to impress Chairman Mao in Peking but to win public opinion in the Shanghai area. The Red Guards' description of how the leaflet was circulated shows the importance of public-relations techniques in China:

> That night, several hundred thousand copies of the leaflet were run off, and the Work Team quickly organized their distribution.
>
> At noon on September 6, the Work Team officials took Red Guard workers from the factory and drove in three-wheeled vans to Shanghai's satellite towns . . . delivering the leaflets to the big factories.
>
> They also got 300 teachers and students from the factory school to take the leaflets around to all ten districts of the Shanghai munici- pality. Their travel and food expenses, which must have amounted to some 200 yuan, were all paid. This was a fine way to carry out the slogan "Make Revolution: Boost Production!"
>
> They also mailed a lot of the leaflets, thus spreading their evil influence all over the country. (Later, when the ax was about to fall, they secretly tried to get these back. We do not know how far they succeeded.)
>
> Even more infuriating, they persuaded revolutionary teachers, students, and Red Guards to take thousands of the leaflets with them on their liaison around the country and distribute them on the way. This not only spread the poison but also made a mockery of the revolutionary liaison that Chairman Mao is so keen on.

We do not know the wording of the telegram, but Red Guard references to it in this leaflet reveal that the Peking students were accused of having "climbed onto the roof," "smashed windows," and "broken into the building." They were also said to be "still making a disturbance." The Municipal Committee, on the other hand, had "upheld the great red banner of Chair- man Mao's thought throughout," a policy that had proved "highly successful."

The leaflet provides another clue to the text in this statement by someone who was present at the discussion:

> I have a little education, so they asked my opinion. I told them: "It's fine the way it is. Three paragraphs, a clear development of

the theme. I would just add 'Shanghai people know best about Shanghai affairs.'" Later, this sentence was added.

Even the left wing acknowledged that the Municipal Committee had pulled off a very clever coup in giving such wide publicity to this telegram. According to this leaflet,

Telegrams, leaflets, and wall posters appeared by the thousand. No. 2 State Cotton Mill came up with its "We Old Workers Want to Have Our Say," No. 5 State Cotton Mill put out its "Urgent Protest," and there were many others. The word spread like wildfire through the country. Yang Fu-chen's telegram was the most influential of all and did the most damage. . . . It had a most deleterious effect on Shanghai's workers, peasants, and townspeople. It turned them against the Peking Red Guards and created the kind of public opinion that led to these students from the North being set upon and driven away.

For the radicals, Mayor Ts'ao Ti-ch'iu symbolized the revisionism of the Municipal Committee, so it was not long before he was getting all the blame:

On September 4, in the guest room of Kangping Street Secretariat, Ts'ao Ti-ch'iu said: "These Peking students have already reported many things to the Central Committee. Now, there are a lot of ordinary people in Shanghai who want to send telegrams to Chairman Mao, to set the record straight. We should not hinder them."

He also repeatedly urged Secretary-General Fang Yang [of the Municipal Party Committee] to telephone various places and get them to send telegrams criticizing the Peking Red Guards to the Central Committee. Before the day was out, Shanghai's walls were fairly plastered with copies of telegrams vilely slandering the Peking students. This caused a number of misguided Shanghai workers, students, and townsfolk to harass the Peking Red Guards, and a serious state of affairs prevailed.

On September 4, Ts'ao Ti-ch'iu even had the audacity to get in touch with Ts'ai Tsu-ch'uan [a scientist at Futan University, famous as the inventor of new sources of light] and ask him to bring the Peking students who were staying at Futan to the Municipal Committee offices, so that they might "dissuade" the Peking Red Guards from their sit-in. (RG 9:4.1)

This is an interesting passage, for it distinguishes between two groups of Peking students. There were some at Futan who did not participate in the demonstrations at the Municipal Committee building. They could have been in Shanghai for purely academic reasons, but then why would the Mayor recruit them? Or they could have been political opponents of the demonstrators, which would make more sense. This might be evidence of an early split in the Peking Red Guard ranks.

There are two possible reasons why most Shanghai students withheld support from the Peking Red Guards: First, they had no clear evidence of revisionism in the Shanghai Municipal Committee nor were they even looking for it at this stage; second, many of the leading Shanghai Red Guard groups were already effectively controlled by high Party cadres. The radicals had no doubt that the second of these reasons was the operative one:

The Shanghai Municipal Committee hastily set up the first Red Guard federation—the General Headquarters of Red Guards from Shanghai Schools and Colleges. With the help of the East China Bureau, it soon controlled this organization through the children of leading officials. . . .

Nan Mo Middle School, for example, was connected by a direct phone link to the East China Bureau Administration Office. . . . Nan Mo was one of the first schools to start a Red Guard organization. Many of the students there were sons and daughters of high cadres in the Shanghai Municipal Committee and the East China Bureau. The son of Han Che-yi [one of the top men in the East China Bureau], for example, was a Red Guard leader at Nan Mo. . . .

On the afternoon of September 4, more than 100 Peking students went to the East China Bureau and demanded to see Ts'ao Ti-ch'iu. The officials were scared stiff. They not only got their own Red Guards to defend them but also rang Nan Mo Middle School for reinforcements. . . . 100–200 Red Guards from Nan Mo came.

The Red Guards are supposed to be spontaneous revolutionaries, springing of their own accord from the masses. Yet here we have the East China Bureau controlling both its own and outside groups and using them to put down genuinely popular revolutionaries who had come to the East China Bureau precisely to oppose its bureaucraticism.[3]

3 From a leaflet entitled "Open Fire on the East China Bureau!" dated December 22, 1966.

A further accusation that the East China Bureau played an active part in opposing the Peking Red Guards was contained in a poster that appeared on a Shanghai wall much later, in November. The writer was a worker from a railway machine shop who claimed that, on September 5, sixteen workers from his factory had seen Peking Red Guards being harassed by a big group outside the Municipal Committee building. They had immediately rushed to tell the East China Bureau and get help for the Peking students. To their astonishment, they were detained for questioning and not released until the following morning. They had asked to be able to telephone the Central Committee in Peking but were told there was no direct line.

The next day, sixty "misguided" Red Guards came to their factory and proceeded to beat the radical workers with "army-type leather belts, leather whips, and iron bars, until their clothes were soaked in blood."

This sounds like a fabrication. For one thing, running to the East China Bureau for help in stopping a street fight is like going to the governor's residence to report a barroom brawl. For another, stories of violence were inevitably exaggerated. I cycled around Shanghai day and night during the worst part of the Cultural Revolution, and I never saw a weapon of any kind. Yet wall posters would repeatedly claim that a peaceful debate between opposing Red Guard groups was suddenly turned by evil backstage manipulators into a full-scale battle with clubs and iron bars. No one ever explained where these instruments came from. They are not more common props in Chinese streets than in the cities of the West, and rather difficult to conceal under a jacket. Furthermore, these lethal skirmishes never seemed to result in death, for the Red Guards would have been the first to scream if they had. This leads one to conclude that the weapons were largely rhetorical and that most of the blood was added afterward to lend color.

The significance of this particular tale lies in its reference to factory-workers who were openly sympathetic to the Peking Red Guards. Subsequent events showed most dramatically that such groups did exist at that time; they became most important when the Shanghai factory-workers entered the movement with a vengeance in November.

At the beginning of September, however, sympathy for the Peking Red Guards was minimal. The Municipal Committee had every reason to be pleased with itself. It had weathered an "invasion" from Peking and emerged with the vast majority of its people behind it. For some time after the September 4 incident, the people of Shanghai looked on the Peking Red Guards in much the same way as white Americans regard black militants —as sincere, perhaps, but somewhat fanatical. The members of the Shanghai Municipal Committee no doubt had their own adjectives.

September was a month of great activity in the streets, as well-organized bands of local Red Guards methodically searched the houses of the middle class. The youngsters enjoyed themselves thoroughly, digging up the gardens, draining the wells, poking around the chimneys and behind the walls of the well-to-do. They came up with enough arms and ammunition, hoarded goods, old land titles, gold, silver, and Kuomintang flags to justify—in their eyes—the raids.

September was also the month of student liaison, when millions of Red Guards traveled the country to "make revolutionary contacts." This was dangerous for the local Party authorities, for it brought new enemies into their area. The Shanghai Committee's fight with the Peking Red Guards was the first step in a campaign to discourage liaison. Mayor Ts'ao Ti-ch'iu, according to the radicals, was to blame:

Ts'ao Ti-ch'iu, in meetings of the Secretariat and the Standing Committee, condemned the "criminal actions" of the Red Guards. Of the Peking students, he said: "They are not interested in arguing pros and cons. They are interested only in violence. They want to bring everything and everyone down."

On September 13, at a Standing Committee meeting, Committee member Yang Shih-fa called the Peking revolutionaries "hoodlums" who "attacked people without cause" and went on to say that they were simply itinerant troublemakers with no experience of revolution whatsoever. . . . "They go around stirring up trouble and call it 'making revolution'; we get on with our normal work and they accuse us of "suppressing the Revolution.'"

Whereupon Ts'ao Ti-ch'iu remarked cynically: "We must examine these people and find out exactly who they are." And later he said: "Ring the Peking Cultural Revolution Office and get them to order these students home!"

On September 30, the Shanghai Municipal Committee cabled the Central Committee, complaining that the Peking students had used violence in Shanghai and asking that they be recalled. (RG 8:3.1)

Perhaps some such request was made, for, as National Day (October 1) drew near, the Peking Red Guards did in fact go back to Peking. This may have reflected a shift in the power balance in the capital, or it may have been an acknowledgment by the Mao group that the Shanghai Committee had won the first round.

Mayor Ts'ao, said the radicals, was delighted and spread the word that the Peking Red Guards had gone home because they were in trouble with the Central Committee:

When the Peking revolutionaries went back to the capital to act as inspection teams for National Day, Ts'ao Ti-ch'iu and the rest slandered them abominably, saying they had returned for a "rectification" of their ideas. He also called on Shanghai to "clean out the noxious influence" they had left behind them. (RG 8:3.1)

The Mayor's main argument against student liaison was that it interfered with production:

Ts'ao Ti-ch'iu said liaison would affect production, disrupt "normal order," and "corrupt the youth by exposing them to evil influences."

On September 24, the Shanghai Municipal Committee sent a telegram to the Central Committee that ran as follows:

"Since the end of August, some most unhealthy tendencies have appeared in the field of production. The worst of these stems from students traveling around the country making revolutionary contacts. This has already had quite an effect on industrial output. If it is allowed to continue, normal production levels will be hard to maintain." (RG 8:3.1)

But, the radicals claimed, "Chairman Mao and the Central Committee refused to call a halt to liaison" and Mayor Ts'ao got up at a meeting of the Secretariat on October 5 and said:

> Revolutionary liaison has already affected our industrial production plan, and we estimate that the problem will be even greater in the month of October. Reports have been sent to Peking from all over the country, requesting that liaison cease, so it's no use saying the Central Committee doesn't know what's going on. They know all right. The question is, do they see it in the same real terms as the people at the grass roots? At any rate, they have decided, in their wisdom, to continue with liaison. (RG 8:3.1)

This statement attributed to Mayor Ts'ao has the ring of truth around it. Once again we get the picture not of an evil man conspiring against the students or the Mao group but of a sincere administrator, genuinely concerned about the impact of the Cultural Revolution on Shanghai's industry and earnestly trying to make the Central Committee see reason. This was probably not the whole picture, but it was a side that the radicals refused to contemplate. For them, the Mayor was vice and cunning incarnate.

It seems Mayor Ts'ao opposed not only Red Guards coming to Shanghai but also Shanghai students and teachers going off to make liaison elsewhere. His opposition to the latter may have been milder, for in some ways it suited him to have potential enemies away from town. Sooner or later, however, they would return, and who knew what ideas they might bring with them? So perhaps there is some truth in a subsequent Red Guard accusation that he "got the Department of Higher Education to have the students at Chiaotung University write a wall poster entitled 'We Do Not Support Liaison Outside Shanghai.'" Its text was "widely disseminated." Ts'ao was also said to have "repeatedly asked the State Council in Peking to keep liaison within provincial boundaries" (RG 8:3.1).

The liaison of Red Guards caused trouble everywhere. During September, Shanghai's walls carried protest and counterprotest from towns near and far, describing local resistance to Red Guard incursions. Places that were featured prominently were Hofei (capital of Anhui Province), Yangchow (a town near the junction of the Grand Canal and the Yangtze), Soochow (about 40 miles inland from Shanghai), and Wenchow and Chinhua (towns in Chekiang Province). In Chinhua alone, there were clashes between Red Guards and local peasants on September 8, 9, 12, 14, 15, 16, and 17. The whole thing seems to have started when some Red Guards tried to put a high hat on the 17-year-old son of a poor peasant and other peasants retaliated by throwing dung at the Red Guards' wall posters.

Shanghai was very crowded during this time, and the colleges, where most of the influx was housed, must have been bursting at the seams. Big private homes were used as reception centers, but visitors stayed in them only a few days. Our hotel looked down on two of these. In one, the original occupant was still in residence though in much reduced circumstances; in the other, the family had been moved out. In both houses, the boy Red Guards slept upstairs and the girls downstairs. And they kept all the lights on right through the night!

Despite the shifting population, the city was still safe. Many of the new Red Guards had never seen a foreigner, so we got a lot more curious stares than usual, but there was never any feeling of danger. The cadres in charge of us were not so sure and twice advised us to stay off the streets. The first time was on September 5 and was prompted perhaps by fear of a backlash after the trouble of the preceding few days. The second was September 25. This time the advice was accompanied by a warning that a "new movement" was about to start. Another teacher and I immediately sallied forth on bicycles, but the only activity was in People's Square, where preparations were being made for National Day.

National Day was a boon for the Municipal Committee. During this traditionally festive occasion, they had the whole city decorated with huge red slogans. This seemed very revolutionary of them, but the radicals pointed out that it also effectively curtailed the use of wall posters, since the people's ingrained respect for the written word made them reluctant to paste their amateurish calligraphy over beautifully executed signs reading "Long live Chairman Mao!"

On the last day of September, the foreign teachers were invited to a banquet in the Sino-Soviet Friendship Building. All the city's notables were present, and Mayor Ts'ao himself made a speech. We felt awkward, since we knew this man had been under attack from the left, and we had no idea of his chances of survival. But he showed no trace of uncertainty. Afterward, while waiting for the bus to pick us up, we noticed that the Municipal Committee members went off one man per car. We sympathized then with the radicals' indignation.

The next day, the big parade took place in People's Square. Again the Mayor spoke, and the crowd roared slogans whenever he paused. As they passed in review, there seemed to be far more Red Guards than workers and peasants; it occurred to us that the Party authorities might have stacked the procession with students loyal to them.

On the whole, the Municipal Committee came through September well. The Peking Red Guards and their left-wing Shanghai allies had every reason to be dismayed as they saw their attacks skillfully parried or turned against them. They could not be sure of the outcome of the movement. If they failed, they would be held responsible for their rebellion; the title of "counter-revolutionary" was never far behind them. Perhaps it was sheer political naïveté that carried them through this period. They were so utterly convinced that they were doing Chairman Mao's will that they never stopped to consider the extent and depth of the power structure facing them.

What could they do, for example, against the might of the press? On September 2, the very day the Peking Red Guards began their sit-in, *Liberation Daily*, the Party organ of Shanghai, ran an editorial warning Red Guards that they disobeyed the Sixteen Points at their peril. And no doubt was left as to which point the paper meant: It was the injunction to "use nonviolent methods in the struggle; do not resort to violence."

Undaunted, the radicals hit back in wall posters. How can we be accused of violence, they cried, when we merely sit down in protest? Surely the violent ones are those who, at the bidding of the authorities, try to drive us away.

On September 8, *Liberation Daily* again stressed obedience to the Sixteen Points. Then it carried a series of articles against bourgeois academics, analyzing their faults in great detail. This, the left wing pointed out, was by that time irrelevant. When the paper did mention the Red Guards, it was always the groups that supported the Shanghai Party. No less than nineteen articles were published in praise of an East China Normal College group called Our Hearts Are Turned Toward the Party. These students had gone out of their way, the leftists claimed, to protect the head of the Shanghai Party's Education Department—Ch'ang Hsi-p'ing—from censure.

What the press did *not* write about was the really newsworthy topic of the time: the Peking Red Guards and the Shanghai radicals. The newspapers in September barely even hinted that the Municipal Committee had enemies. The key phrase of the Cultural Revolution—"Party authorities leading the country back to capitalism"—hardly ever appeared.

This situation was to change very soon.

6. The Party Black Books

September had come and gone with no significant victories any-where for the Mao group. Three major offensives—the original June campaign, the Eleventh Plenum, and the Red Guard move-ment—had all been absorbed in the Party's thick padding of prestige. The Red Guards were meant as a shock force, but the Party establishment had deftly organized other Red Guard units that were loyal to the local committees. These moderates quickly outnumbered the radicals, thus denying them the right to claim mass support.

The Mao group reacted with yet another escalation. On Octo-ber 5, an "Urgent Directive from the Central Military Com-mittee" was issued. Unlike the Sixteen Points, it received very little publicity. The establishment had welcomed the Sixteen Points, because it could be used in the Party's defense, but the Urgent Directive was a clear threat to the hierarchy.

The Urgent Directive introduced new dimensions into the struggle. Its military origin was, of course, very important. It suggested, for one thing, that Defense Minister Lin Piao was behind it; it also implied that the Central Committee was now so badly split that the Military Committee had become the motive force in the Cultural Revolution; finally, it represented an intensification of the struggle—an order from the Military Com-mittee would naturally elicit a military or paramilitary response from the radicals.

It also clarified for the first time that the Cultural Revolution was a fight to the death between two distinct Party lines. It did not call them "Mao's line" and "Liu Shao-ch'i's line"; it was only much later that people would see the movement in these terms. At this stage, the distinction was between "the proletarian and revolutionary line of Chairman Mao" and "the bourgeois and reactionary line of Party authorities taking the capitalist road."

This was news to most of the students, and it complicated the situation considerably. By destroying the comfortable concept of the Party as a monolith, it threw into question the authority of *any* Party member, even a member of the Central Committee itself. It also made participation in the Cultural Revolution a much more risky business. Up to this time, it had been considered natural for student groups to have differences of opinion. These would eventually resolve themselves through debate. Now, with the existence of a revolutionary line and a *counter*revolutionary line, the students would have to be much more careful. The prospect of being involved, even unwittingly, in a counterrevolutionary movement, made many Red Guards—especially those who had supported their local Party authorities—reconsider their stand.

The Urgent Directive, besides redefining the strategy of the Cultural Revolution, also offered precise tactical instructions to the Red Guards. The best way, it said, to expose the purveyors of the bourgeois reactionary line was to concentrate on one of the Sixteen Points—namely, point seven, which explicitly forbade Party authorities to suppress student activists by labeling them rightists, counterrevolutionaries, or anti-Party elements. Party members who had classified students in this way must certainly be bourgeois reactionary authorities who deserved to be brought down.

We have already seen how the students and teachers in the Shanghai Foreign Languages Institute were classified as leftists, middle-of-the-roaders, and rightists. There is no reason to doubt that this process was organized by the opponents of the Mao group, that it went on all over the country, and that the establishment's most outspoken critics were "rightists." The Mao group knew that these lists had been compiled. It also knew that they constituted almost the only written evidence against the establishment, which had been careful throughout the movement to hint and suggest rather than commit things to paper. The Urgent Directive ordered the Party authorities to produce these lists or "black books" and immediately burn them in full view of the masses. It also stipulated that those who had been falsely classified as rightists should receive a formal apology and have their good names completely restored.

This was a clever stroke, for it put the whole Party hierarchy on the defensive. Even Party committees that had not kept black books were forced to prove their innocence. Those that *had* kept lists found themselves confronted by unpleasant alternatives: (1) They could make a clean breast of it, thereby losing untold prestige and endangering the higher levels of the Party, where the idea had originated; (2) they could deny everything, thus inviting student investigation—and woe betide the Party committees should the truth ever come out!

According to a statement by Chou En-lai, the Mao group had hesitated before deciding that the black books should be burned:

> Some comrades say that if the lists are burned their evidence against the bourgeois reactionary authorities goes up in smoke. We do not agree with this view. The students know by now most of the mistakes that the Party committees and the Work Teams have made. . . . These will become even clearer as they keep up the pressure and begin to see the full consequences of such mistakes. . . . Chairman Mao and Vice-Chairman Lin, the Central Military Committee, and the Central Cultural Revolution Group considered this question over and over again and finally decided it was best to burn this evidence.[1]

The radicals claimed that the Shanghai Municipal Committee had ordered all cadres to deny the existence of black books and to destroy material that could be called repressive:

> Ts'ao Ti-ch'iu stubbornly resisted the Urgent Directive. He refused to hand over any "black" material but continued to investigate and denounce members of the masses.

[1] Chou En-lai's speech in the Great Hall of the People, November 27, 1966, as reported in a Red Guard newspaper.

At a meeting of university Party Committee secretaries called by the Municipal Committee, it was suggested that public utterances by school officials and records of enlarged meetings of Party committees be handed to the masses for examination and criticism.

This was not much to ask, but the counterrevolutionary revisionist Yang Hsi-kuang opposed the idea with all his might. Ts'ao Ti-ch'iu supported Yang Hsi-kuang and would not permit this material to be made public. It was even decided that, for "security reasons," cadres' notebooks should be destroyed. This was done to remove proof of their guilt.

As a direct result of this policy, fighting broke out in several colleges; there was even bloodshed, as large groups clashed over "black" material. (RG 8:3.1)

To get an idea of what this fighting meant, let us take another look at the Shanghai Foreign Languages Institute.

The strife in August had carried over into the Red Guard groups. Two main student organizations had come into being, both of which included in their ranks some teachers and Party members. There were also many minor groups formed by people who did not totally agree with the policies of the larger bodies. They had less power, of course, though they sometimes served as a catalyst.

The larger of the two main organizations was the Red Guard Regiment. It had responded to the Shanghai Municipal Committee's call to form Red Guard groups and was therefore part of the city-wide First Headquarters, a body loyal to the Party establishment. In our Institute, the members of the Red Guard Regiment tended to be third- and fourth-year students—many of whom were the children of petty-bourgeois Shanghai parents. They had been admitted to the Institute before 1964, when a policy change had raised the proportion of proletarian children.

The smaller group called itself the Field Army. Most of its members were first- and second-year students, and its leaders were the handful of radicals who had been hitting the administration hard during the first stages of the movement. Like the Red Guard Regiment, the Field Army was also affiliated to a Shanghai-wide student organization. Theirs was known as Second Headquarters, though they preferred to call themselves "Red

Revolutionaries," instead of using their full title: The Revolutionary Committee of Red Guards from Shanghai Schools and Colleges. The Second Headquarters was set up after the first, precisely to prevent the Municipal Committee from dominating the Red Guard movement. Its leaders were Peking-oriented (if not actually from Peking), and they considered the Shanghai Committee a stumbling block in the path of the Cultural Revolution.

At our Institute, the Red Guard Regiment seems to have outnumbered the Field Army roughly two to one. In some respects, the Field Army had only itself to blame for this disparity. It had managed to alienate the majority by its extremism, as in the clash between exorcists and the student body on August 12, and by its exclusivity. Copying a Peking left-wing slogan: "If your father was a reactionary, you're no good; if your father was a revolutionary, you're automatically a good fellow!" it had refused membership to people not of proletarian origin. This slogan, which was current for a time throughout the left wing, was quickly repudiated, but the memory of its use lingered on, and did a lot of harm to the radicals.

Judging from our Institute's Field Army, the left-wing students were very disappointed at being in a minority, and they spoke and acted larger than life to make up for it. My wife taught second-year English, and 11 of her 15 students were Field Army members. (Three of the remaining 4 had a little authority, which would explain their decision to go with the pro-Party majority.) These boys and girls often came to keep us informed during the movement. They were as cheerful as ever during the preliminary small talk, but as soon as the subject of the struggle at the Institute was broached, they would get very serious, even a little bitter, and soon epithets would rain down on the Party authorities. Why was it, they would ask, that, of 200 Party members in the Institute, only 7 or 8 were in any way affiliated with the Field Army? Why was it that only 6 of the 24 representatives on the students' own Provisional Revolutionary Committee were Field Army members? Clearly, they said, the radicals were the victims of a Party Committee conspiracy.

These youngsters were patently sincere in their indignation.

They saw themselves as "Chairman Mao's good children" and believed that their Field Army was the only group in the Institute that was truly responding to the great call to "carry the Cultural Revolution through to the very end." They were convinced that time would justify them and that the majority would eventually join them.

My students were equally sincere, but they held different views. They were third-year English students, and all fifteen of them were stanch Red Guard Regiment members. They did not despise the Field Army, but they felt a rather elder-brotherly sadness that the younger students had taken an erroneous course. They too looked forward to the reunification of the student body, but they were quite sure that *they* were the mainstream of the movement.

What the Red Guard Regiment disliked most about the Field Army was its violence. My students were prepared to admit that revisionism did indeed exist in our Institute, but they maintained that the proper way to expose it was to follow the Sixteen Points and "use peaceful methods, not violence." The Field Army, they claimed, was essentially violent in language and action, and the behavior of its members showed no respect for the Party. My students felt that the Party—not only in the Institute but throughout the country—deserved credit for its achievements. If revisionists and bureaucrats had usurped important positions, they were to be rooted out, but, as the Central Committee had consistently emphasized, the guilty were only a handful, and there was no reason to suspect all Party members of heinous crimes.

An intense ideological debate went on behind the scenes, and both the Red Guard Regiment and the Field Army produced masses of documentation to support their positions. My students mimeographed a substantial booklet entitled "100,000 Ways of Looking at Things," containing abundant quotes from Mao Tse-tung, Lin Piao, Marx, Engels, Lenin, and Stalin, all of them skillfully chosen to refute the arguments and attitudes of the radicals. Here are some selections:

What should our attitude be to words and actions that *seem* revolutionary but are in fact reactionary?

Stalin says ("On the Struggle Against Rightists and Extreme Leftists"): "We should not forget that right-wingers and extreme left-wingers are birds of a feather. They both start from a position of opportunism. The difference between them is that the right-wingers do not generally disguise their opportunism, whereas the extreme left-wingers normally give theirs the euphemism of 'revolution.'"

What should our attitude be to people who quote Chairman Mao in support of erroneous ideas?

Lenin says ("A Letter to the Comrades"): "Marxism is an extremely profound and universal subject. It is not surprising, therefore, that in the 'reasoning' of people who have betrayed Marxism one often comes across a quotation from Marx—usually taken out of context."

What should our attitude be to the slogan "If your father was a reactionary, you're no good; if your father was a revolutionary, you're a good fellow!"?

Mao Tse-tung says ("On Strategy Against Japanese Imperialism"): "In the world of adults, one sometimes runs across 3-year-old children. Now, 3-year-old children are fine for their age; they already know quite a lot of things. But they are not capable of governing a nation, for they do not understand the principles that are involved. Marxism-Leninism is against infantilism in the revolutionary ranks. One manifestation of infantilism is when people cling to rigid and exclusivist tactics."

What should our attitude be to those who quote from Chairman Mao's "Report on an Investigation into the Hunan Peasant Movement," in order to justify the practice of putting high hats on people as a form of struggle?

Lenin says ("On the Rights of Peoples to Self-Determination"): "In analyzing any social problem, Marxist theory absolutely insists that the problem be put in a definite historical context."

What should our attitude be to people who say, "The grass roots organizations of the Party cannot lead this movement but must stand to one side"?

Mao Tse-tung says ("On Strategy Against Japanese Imperialism"): "The Chinese Communist Party—its leading administrators, its cadres, its ordinary members—is not afraid of any hardships. Those who doubt our ability to lead the revolutionary war run the risk of sinking into the mire of opportunism."

Someone had devoted much time and careful research to find
neat answers to the problems posed by the militant left wing.
My students had an excellent grasp of Marxist political principles, drawn, for the most part, from the study of Mao Tse-tung's
works. Their direct experience of basic Marxist texts was comparatively limited. This work, then, was probably compiled by
a special research team, commissioned by the Party at the municipal or even the national level to present ideological alternatives
to the radicals' tactics.

The effect of such sound theoretical justification for the moderate position was to convince my students—and hundreds of
thousands like them through the length and breadth of China—
that *they* were the true defenders of orthodox Marxism and, more
important still, that they were the real *Maoists*. The Cultural
Revolution was a fight between two interpretations of Maoism,
and not, as the mass media in the West made out, a struggle for
supremacy between "Maoists" and "anti-Maoists." Almost everyone in China is pro-Mao, just as almost everyone in Britain was
pro-Churchill during World War II; commitment to the name
ranges all the way from superstitious faith to a critical appreciation of the man's contribution to his country. Most Chinese have
a mixture of ingredients in their attitudes, but few could rightly
be labeled anti-Mao.

In the Red Guard movement, it was precisely this universal
admiration of Mao that made the struggle so bitter. The students'
views coincided on so many essential points that they had to keep
their eyes peeled for the characteristics they *thought* they should
find in their opponents. Only by magnifying their differences
could the students distinguish between the groups that were
genuinely carrying out the Chairman's policies and those that
were being manipulated by reactionaries.

The same principle applied to the radicals' attacks on the
Party. They snatched at straws. In our Institute, for example, the
Field Army suspected that the Party Committee had kept black
books on them. But the only evidence was so slight as to be
worthless. A radical student had written a poem on the black-
board—a quatrain composed by a Communist martyr before
1949. The lines vowed revenge on "the king" who had caused

his people so much suffering. The allusion was to Chiang K'ai-shek, but some of the moderate students, who were looking for material to use against the Field Army, reported that a poem against Chairman Mao had appeared in the Institute. The Party Committee promised to investigate, but by October nothing had been done, and the radicals charged that the authorities were keeping the information to use against the student—and, by extension, against the Field Army—at a later date. This flimsy "evidence" was all the Field Army had, and they clung tenaciously to it. The issue was the center of quite a controversy during September.

In October, after the Urgent Directive, the Field Army decided to take "revolutionary action." On October 15, using the poem as a pretext, though obviously hoping to capture more damaging material, Field Army Red Guards methodically sealed desks and filing cabinets in the Institute offices of the Party Committee and the Cultural Revolution Group and in the departmental Party branches. In typical Chinese style, the seals were nothing fancy—simply strips of paper, an inch or 2 wide and 2 to 3 feet long, with the date of sealing and the name of the group responsible. They were a common sight in Shanghai around this time; as I cycled through the city, I could tell at a glance, by the St. Andrew's crosses of white paper on the windows and doors, which houses had been searched and closed by Red Guards.

Once the seals were put on, no one dared to remove them. The writer of the seal would know immediately if someone had tried to replace his original with a forgery, and removing or tampering with a seal was a sure proof of guilt. To the indignant protests of the Party authorities, the radicals would say: "If you have nothing to hide, why should you object to our sealing your files?"

This was an awkward question to answer. The authorities could only retort, as they did immediately, that some of the information in the files was classified material and that to touch it would constitute a serious breach of the laws regarding state secrets. This threat worked for the time being; it was made by the Party officials in all the colleges where files were sealed and was repeated when the practice spread to factories and government departments. It was a coordinated response by the Party to what was obviously a coordinated attack by the left wing.

In our Institute, most of the students deplored the sealing and supported the Party's warning about secret material. Once again, their ingrained sense of discipline and respect for the Party strongly influenced their judgment.

The result was a brief stalemate. The Municipal Committee tried to relieve the pressure by spreading the word that no less than 370,000 middle-school students and 70,000 college students would be sent to the countryside to help with the autumn harvest. But there was a change of plan at the last minute, and our students did not go.

On October 18, the Field Army published a statement formally accusing the Party Secretary of possessing "black" material and demanding that he produce it at once and admit that he had been keeping it as evidence against the radicals. The Party Secretary refused point-blank, and the Red Guard Regiment, along with other smaller groups, supported him. The Field Army, after many meetings and discussions, decided to stage a hunger strike. On October 26, thirty-six Field Army students vowed not to eat until the Party Secretary signed their demands. Despite the small number of participants, the hunger strike caused quite a stir. Not since the really bad old days, before liberation, had Shanghai students used such a method against the authorities. Nor was it confined to our Institute; radical Red Guards in several other Shanghai colleges launched simultaneous hunger strikes.

Wall posters then appeared in profusion, condemning the hunger strike as "a bourgeois weapon" that was "entirely unnecessary in a socialist society" and "an illegitimate method of struggle" that "damages the health for no reason." Our Institute's Red Guard Regiment, along with the students' Provisional Revolutionary Committee and other groups, staged a counter sit-down strike in front of the Municipal Committee offices for the duration of the Field Army hunger strike. This event was discussed in buses and shops and on the walls, thus bringing the Institute into the limelight for the first time.

Perhaps the incident drew too much attention, for the Party Secretary suddenly agreed to sign the radicals' demands. The joy in the Field Army was short-lived; no sooner had the hunger strikers broken their fast than the Party Secretary promptly retracted his signature. He wrote a wall poster by way of explanation:

At 2:30 P.M. on October 26, the Field Army Red Guards of our Institute held a meeting about so-called black material. . . . They demanded that I admit that the material came within the scope of the Military Committee's Urgent Directive—in other words, that it was information kept for future use against the students. They also insisted that I start rehabilitating the students who had been classified as rightists during the movement.

At first, I refused. Then I saw that this was only a minor contradiction, that these few hundred revolutionary students had boundless love for the Party and Chairman Mao and that their revolutionary emotions were running at full spate. I decided to support their spirited attack on the bourgeois reactionary line.

Then they refused to eat. To make matters worse, the weather was cold. It struck me that, if they went on like this for long, they would damage their health. So, to settle the issue quickly, I took the step of signing a statement prepared by the Field Army comrades. This was at 2:20 A.M. on the night of October 27.

But the broad masses of revolutionary teachers, students, and staff at our Institute were most upset when they heard what I had done, and they criticized me severely. So I had another look at the Urgent Directive of the Military Committee. . . . On rereading it, I realized that I had made an extremely serious mistake. In the first place, although some fourth-year French students had told me certain things orally, I had not seen any actual document that could be interpreted as a threat to any students. I therefore had no right to decide on the nature of this material. Secondly, since the movement began, no student at this Institute has been classified as counterrevolutionary nor has any student been forced to write a confession or coerced in any way. Therefore, the question of restoring the good name of students simply does not arise.

It is true that early in the movement the German-French Department Party Branch reported on some students. This document is at present being examined very carefully by a fourth-year French group, to ascertain its true nature. I hope the broad masses . . . will continue with this investigation and find out the truth of the matter.

I am perfectly willing to accept criticism, regardless of who makes it. Chairman Mao says: "A Communist must be prepared to uphold the truth at all times, because the truth is to the advantage of the people. A Communist must also be prepared to correct his mistakes at any time, because mistakes are to the detriment of the people."

. . . I am determined to do as Chairman Mao says and correct my mistakes. I shall make a public self-criticism at an appropriate time. Meanwhile, I trust that everyone will act on the Urgent Directive and continue to expose and denounce the shortcomings and mistakes made by me and the Party Committee during the movement so far.[2]

This statement by the Party Secretary did little good. By signing in the first place, he had alienated many members of the Red Guard Regiment; by then retracting his signature, he had convinced the whole Field Army of his treachery.

His predicament was relieved somewhat by a sudden upsurge in the movement of revolutionary liaison. Throughout September, students had been traveling a great deal, but most of the traffic was of Peking Red Guards going out to the provinces and provincial Red Guards making the trip to Peking to "see Chairman Mao."

Then, in October, "long marches" became fashionable. Some students from Dairen in Manchuria started it all by walking to Peking, and, before long, thousands of Red Guards were packing their knapsacks for unheard-of journeys. In parties of a dozen or so, boys and girls set off not only for the capital but also for Mao's old guerrilla bases, for Manchuria, for barely civilized areas of the southwest, even for Tibet and Sinkiang. Some boasted they could cross the Great Snow Mountains or the terrible marshlands of the Northwest, as the Red Army had done in 1935. Others were content to do a round trip of a few hundred miles.

They carried a bedroll, a change of clothes, a picture of Chairman Mao, the little red book of quotations, a portable mimeograph machine, and precious little else. The idea was to preach the word to the peasants as they went, but many of the students stuck to main roads or railroad tracks; others did go to the villages but, after their day's march, they were often too tired for propagandizing.

[2] From "An Anthology of Wall Posters," published by the Field Army Red Guards of the Shanghai Foreign Languages Institute.

The long marches gave the establishment in the cities a short breather. Many of the local students went off on safari, and the colleges and schools were crammed with comparatively unsophisticated visitors from the provinces. At our Institute, there were some 4,000 "outsiders" late in October. Since the place was designed to hold a maximum of 2,000 students, the excess population had to sleep wherever it could find space.

Whatever practical purpose the long marches were meant to serve, their effect was to slow down the movement. Visitors were permitted to sit in on meetings and contribute from their own experience, but they were forbidden to take an active part in the host college's internal struggle. As a result, visitors were often nothing but a nuisance. At our Institute, the students, staff, and administration were all kept busy avoiding strife, for their young guests were quick to complain of overcrowding, unusual or unpalatable food, and discrimination of any kind.

It was several days before the students began to realize that the idea of tramping around the country was not exactly calculated to bring the Cultural Revolution to a head. The Field Army was the first to try to get all its wandering members back to the Institute to strike again.

On November 8, they staged a midnight raid on the Party branch offices, breaking their own seals and rifling the files. Up to this time, they had not dared to take such a drastic step, because of the warning about state secrets. They acted now for fear that the Party authorities were about to break the seals themselves and remove the evidence. After the raid, the Field Army claimed they had found what they were looking for, but nothing concrete was advanced to support this boast. The Party Committee, of course, protested loudly, denying the very existence of "black" documents and deploring the "fascist violence" of the minority.

Meanwhile, telegrams were flying all over the country, urging the Red Guard Regiments to return "The Field Army is taking state secrets," the message ran, "come back immediately and stop this." By November 10, enough students had rallied to worry the Field Army. Perhaps the radicals underestimated their opposition, or perhaps they felt it was then or never. In any case, they struck again, this time at the office of the Party Committee itself.

The battle of November 10 was the most spectacular incident of the movement at our Institute. Late at night, the Field Army approached the three-story building that housed the administrative offices, only to find it defended from ground floor to roof by the Red Guard Regiment and allied groups of moderate teachers and workers.

If anyone had suggested in May that by November the whole Institute would be engaged in a nocturnal slugging-match, the students would have laughed themselves sick. Yet here they were, several hundred of them trying to get into a building occupied by several hundred others, and only the small print on the Red Guard arm bands to distinguish one side from the other.

Many a punch must have bounced off the wrong chin that night, as the students wrestled and shoved at the main entrance, fought each other through the corridors, scaled the walls, stove-in windows, and pelted each other with anything that came to hand.

The next day, the usual long lists of minor injuries appeared on the walls, plus the recriminations and exaggerations that always followed a Red Guard clash. The battle was inconclusive. The Field Army again claimed to have found "black" material; the Red Guard Regiment again vehemently denied it. Both sides brought charges of violence, with each claiming that the other had provoked it. The violence gave way to ideological debate, which centered on whether or not the radicals had the right to use force to find evidence against Party authorities. This argument was by no means limited to our Institute, as the following quote shows:

> Recently, in Futan University, Shanghai Engineering College, Shanghai Foreign Languages Institute, Chiaotung University, and other places, "black" material has been taken by force. Since this is an unprecedented phenomenon, it has now become the topic of all conversation and a source of debate whenever it is mentioned. No two people see it alike. One person says it is an excellent revolutionary device; another condemns it as disruptive of law and order; still another argues that it is neither wholly good nor wholly bad, because it uses the wrong means for the right ends.

This passage is from an interesting pamphlet entitled "Should 'Black' Materials Be Taken by Force?" that was circulated in

Shanghai by a radical group from Peking Aeronautical Institute. It quotes Chou En-lai's July 22 definition of "black" material [see page 62] and castigates Party officials who used such repressive measures as no better than the Kuomintang reactionaries with their theory of "political tutelage." Any form of paternalism is equally undesirable, it points out; the students of China are not to be treated as children. On the contrary, the students must act according to the Sixteen Points and "educate and liberate themselves." Therefore, the pamphlet concludes, force *can* be used in this particular situation:

> It is already more than a month since the Military Committee's Urgent Directive, yet not a single Shanghai college has handed over a scrap of "black" material. There are many factories, administrative offices, and artistic and literary circles where people do not even know of the *existence* of instructions from the Military Committee. In the last 4 weeks, the Shanghai Municipal Committee has made no attempt to publicize the Urgent Directive. Instead, it has stubbornly tried to suppress it. . . .
>
> Under these intolerable circumstances, we revolutionaries have no choice but to take the "black" material by force!
>
> . . . They will say: "You are stealing state secrets!" But this is a lie. It is the oppressed revolutionary masses who are most concerned with the affairs of state. They are the true revolutionaries, the ones who have the welfare of the Party and the people at heart. It is precisely to root out counterrevolution and revisionism, to protect the security of the state, and to ensure that secrets are *not* betrayed that they fight so bravely. When the "monarchists" scream "You must not steal state secrets!" it is a perfect case of the pot calling the kettle black.

These raids on Party files were obviously coordinated. In our Institute, the original sealing was done on October 15, and the frontal attack took place on November 10. Compare these dates, and the nature and sequence of events, with the following account of what happened at the Shanghai Engineering College:

> There is ample evidence that the College Party Committee . . . practiced a thoroughly bourgeois and reactionary line. Even after the Military Committee's Urgent Directive, they still refused to hand over "black" material. In order to show them up, as well as to pre-

vent them from moving or destroying the material, we took revolutionary action on October 18, sealing the files in the administration office and in all the departmental Party branch offices.

This reduced certain people to tears of rage. . . . One group . . . tried to counter our revolutionary action by secretly removing our seals. A man named Tu, an Assistant Secretary-General of the Shanghai Municipal Committee and its representative in our college, made inflammatory statements such as "If it is a revolutionary act to put seals on things, it is an equally revolutionary act to take them off!"

. . . When they had removed our seals, they started shifting the "black" documents. On the night of November 4, a fire was seen in the Party Committee's archive office. Realizing that state secrets and "black" material were in danger of being destroyed, we demanded permission to enter the office and save them. The Party Committee not only refused this just request but sent the Workers Scarlet Guards and the Proletarian Revolutionary Rebels Headquarters[3] to defend the building, inside and out, right up to the third floor. They kept shouting slogans like "Use peaceful means, not violence!" but they were kicking and punching as they spoke.

. . . On the night of November 9, we revolutionary rebels took further revolutionary action and entered the building to look at the "black" material. This aroused the fear and hatred of the political cadres, who . . . got together a big gang of supporters and prepared to defend the place to the death. . . . (RG 1:2.2)

Then follows a typical description of a Red Guard battle, with all the stereotypes of horror that the writer could summon up: Students are beaten with clubs and whips, hurled out of second-floor windows, dragged by the hair, kicked unconscious, bound and imprisoned in underground caverns, and so on. If one had not seen the same phrases used to describe a dozen other skirmishes he would have feared dreadful carnage. In fact, the Chinese are so appalled by physical violence that a few noses bloodied or eyes blackened immediately assume the proportions of "bloodshed" and "murder."

One important point that emerges from this description is that the attackers were a composite group. The radicals of the Engineering College were accompanied in the raid by allies from the

[3] The latter was a very minor local group; the former, a branch of what later became Shanghai's largest Moderate workers' organization.

Shanghai First Medical College, Futan University, and the Marine Products Institute. This implies a considerable amount of prior organization.

Another interesting aspect is that the defenders of the building, having managed to cut off the besiegers' loudspeaker system, then broadcast their own message at full volume. Their theme: "We are not going to have a repetition of the Hungarian uprising!" As we have seen, this was a common charge brought against the left wing.

The radicals at the Engineering College succeeded in occupying the building, and the Party authorities called up the Municipal Committee:

> The "solution" of the Municipal Committee was to say to us: "If you leave the building, there will be no further problem." This remark was laughable. What about all the people who had been inside the building for days, defending the "black" material—why had they not been asked to leave?
>
> . . . Later some so-called officials from the Municipal Committee arrived. After "conferring" with the Party Committee, they asked us to "negotiate withdrawal." We replied: "If the Party Committee wants to negotiate, why did it not negotiate earlier? Why didn't it hand over the 'black' material while there was still time?" (RG 1:2.2)

If the left-wing students sound violent and intransigent, we must remember that they felt they had cause for anger. Not only in the colleges but in factories, civil administration, urban neighborhoods, and suburban communes radicals had been persecuted by appointees of the pragmatists. Here is an article written by workers in an automobile service station near Shanghai, which shows very clearly what kind of repression had existed:

> The leader of the Socialist Education Movement Work Team, who is now head of the Cultural Revolution Work Team sent to our station by the "black" Shanghai Municipal Committee, is an out-and-out purveyor of the bourgeois reactionary line. . . .
>
> In the Socialist Education Movement, he used all kinds of spy tricks to get information against those he called "the main targets." He watched them like a hawk, asked thousands of questions, and coaxed and coerced people into telling him things. He watched them

eating, walking, and working. He set up a reign of white terror, so that everyone was jumpy and scared to talk to each other.

When the Cultural Revolution started, he stirred up quarrels between people, suggested targets for wall posters, had individuals whom he did not even know branded "antisocial freaks." . . .

Later he held "black" meetings, made "black" speeches, drew up "black" name lists, collected "black" evidence. . . . Any revolutionaries who dared to speak out or take action were labeled "counter-revolutionaries," "anti-Party elements," "dangerous people," "cliques," and "black gangs." And all this he entered in the personal dossiers. . . .

We demand:

1. That he immediately carry out the Central Committee's orders by conscientiously and thoroughly restoring the good names of all revolutionaries falsely accused of counterrevolutionary attitudes.

2. That all the "black" material he used to intimidate the people, including passages from wall posters, be burned in front of everyone and that repressive entries in personal files be cut out and burned and that any information gathered during the Socialist Education Movement, unless it is acknowledged to be true by the person concerned, be henceforth null and void.

3. That all "black" classifications of workers and cadres into such categories as "stanch," "active," "average," "backward," and "hostile" be considered without effect and that they be burned in front of everyone. . . .[4]

Such documents show in a very real way the grave risks run by the radicals in the Cultural Revolution. Their one fear was that something would go wrong, that the authorities would survive the movement and wreak vengeance on them later. This explains the importance they attached to the destruction of any records against them that might be used in "settling accounts after the harvest."

The Field Army students at our Institute were equally obsessed with this possibility. After their unsuccessful raid on the Party archives, they were very vulnerable. The Party Committee seems to have taken the initiative; the radicals claimed that it ordered all the damage caused by the raid to be left exactly as it was, so

[4] From a leaflet dated February 16, 1967, signed The Chinchiang Rebel Branch of the Automobile Service Station Rebel Brigade of the Shanghai Workers Headquarters.

that everyone in the Institute could see proof of the Field Army's violence. It even had the whole scene photographed in detail, they said, and kept certain articles as evidence. This was precisely the kind of blackmail the radicals had been talking about.

Several months later, when the Institute held a long and detailed investigation into the events of October 15, the top men on the Party Committee repeatedly denied the Field Army's charges. Several dozen Party members, workers, students, and teachers, however, testified to receiving or overhearing orders that the damaged building was not to be repaired until photos had been taken. Here is one scene from the "inquest":

> *A Worker*: We were going to fix the windows and doors of the office building, but a workmate came along and said that Liu, the head of the Institute's Cultural Revolution Group, had given orders to leave everything as it was.
>
> *Liu*: It wasn't me. It was someone else. . .
>
> *The Audience* (that is, everyone in the Institute): Down with Liu!
>
> *Another Worker*: I was told not to repair anything. Liu was the one who told me. He said the building should be sealed and nothing touched.
>
> *The Audience*: Down with Liu! (Liu halfheartedly joins in the cry against him.)
>
> (One of the five chairmen, a Field Army student, walks up to Liu, snatches off his blue cap, and throws it across the stage.)
>
> *The Chairman*: Tell us the truth and be quick about it! Did you want this evidence so you could "settle accounts after the harvest"?
>
> *Liu*: No, I did not!
>
> *The Audience* (quoting from the little red book): "We must have faith in the party; we must have faith in the masses. . . ."
>
> *The Chairman* (angry now, waving a finger in Liu's face): Did you? Answer!
>
> *Liu*: No, I did not!
>
> *The Chairman* (turning to the audience): What should we do with him?
>
> *The Audience*: Down with him![5]

It is hard to gauge the success of the radicals' quest for "black" material. On the whole, it seems to have backfired, for, on November 16, the Central Committee was forced to issue a

[5] From the author's notes.

Supplementary Ruling on the Question of Personal Files in the Great Proletarian Cultural Revolution—a document that explicitly forbade the use of violence to get hold of student records.

This raised a laugh in, of all places, the Soviet Union. Radio Moscow commented archly:

> The Supplementary Ruling . . . is a nice example of closing the stable door after the horse has bolted. In Shanghai, for example, there are more than thirty institutes of higher education. It appears from a Red Guard newspaper called *Revolutionary Rebel News* that the Party Committees in all these institutes refused to hand over so-called black material and that a few people with ulterior motives therefore broke in and stole it. As a result, there was bloodshed in several colleges. (RG 2:2.1)

Some radical Red Guards monitored this broadcast in Shanghai, and their reaction was in character: "So the Soviet revisionists abuse us for taking 'black' material! What further proof do we need that we are in the right? . . . All revolutionary comrades should ask themselves: What does it signify that the Soviet revisionists get such a kick out of abusing our party and our Red Guards and support the position of the Shanghai Municipal Committee?"

The Central Committee appears to have been embarrassed by the widespread and often abortive use of breaking and entering as a revolutionary tactic. The Supplementary Ruling was an attempt to halt a dangerous trend. The brains behind the Cultural Revolution knew that if they tolerated or encouraged violence there was no telling how or when it would end.

Nor would it be easy to restrain the radicals once they got into the Party's files. A leaflet dated December 1, 1966,[6] makes this clear in its account of a telephone conversation that reportedly took place between some Chapei retail-workers in Shanghai and a representative of the Central Cultural Revolution Group in Peking:

> *Question*: Can we look at the personal files before we destroy them?
> *Answer*: You can look only at your own dossier. The rest must be

[6] The leaflet's signatories were from the State Textile Store, the State Department Store, and the State Hardware Store in Chapei District.

collected together and burned. The Politburo studied this question and decided it was best not to look at the files of others. Some people might use the information for their own purposes, and this could be detrimental to the unity of the masses and the development of the Cultural Revolution.

Question: The Central Committee's Supplementary Ruling does not actually *say* we can't look at them. What if some people are determined to?

Answer: The Supplementary Ruling, which was approved by Chairman Mao himself, distinctly says you *cannot* look at them. If people are determined to, then their superiors should do some ideological work on them and see that principles are not flouted.

Question: Some people say that if they look at the files and see how the masses and the students have been falsely classified, they'll be better equipped to denounce the bourgeois reactionary line.

Answer: The masses can recognize the bourgeois reactionary line by now. They can condemn it on ideological and political grounds, without looking at the files.

Question: Some say that if they're not allowed to look at the files, they'll take them by force. Is this attitude correct?

Answer: According to the Supplementary Ruling, it is absolutely forbidden to take files by force.

Question: But they say that, in this case, they wouldn't be taking files; they'd be taking "black" material. What about that?

Answer: The Supplementary Ruling speaks only of material used to classify or restrict the masses or the students. It does not mention "black" material.

It seems, then, that the Military Committee's Urgent Directive of October 5, which was meant to give the radicals the upper hand over the Party authorities, did not have the desired effect but only complicated the issue by stirring up endless arguments about the use of force.

This was the last time the Mao group tried to work through students alone. From November on, the movement expanded to include the industrial workers. Whether Peking wanted this to happen or not, it was inevitable. We shall see that, from this time on, no group had full control over the Cultural Revolution. It developed a momentum of its own and did not stop until it had swept through all resistance.

7. The Workers Join In

At the beginning of November, there was a distinct change of mood in Shanghai. October had been a month of bitter confrontation, but most of the action had gone on behind the walls of schools and universities. The public side of the Cultural Revolution—the coming and going of Red Guard groups, the continuing raids on bourgeois houses, the campaign against feudal or foreign relics—was more spectacular than significant. The cutting edge of the movement was the attack on Party officials, and this had rarely gone into the streets.

True, the Municipal Committee building was plastered with wall posters and had been ever since the September 4 incident. But these were selective, cautious, and detailed investigations into the administration rather than a wholesale condemnation of the Party leadership. The strongest headings never went beyond "Something Is Rotten in the Municipal Committee!" or "Those Municipal Committee Members Who Are Trying to Lead Us Back to Capitalism Should Be Sacked!"

This was a mild forerunner of the spate of sloganeering that began in November. Characters 3 feet high, painted in bold black strokes, shouted "Bombard the Municipal Committee!" and "Burn Mayor Ts'ao Ti-ch'iu!" And soon it became quite common to see breathtaking threats like "Any Rat that Dares to Try and Shift the Revolutionary Pacemakers Half a Hair's Breath off Course Will Be Smashed to a Pulp!" I asked some of my students (who had taken a moderate position) what they thought of this language. They laughed uncomfortably and mumbled that the slogans, though "admirably strong," were "of course not to be taken literally."

The new belligerence can be explained by the return to Shanghai of powerful Red Guard groups from cities in the North. The first onslaught of "outside agitators" had been successfully countered by the Shanghai authorities, and the "young daredevils straight from Chairman Mao" had been forced to return to Peking. In November, however, they came back with a vengeance, and they came armed with a new identity and new tactics.

Their identity could be summed up in a word: rebels. So many student organizations had fallen under Party control that the term Red Guards no longer had much revolutionary content. Of the millions of Red Guards in China, only a minority were radical. The title Rebels was introduced to identify those who were truly out to change the system. The motto of this new unity was "Revolution Is No Crime; Rebellion Is Justified!"

The arrival of the Rebels meant a new lease of life for the Shanghai radicals, who immediately joined forces with the newcomers. In our Institute, for example, the Field Army supported the tactics of the Rebels, while the Red Guard Regiment found ideological reasons to reject them.

But it was the tactics themselves that really changed Shanghai. The Rebel policy was to abandon the idea of a purely student movement and take advantage of the growing restlessness of the workers. Employees in Shanghai's factories and offices had put up with half a year of student agitation. They had heard themselves described again and again as "the main force in the revolution," yet they had not been allowed to play a major part. The students, on the other hand, who were merely "the vanguard of the movement," had been acting as if they were the only people in the country.

The left-wing workers were particularly anxious for the Cultural Revolution to succeed. During the first months, when the radical students were criticizing the Party authorities, some workers and factory cadres had also taken a stand and spoken out. If the student movement stopped here—and there were signs that it would—the radical workers might well be classified as rightists and suffer persecution later. Especially concerned were cadres and Party members who hoped that the Cultural Revolution would win them back positions that they had lost during the Socialist Education Movement.

The Shanghai Party authorities knew full well what could happen if the Cultural Revolution got going in the factories and offices. Even the Central Committee in Peking seems to have been reluctant to take the lid off the urban proletariat. Most instructions from the Center were cautious or ambiguous; workers were urged to "stay at their jobs but take part in the movement after hours," and the slogan coined for them was the practically meaningless "Make Revolution: Boost Production."

By November, the movement had been going for 6 months, yet in a city like Shanghai not a single high Party official had been discredited. Some—like the head of Education, Ch'ang Hsi-p'ing, and the man who controlled Propaganda, Yang Hsi-kuang —had occasionally been forced to attend Red Guard rallies and read out self-criticisms to "the masses." But, as long as Mayor Ts'ao and the Committee were behind them, and as long as the press printed glowing reports of the doings of the moderate Red Guards and almost nothing at all about the radicals, these men were safe.

As for the heads of universities, only one man in the whole of East China had lost his job. That was back in June, when the President of Nanking University, K'uang Ya-ming, was dismissed. Since that time, the Party's East China Bureau had seen to it that no one followed in his footsteps.

There had been close shaves, of course, as we have seen from what happened at the Foreign Languages Institute. But disaster had been avoided, usually by pitting student factions against each other and thus preventing them from uniting against the Party. The left-wing students called this tactic "standing on the mountain, watching the tigers fight."

The Rebels from the North were going to change all this. They preached unity with the workers and all-out war on the Party authorities. At first, they had trouble persuading even their own supporters; some said they were too busy with the question of "black" material in their own colleges; others pointed out that they were totally unfamiliar with the problems of workers. Splits developed among the local radicals, but, as the Rebels themselves said, this purified their ranks of wavering elements.

The Municipal Committee watched these developments carefully. At this stage, however, the Party had other urgent problems. There were ominous signs of disaffection in the press, the one place where loyalty had to be maintained at all costs. On October 26, five employees of *Wen Hui Pao*—the paper that had published the article by Yao Wen-yuan that triggered the Cultural Revolution—put up a wall poster criticizing the heads of Shanghai's Propaganda Department (RG 5:4.1). And on November 1, some *Wen Hui Pao* journalists made four demands of the Municipal Committee:

1. The employees of Shanghai newspapers should be allowed to make liaison with each other and exchange experience.
2. We should be permitted to put up wall posters against the Municipal Committee in public places specified by the Committee.
3. Our Rebel group, called The Spark that Sets the Prairie Grass on Fire, has prepared a pamphlet exposing the crimes committed against Chairman Mao's ideas by certain Municipal Committee members. This should be published.
4. We should be told whether the questions and mistakes that came out during our debates on the play *The Dismissal of Hai Jui* are secret or whether they can be made public (RG 5:4.1).

These demands were passed on to the Municipal Committee by a Vice-Director of Propaganda who attended the meeting at which they were formulated. He is said to have dashed straight off to report—at 2 o'clock in the morning! The Municipal Committee's answer was typically evasive and cannot have done much to pacify the Rebels:

1. As the press is an instrument of the dictatorship of the proletariat, the responsibility of each newspaper is heavy. We therefore feel that an exchange of experience between the employees of different papers is undesirable at this time.
2. We also feel it is unnecessary to put up wall posters in public. You can continue to put them up inside the Municipal Committee building. This is our opinion. How does it strike you?

3. The question of publishing a pamphlet is related to that of putting up wall posters. Once a thing is published, it is no longer confined to press circles. Other people read it. Think about this. It's not necessary to publish things when you are free to say all you want to in wall posters.

4. On the question of *The Dismissal of Hai Jui,* you should have faith in the Municipal Committee. We follow Chiang Ch'ing very closely in this matter. You should not worry about it. (RG 5:4.1)

The reference to Chiang Ch'ing (Mao's wife), who had pressured *Wen Hui Pao* into publishing Yao Wen-yuan's first article, suggests that her influence in Shanghai publishing circles was still strong.

Mayor Ts'ao Ti-ch'iu's reaction to the four demands was blunt and threatening, if we can believe the Rebels: "I hear you've been causing strife in *Wen Hui Pao.* Your paper is a part of the dictatorship of the proletariat. You can't carry on like that. If you do, there'll be trouble" (RG 5:4.1). And the Party Branch Secretary of *Wen Hui Pao,* in remarks attributed to him by the Rebels, gave a summary (if not a caricature) of the conservative position:

What you've got now is a few people shouting "Long Live Chairman Mao!" and bellowing all sorts of slogans good and loud. This is a new sort of class struggle—these days people wave a red flag while they're actually attacking the red flag. . . .

When the movement is over, we'll see who's been opposing Chairman Mao from behind a left-wing banner. . . .

These Rebels are suspicious of everyone. They're nihilists. . . . We're approaching a state of anarchy. . . .

We must organize the majority . . . we must put this maverick thinking to the test. (RG 5:4.1)

The trouble in the press was symptomatic of a more widespread unrest. The Municipal Committee managed to keep the journalists quiet, at least for another month; but the ferment in the workers' ranks was not to be contained. To make matters worse, groups of Rebel students were making the rounds of the factories, urging a coalition against the authorities.

A Shanghai-wide organization of Rebel workers was quickly

formed. At first it functioned underground; then, on November 9, a big inauguration rally was held in Culture Square, attended, some reports said, by as many as 20,000 people (RG 17:3.1).

The organization called itself Shanghai Workers Revolutionary Rebel Headquarters—a title that was immediately abbreviated to Workers Headquarters. It was opposed from its inception by the Municipal Committee, which had nothing to gain and everything to lose from the formation of such a body. Some idea of its birth pangs was provided by a Rebel source:

On November 8, representatives of the Workers Headquarters went to the Kangping Street Secretariat of the Municipal Committee and asked to see Mayor Ts'ao Ti-ch'iu to talk over the inauguration rally of the following day. Ts'ao was skulking in the Hengshan Hotel and refused to see them. Instead, he sent a Vice-Director of the Municipal Office to handle them. The workers' representatives confronted this man with three demands: (1) that their organization be recognized, (2) that Mayor Ts'ao attend the inauguration rally, and (3) that they be provided with finances, propaganda equipment, and so on.

They asked that these demands be relayed to the Mayor and set a time limit of 2 P.M. the same day for his reply. Party Secretary-General Li Chia-ch'i immediately telephoned the Mayor's private secretary and told him what had transpired.

Mayor Ts'ao phoned his reply that afternoon. The Vice-Director of the Municipal Office was to tell the workers that their demands could not be met. He was also to convey to them (as his *own* opinion, not the Mayor's) that they should behave in accordance with the slogan "Make Revolution: Boost Production!" (RG 8:3.2)

Another delegation went to see Ma T'ien-shui, the Municipal Party Committee Secretary of Industry. His reaction was said to have been: "I'll think about it" (RG 8:2.1).

The Rebels claimed that the Municipal Committee did everything it could to deter workers from attending the inauguration:

On the morning of November 9, the Municipal Committee was besieged by phone calls from cadres, reporting that many workers and office staff wanted to attend the rally and asking for suggestions on how to proceed. The Municipal Committee told them to issue the following advice: (1) don't attend the rally, (2) don't recognize it,

(3) don't support it. The workers were also to be warned that they must obey the slogan "Make Revolution: Boost Production!" and not leave their jobs. (RG 8:3.2)

Another account accused the Municipal Committee of having sent spies to the rally. Two men pretended to be Culture Square officials, hid backstage, listened to what was said, and phoned in hourly reports. Elsewhere the Rebels complained, somewhat contradictorily, that the Municipal Committee was not interested enough in the rally even to send representatives (RG 8:2.1).

All Rebel sources agreed, however, that the rally was a swinging success. The workers' main act that day, apart from establishing themselves as an organization, was to present the Municipal Committee with five new demands.

With the rejection of these demands, Shanghai entered a new phase of the Cultural Revolution. Workers Headquarters was determined to prove that it was no milksop student group. The very next day, November 10, 2,500 of its members descended on the Shanghai railway station, commandeered a Peking-bound train, and steamed out of the city. They were going, they said, to see Chairman Mao in the capital and tell him how the Shanghai Municipal Committee was trying to keep the workers out of the movement.

Shanghai is not the easiest place to hijack a train, even at the best of times. When the Rebel workers made their move, the station was packed with Red Guards seeking to "make liaison" with other parts of the country. I had been at the station on November 9, and it was clear from the thousands of students waiting for trains, the stench of urine rising from the tracks, and the general air of a campground that the transport system was unable to cope and that travelers had been sleeping on the platforms.

Yet somehow the workers managed to clear a whole train of Red Guards, take their places, and set off for Peking—without provoking any violence! This strongly suggests that they had powerful friends in the Railways Department, without whose help they could not have pulled off the coup. If this was the case, their allies' influence did not extend far beyond Shanghai, for the train was stopped, on the orders of the Municipal Committee, at Anting East, a small siding a few miles beyond the city limits.

This was an emergency for the authorities. If the Rebels got away with their maneuver, the Municipal Committee would lose a lot of prestige. Instead of making a show of force, however, the Party leaders went to work in a typically Chinese way: "They got an Assistant Director of the Political Bureau of the Department of Industry to mobilize 'trustworthy' people—relatives and workmates of the Rebels—and send them to Anting . . . ostensibly to 'look after their friends' but actually to divide and weaken the Rebel ranks" (RG 8:3.2). This method, combined with an official plea that Shanghai's industry would suffer if the workers did not return, was quite successful. More than half the hijackers went back to their jobs.

But 1,000 hard-core Rebels refused to leave the train and settled in for a siege. Some wall-poster accounts described their sufferings, dwelling on the 3 days spent in packed carriages without food or water. Others declared that they had been given food but had thrown it to the ground with a cry of "This is revisionist! We won't eat it!"

Every minute that the Rebels remained in the train the prestige of the Shanghai authorities drained further away. It was imperative for them to get the men back to the city, but the only way to do it was to sign their demands, which would be tantamount to complete surrender.

Help came from Peking. The Municipal Committee must have contacted the capital as soon as the affair began. One might have imagined that they would get little sympathy from the Mao group, but perhaps some bargain was made, for a telegram arrived from no less a person than Ch'en Po-ta. This man, as head of the Central Cultural Revolution Group, was one of the most powerful people in the country at the time, and it was widely assumed that he as much as anyone was running the Cultural Revolution. His telegram read approximately as follows:

I hear that a lot of Shanghai workers wanted to come to Peking and that they have since occupied the Anting East railway station. When the situation was explained to them, many went home of their own accord. This is very good; this is the correct thing to do. I hear there are others, however, who refuse to leave the station.

Now, I understand their enthusiasm in wanting to come to Peking. It is right for them to join in the Cultural Revolution. But they must also follow the instructions of Chairman Mao and the Central Committee. There are two principles involved here, and the minor one must be subordinated to the major one. As workers, their main job is to work. Joining in the Revolution is only secondary. They must therefore go back to work. They can take part in the Revolution outside working hours. They should go back immediately. It is a serious matter to disobey Party instructions.[1]

The remarkable thing about this telegram was its mildness. More than 1,000 workers had walked off the job, stolen a train, and snarled up the whole railway system of East China, yet Ch'en Po-ta reasoned paternally with them. Perhaps he, too, was alarmed at the prospect of the workers entering the movement.

The Municipal Committee seemed to have won another round. All Mayor Ts'ao had to do was read the telegram to the Rebels. Ch'en Po-ta's name would do the rest. And, once the workers were safely back in their factories, the press could print the telegram, contrasting the moderation of Ch'en Po-ta with the extremism of the Rebels and pointing to the disorder that ensued when workers disobeyed the Party. At this point, the authorities had every reason to congratulate themselves for standing firm and refusing the Rebels' demands.

But the Mayor never got to Anting to read out his telegram. Before he could move from Shanghai, a member of the Central Cultural Revolution Group arrived from Peking by plane, went straight to Anting, and told the workers that he supported their action and would sign their demands!

This was Chang Ch'un-ch'iao, a man most people had forgotten about. He had left Shanghai in July to attend the Eleventh Plenum in the capital. Unlike the Mayor and the others who attended this conference, Chang did not come back when it was over. Abandoning his dual role as Secretary of the Municipal Party Committee and head of its Propaganda Department, he

---

[1] Copied from a wall poster.

stayed in Peking to become a Vice-Director of the Central Cultural Revolution Group. This meant leaving Shanghai in the hands of his enemies, but it also put him right in the heart of the Mao group.

His dramatic return to Shanghai on November 12 revealed a serious split in the Mao group. He seems to have come for the precise purpose of forestalling Ch'en Po-ta's telegram. Ch'en had urged the workers to return to their jobs but had made no mention of their demands. Chang also asked the Rebels to go back to work but first promised to meet their demands. The difference was crucial, for the role of the workers in the Cultural Revolution depended on which approach prevailed.

Early the next day, at a hastily called meeting in Culture Square, Chang Ch'un-ch'iao formally signed the five Rebel demands in the presence of the workers who had come back from Anting. He signed, not as a member of the Shanghai Municipal Committee, but by virtue of his position in the Central Cultural Revolution Group—a body supposed to have been set up by Mao himself.

In one stroke, Chang Ch'un-ch'iao had done the Mayor and Municipal Committee more harm than the left-wing students had managed to do in 6 months. Here is a Rebel account of how Ts'ao took the news:

> When Chang Ch'un-ch'iao left Culture Square and went back to the Secretariat, Ts'ao Ti-ch'iu, who had been hiding there, was furious with him and told him with hatred in his voice. "What you're saying is that all of us—all the members of the Municipal Committee—are in the wrong on this matter!" (RG 8:2.1)

Another remark attributed to the Mayor was: "Ch'un-ch'iao signs and catches us all with our pants down!" (RG 8:2.1) The irony of this lament is in the Mayor's use of "Ch'un-ch'iao," Chang's personal name; such familiarity is common among Party officials in China but seems misplaced in regard to a man who had just betrayed all his colleagues.

The Mayor had no choice but to stand firm. Having refused to meet the Rebels' demands, he could not now change his mind without sacrificing his whole position. Two Municipal Commit-

tee secretaries—Ma T'ien-shui and Wang Yi-p'ing—were therefore instructed to issue a statement that Chang Ch'un-ch'iao's
action did not have the support of the Municipal Committee.

Meantime, Chang was in the Secretariat, telephoning Peking.
According to Rebels who claimed to have been eyewitnesses, he
spoke to Ch'en Po-ta himself. He first told him what he had done
and then read out the text of the demands he had signed. This
would confirm the suggestion that Ch'en Po-ta had not known of
Chang's intentions. According to the Rebels, the Central Cultural
Revolution Group, after hearing Chang's report on the phone,
then held a conference. After a while, they rang back to say they
entirely agreed with the action Chang had taken.

It was probably a good deal more complex than that, with the
lines buzzing between Peking and Shanghai. The Rebels described one conversation in which Ch'en P'ei-hsien, First Secretary of the East China Bureau of the Party and the highest
authority in Shanghai, rang Ch'en Po-ta on behalf of Mayor
Ts'ao, Wei Wen-po (a secretary of the East China Bureau) and
himself:

> His manner was extremely rude. Every sentence started with "Why?"
> He heaped accusations on the Central Cultural Revolution Group,
> saying things like: "How much power was Chang given anyway?"
> and "Why the devil didn't he discuss it with us first?"
>
>   Ch'en Po-ta answered sternly that Chang Ch'un-ch'iao had been
> given the authority to settle the matter boldly and that he had faith
> in him.
>
>   Ch'en P'ei-hsien and Ts'ao Ti-ch'iu were so shocked by these words
> that they did not report them to the Standing Committee. It was
> only 10 days later, under pressure from Chang Ch'un-ch'iao, that
> Ts'ao made a reference to them in a Committee meeting. And even
> then he dismissed them in two sentences. (RG 8:2.1)

If there is any truth in this description, it would seem that Ch'en
Po-ta, confronted with Chang Ch'un-ch'iao's *fait accompli,* decided to cover up for him. The Shanghai leaders not unnaturally
interpreted this as a double cross—hence their surprise.

The charge of concealing information was to become quite
common. The Rebels claimed that the Politburo in Peking rati-

fied Chang Ch'un-ch'iao's signing almost immediately and that Mayor Ts'ao and Ch'en P'ei-hsien knew of this, but did not report it to the Municipal Committee. Mayor Ts'ao and Ch'en were even said to have suppressed the news of Mao's own reaction. Mao, the Rebels maintained, was told of the affair 2 days after it had happened, but he said he already knew about it. His reported comment was classically Chinese: "This is one of those cases where it is all right 'to behead the felon first, then tell the throne.' Actions always precede ideas anyway" (RG 8:2.1). This sounds so like Mao that it could be true.

Meanwhile, Chang Ch'un-ch'iao had problems of his own. Although his signature had satisfied most of the Rebels, 474 workers had refused to follow the rest back to Shanghai and had decided to continue to Peking. They called themselves a "protest brigade" and said they wanted to have a word with Ch'en Po-ta about his "repressive" telegram (RG 19).

This band reached the town of Soochow on November 14 and started canvassing for support. Chang Ch'un-ch'iao and Mayor Ts'ao Ti-ch'iu argeed on one thing at least: The expedition had to be stopped. They postponed their differences long enough to go to Soochow, taking with them Han Che-yi, a secretary of the East China Bureau. The Mayor thought it would simply be a matter of persuading the workers to return, but the Rebels presented the three leaders with another set of five demands and refused to go back until these were met.

Once again, Chang Ch'un-ch'iao was prepared to sign. Mayor Ts'ao, appalled at the trap he had blundered into, refused. "They can drag me all the way to Peking," he was quoted as saying, "but I will not sign!" Chang Ch'un-ch'iao "argued with him fiercely for about 2 hours" and finally exclaimed: "All right. If you won't sign, that's your affair. *I'm* going to." At last, presumably after striking some bargain with Chang, Ts'ao gave in and signed (RG 8:2.1).

Back in Shanghai, the Rebels were accusing the Municipal Committee of trying to gather intelligence on the leaders of Workers Headquarters, especially those who had acted as chairmen and made speeches at the inauguration rally. This charge of collecting "black" material was emphatically denied by the authorities concerned, who preferred to call their investigation "summing up what we can learn from the experience."

It must be admitted that the Party hierarchy stuck together with admirable tenacity throughout. One gets the impression that what really irked the leaders was Peking's further interference in Shanghai's affairs. A Rebel story relates how Wang Li, an important member of the Central Cultural Revolution Group, rang the Shanghai Municipal Committee to say that he supported Chang Ch'un-ch'iao's action. The official who took the call had no sooner put down the phone than he turned to his colleagues with an oath and added: "So Wang Li supports Chang Ch'un-ch'iao, so what? It makes you laugh. I'd like to see a few of these old fogies in the Central Cultural Revolution Group come down here and try solving some of our problems!" (RG 8:2.1)

When Chang Ch'un-ch'iao returned from Soochow, he had to run a gantlet of disapproval from his fellow Committee members, who censured him for destroying unity and embarrassing the Party authorities. Ma Ta, editor of *Liberation Daily*, in a speech to Rebels in *Wen Hui Pao* on November 17, declared:

> These last few days, Chang Ch'un-ch'iao has been under fire from all sides. The minority has criticized him for not giving it enough support; the majority has criticized him for helping the minority out of all proportion to its numbers; the cadres have criticized him for going around signing demands all over the place. (RG 6:4.1)

In the same address, Ma warned: "Once the Cultural Revolution gets going in the factories, there'll be no end to it." This, he said, was why the Politburo had debated the Anting affair and decided that Chang Ch'un-ch'iao had been *wrong* to sign the workers' demands (RG 6:4.1).

The Rebels retaliated by accusing Ma Ta of having commissioned a strongly worded wall poster against Chang Ch'un-ch'iao that appeared in Shanghai at this time. It was said to have been written by Hsü Hsüeh-ming, head of the News Department of *Liberation Daily*, and it was the forerunner to a whole series of attacks on Chang's position (RG 5:2.2, RG 6:4.1[2]).

---

[2] This newspaper attributes the poster to the head of *Liberation Daily*'s industry section.

The poster was entitled "Why Barter Away Principles?—A Criticism of Chang Ch'un-ch'iao." Chang's surrender to the workers' demands was described as "a mistake of principle, a mistake of stand"; he was accused of promoting "a bourgeois kind of democracy, the kind that opposes centralized control and ignores the welfare of 700 million people." "He has thrown away the whole position; he has bartered away principles and sacrificed the well-being of the vast majority for the unreasonable demands of a tiny few. The logical question to ask is *why* he has done this." The most serious accusation included a reference to Ch'en Po-ta's telegram: "He has openly gone against the instructions of the Chairman, the Central Committee, and Comrade Ch'en Po-ta." And the final flourish read:

> You granted Shanghai's workers the right to form a Rebel Headquarters, but did you even stop to think what effect this might have on the country as a whole? Your influence has been detrimental. To make up for this, you must immediately make a thorough-going self-criticism before the Party, before the people of Shanghai, and before the people of the whole country. You must return to a correct class stand. (RG 5:2.2)

There is no need to doubt the sincerity of this attack. The conservatives saw workers' involvement in the movement as a real threat to the welfare of the Chinese people. In their view, progress required peace and security rather than more revolution.

This is the kindest interpretation that can be put on the resistance to the workers' movement. The Rebels, of course, had their own explanations, most of which indicted the Municipal Committee and eulogized Chang Ch'un-ch'iao. The most outspoken of all were Rebels from other cities. The group from Harbin Military Engineering Institute, for example, said:

> Some people are getting quite hysterical about Chang Ch'un-ch'iao's settling of the Anting affair and his actions on behalf of the Central Cultural Revolution Group. They are putting up slogans like "Chang Ch'un-ch'iao should be sacked!" and "Let us rebel against Chang Ch'un-ch'iao!" They are saying things like "He has abandoned the qualities essential to a Communist; to save his own skin, he has bargained with principles and sold the Revolution down the river!"

We do not agree. We feel Comrade Chang acted correctly and that his solution of the Anting incident was a reflection of the Central Cultural Revolution Group's faith in the revolutionary working class.

We would like to ask those who are stirring up antagonism toward him: Whose side you are *really* on? Who are you *really* against?[3]

A great fight must have gone on behind the scenes. The Municipal Committee's trump card was its control of the mass media, which it used as much as it dared against Chang Ch'un-ch'iao. It would have been suicidal to attack him by name when he seemed to have the backing of Peking. But there were other ways; one was to publish front-page articles and editorials on the importance of keeping up production. This was the equivalent of saying: Anting was wrong, and what Chang Ch'un-ch'iao did at Anting was a mistake.

Chang stayed on in Shanghai, trying to persuade the Municipal Committee that Mao, the Central Committee, and the Central Cultural Revolution Group all supported his action. An enlarged session of the Standing Committee met on November 24, at which some home truths came out. A Rebel newspaper recorded part of the meeting:

Ts'ao Ti-ch'iu: As far as the worker's right to organize is concerned, I'm in perfect agreement. It's their *ideology* that worries me, that makes me have reservations.. . . . Why, for instance, did they include in their demands the sentence "The East China Bureau and the Shanghai Municipal Committee are entirely responsible for Anting and its aftermath"?

. . . We must make it very clear to the bulk of the workers that they must not support a bunch of antisocial elements that includes people of landlord, rich-peasant, counterrevolutionary, right-wing, or criminal backgrounds. We should point out to them that, if they do support such a group, they will be putting their own political standing in jeopardy.

Wang Yi-p'ing (Secretary of the Municipal Party Committee Secretariat): That first signing caught us totally unprepared, and we had

3 From a leaflet entitled "We Firmly Uphold the Correct Leadership of the Central Cultural Revolution Group," signed by the Red Rebel Regiment from Harbin Military Engineering Institute and dated November 15, 1966.

only the haziest idea of the possible consequences. That single initiative threw us right onto the defensive. I for one was flabbergasted when Chang Ch'un-ch'iao turned up. . . .

Yang Hui-chieh (in charge of the Municipal Party Committee's Socialist Education Office): Most people in Shanghai support us. They're not at all happy that the Mayor went to Soochow and signed the workers' demands. They're angry with Chang Ch'un-ch'iao. They say he panicked and betrayed the interests of the working class. Most people follow the lead of their Work Teams . . . most of the older workers have strong class feelings and a deep emotional attachment to the Party.

Chang Ch'un-ch'iao (interjecting): Which doesn't mean the Rebel workers are *not* emotionally attached to the Party. . . .

Chou Pi-tai (in charge of the Municipal Party Committee's Industrial Production Committee): Many people are coming out with criticisms of the Municipal Committee. They want to know why Chang Ch'un-ch'iao, Han Che-yi and Ts'ao Ti-ch'iu signed the demands. Was it in the spirit of the Central Committee's directives, of the Chairman's ideas, of the Sixteen Points? They raise these questions in a hostile tone. . . . Some even call for rallies 10,000 strong, to denounce the bourgeois reactionary line of the Municipal Committee. Others demand revolutionary action; they want to liquidate the Rebel Headquarters and debate the whole affair with Chang Ch'un-ch'iao. . . .

Yang Shih-fa (Secretary of the Municipal Party Committee's Organization Department): Our factories and businesses have one important characteristic in common—they're all in the middle of a movement to clean up corruption. The ranks of the white- and blue-collar workers are not pure; there are people of various reactionary backgrounds. Who is to say that some of these will not try to get themselves reclassified? They could use this opportunity to wipe out their stigma and start again with a clean bill. The students know nothing of all this; they have no idea of the facts. Unless they look at it from a class viewpoint, they'll be deceived.

Chang Ch'un-ch'iao (interrupting again): Just because an organization has a few bad people in it doesn't mean it can't be revolutionary. There are evil people in the Chinese Communist Party. And, as we all know, there are monsters in the Central Committee itself! . . .

Sung Chi-wen (a member of the Municipal Party Committee's Standing Committee and Vice-Mayor): We have to make meticulous preparations. Disorder comes in three sizes: full-scale, moderate, and minor. What we have now is minor disorder. It means that production drops 10 per cent. Moderate disorder produces a greater drop, and full-scale disorder affects the very livelihood of the people. Production is paralyzed. . . .

It boils down to a question of whether that worries us or not. If it doesn't, then let's go ahead. Let's have chaos. . . .

Chang Ch'eng-tsung (Municipal Party Committee member and Vice-Mayor): Agreeing to all five demands, or even to any one of them, must mean a drop in production. The question we have to ask ourselves is: Can we go on like this? Where is the thing heading? Logically, it seems we are headed for disorder.

Chang Ch'un-ch'iao (interrupting for the third time): Everyone seems to be hung up on disorder. I want to make it quite clear that the disorder did not arise because of the Workers Headquarters. On the contrary, the Workers Headquarters arose because of the disorder! . . . As for the legitimacy of this workers' organization—it's got nothing to do with what the Constitution says. It's a question of our whole attitude to mass organizations. . . . In the situation as it is now, if you proceed to dissolve this Workers Headquarters, you'll be acting more or less like Ch'en Tu-hsiu [a former leader of the Party, accused of right-wing opportunism in 1927]. (RG 8:2.1)

There is no way of knowing how accurate these quotes are. They were printed in a Rebel newspaper more than a month later and were said to have been supplied by people in the Party administration. If they are reliable, they indicate that Chang Ch'un-ch'iao got little or no support from the Municipal Committee. The Rebels, in fact, said as much: "To the crucial question of Anting and its consequences, the vast majority of Shanghai's Party leaders, from the Secretariat to the Standing Committee, did not take their stand on the side of Chairman Mao's revolutionary line, did not support the Central Cultural Revolution Group, and did not back Chang Ch'un-ch'iao" (RG 8:2.1). The upshot was that Chang Ch'un-ch'iao pulled out. On November 25, the day after the Standing Committee meeting, he suddenly returned to Peking, presumably in disgust.

A few days later, the Central Committee called an important conference in Peking to discuss problems created by the Cultural Revolution in industry and communications. The Shanghai

Party sent Ma T'ien-shui, its Secretary of Industry, to the conference. Before he went, the Rebels claimed, he had the Party
Socialist Education Office prepare him a detailed report on every
workers' organization that had sprung up during the movement,
to show that the Cultural Revolution had damaged production.

A Rebel newspaper reported that Ma had not been in Peking
long before he rang the Municipal Committee to say:

> On the question of the Cultural Revolution in factories and com-
> mercial enterprises, there is a great discrepancy between the opinion
> of the Central Cultural Revolution Group and that of the provincial
> and municipal leaders. A full-scale debate looks unavoidable. I want
> all the information you can get me on factories stopping work, on
> people being beaten up, and on the composition of the workers'
> organizations. (RG 8:3.2)

A little later, he called again:

> Shansi has produced a report that brings all sorts of questions out
> into the open. Comrade Yü Ch'iu-li [Secretary, Shansi Party Com-
> mittee] says now is the time to tell things as they really are. It would
> be a great mistake, he says, to conceal what is happening. He wants
> to collect even more information and write a further report for the
> Central Committee. (RG 8:3.2)

The Rebel article roundly denounced this collaboration
among provincial leaders to oppose the will of the Mao group.
It maintained that an investigation had been conducted into
production damage in every district of Shanghai—with special
reference to the back-street workshops and cottage industries—
and that hardly anything out of the ordinary had been discovered:

> Shanghai's industry at that time was going great guns, so there was
> nothing to report! But the Director of the Socialist Education Office
> got the investigators to concentrate on a very few factories where
> there had been clashes between workers' groups and to write this up
> as the norm. He also limited his report to the period after November
> 9—the date that Workers Headquarters was set up. (RG 8:3.2)

Ma T'ien-shui rang again from Peking, this time asking for information on cases where Workers Headquarters had used harsh methods to settle minor contradictions among the people. What he was really after, said the Rebels, was "material describing how Workers Headquarters had set up kangaroo courts and beaten or imprisoned people." But it seems he was out of luck again:

> The investigators looked everywhere but only came up with some run-of-the-mill abuses. These were sent off to Ma T'ien-shui, who got very angry and said that the Director of the Socialist Education Office was being very dense and not seeing things from a class viewpoint. "You'd better get it into your head," he told the Director on the phone, "that Rebels are not the same thing as left-wingers!" (RG 8:3.2)

These efforts to control the Rebels were doomed to failure. The Party hierarchy, not only in Shanghai but throughout the country, had seriously miscalculated if it imagined that warnings about production losses would divert the course of the Mao group. The Maoists in Peking meant to keep pushing until their enemies in the provincial and municipal committees fell and, if production dropped 10 or even 20 per cent, would consider it worthwhile in the long run. China was going to have a new spirit, said the Rebels, one of daring to think and act outside of conventional formulas, to slough off outmoded cultural forms, to question all people in authority by holding them up to the searing light of Maoism, to smash bureaucratism and revisionism and return to the mass participation of the Yenan period—in short, the spirit of revolutionary rebellion. The Rebels were the midwives of this historical birth. They called for the *spiritual* liberation of the people, who would transmute this freedom into rapid *material* progress. Production might drop during the period of struggle, but it would catch up and surge ahead as the movement went on. This was the true meaning of the slogan "Make Revolution: Boost Production!"

The call to break free from administrative repression sounded good, especially to younger people, who tended to resent the stringent discipline and almost priestly paternalism of the old Party. The mood of the young severely handicapped the authorities, who found it less and less possible to *control* anything without appearing to *stifle* it.

Chang Ch'un-ch'iao's cavalier re-entrance on the Shanghai scene captured the imagination of many people. He seemed to be saying that Mao himself was a Rebel and supported the Rebels, while the Municipal Committee leaders were at best fuddy-duddies and at worst downright reactionaries.

He also alienated thousands. The senior cadres and older workers hated him for destroying discipline—the discipline created so painfully out of China's earlier chaos and to their minds so essential for the nation's future. Opposition to Chang, and to what he stood for, had begun building even before the end of the Anting incident. This opposition was to unite a force of nearly a million people under the banner of the Workers Scarlet Guards for the Defense of Mao Tse-tung's Thought—the Scarlet Guards—of which we shall hear more.

As November drew to a close, the city was tense. The student movement seemed a pale doctrinal squabble in a monastery garden compared to the forces that were moving the people, forces that would soon split Shanghai from top to bottom.

8. Showdown at Liberation Daily

While the Anting affair was still reverberating, Shanghai was hit by another shock, in the person of Miss Nieh Yuan-tzu. The Mao group had widely publicized her attack in May, 1966, on the President of Peking University, which gave a green light to the Cultural Revolution. For a time, she was perhaps the most famous woman in China. Then, in September and October, she dropped from the limelight. Some rumors said she was sick; others that she had been caught in a reverse current and was being held a virtual prisoner at Peking University.

Her disappearance coincided with a comparative lull in the movement—the two months between the Red Guards' first wild fling and the entry of the workers into the fray. In November, when the northern Red Guards renewed their assault on the provinces, when the Shanghai workers began to organize openly, and when it looked as if the Municipal Committee might be seriously tested, Miss Nieh turned up again. She arrived in Shanghai on November 20, accompanied by a few close friends from Peking University.

She was not warmly received. The Party press studiously ignored her, but the living newspapers on the city's walls were quite outspoken. Overnight, Shanghai was plastered with slogans reading "Nieh Yuan-tzu, go home!" "Nieh Yuan-tzu, go back to Peking!" "Nieh Yuan-tzu, Shanghai is not your stamping-ground!" The Rebels claimed this was the work of the Party authorities: One rumor had it that Teng Hsiao-p'ing—who, as

we shall see, stood to lose most by Nieh's visit to Shanghai—
phoned Mayor Ts'ao to warn him of her arrival. Another quoted
Ch'en P'ei-hsien, head of the Party's East China Bureau, as re-
acting to her appearance with the words: "She came to Shanghai
because she had to leave Peking. When she has to leave Shanghai, where will she go?" This sounds like Ch'en, who suffered
from chronic optimism, but his confidence in Shanghai's ability
to resist Miss Nieh was somewhat misplaced.

It soon became clear that, if there were people in Shanghai
who loathed Miss Nieh, there were others who were prepared to
defend her to the hilt. On posters attacking her, one began to
find penciled remarks such as "This is all pure dog-fart!" or "You
snort like a bull, but you have the courage of a rat!" These would
often be opposed in their turn, until the graffiti covered more
space than the original text. At the same time, a crop of posters
appeared with headings like "Welcome to Nieh Yuan-tzu, the
close comrade-in-arms of the Rebels!" And there were detailed
refutations of the charges against her, often under a title like
"Why are some people afraid of comrade Nieh Yuan-tzu?"

Her detractors then discovered that she was staying in a first-
class hotel, where she had special meals prepared for her by the
chef. When this came out· on the walls, Shanghai was scandal-
ized; the Chinese get very emotional about things that smack of
the bad old days, and the quickest way to discredit an enemy is
to accuse him of luxury. During the Cultural Revolution, such
charges were usually fabricated. But in the case of Nieh Yuan-
tzu, they were probably true; I knew some of the waiters in her
hotel, who confirmed every detail.

Her defenders, appalled by the tongue-clucking and head-
shaking of the rather puritanical Shanghai working class, tried
to turn the attack against the Party authorities. Miss Nieh, they
claimed, had been tricked by the East China Bureau into taking
a room in a fancy hotel. As for her special food, that was because
of an old gastric complaint. The argument went on for days.

Meanwhile, Miss Nieh was busy making speeches to the Rebels.
On November 22, she told a rally in Culture Square that the
purpose of her visit was to expose the crimes of Ch'ang Hsi-p'ing,
Shanghai's head of education. Ch'ang, she said, was a member of

the Work Team sent to Peking University in 1964 during the Socialist Education Movement and had ruthlessly suppressed the student left wing. She had been horrified to find that the Cultural Revolution in Shanghai was letting this bourgeois reactionary authority get off scot-free. She swore to remain in the city until he lost his job.

This in itself was nothing new; Ch'ang Hsi-p'ing had been under attack for months. The novelty was that Miss Nieh (claiming that Chairman Mao had personally sent her to Shanghai) charged that Ch'ang Hsi-p'ing was being protected by powerful forces. Nor was she afraid to specify: "The case of Ch'ang Hsi-p'ing is not an isolated phenomenon. It is intimately connected with two sources of authority: One is the Shanghai Municipal Party Committeee under Mayor Ts'ao Ti-ch'iu; the other is the Secretary-General of the Party, Teng Hsiao-p'ing."[1]

This widened the scope of the movement considerably. Before November, most people in Shanghai still thought of the Cultural Revolution as a struggle against a few local reactionaries. The radicals had insisted that the Municipal Committee was involved in a city-wide plot to oppose Mao Tse-tung's ideas and suppress any students who tried to act them out. But no one had dared suggest that a man as powerful as Teng Hsiao-p'ing was actually leading a national campaign against Chairman Mao and his loyal supporters.

On November 1, a *Red Flag* editorial revealed for the first time that one or two people at the top were deeply implicated in the bourgeois reactionary line, but no names were mentioned. Then, beginning around November 16, isolated posters in Shanghai accused Liu Shao-ch'i and Teng Hsiao-p'ing by name.

Most people, I feel, had dismissed this notion as absurd. Yet here was Nieh Yuan-tzu, a woman who had received high praise from Chairman Mao, saying more or less the same thing. If there really was a nationwide plot against Mao, it would not do to find oneself involved. And if the Shanghai Municipal Committee was part of it, maybe these Rebels had something after all. Some began to think like this, but by no means all. The general at-

[1] Copied from a wall poster.

mosphere in the city was distinctly hostile to Nieh. Those I spoke to had one of two reactions. Some said: Nieh has every right to criticize Ch'ang Hsi-p'ing for what he did in Peking University in 1964, but she knows nothing whatever about the Shanghai Municipal Committee and is therefore totally unjustified in maligning it. That is why so many people here are against her. Others put it this way: Mayor Ts'ao has admitted that Ch'ang Hsi-p'ing might have made mistakes in Peking. But he has worked as a Shanghai Party official for 17 years, and the Municipal Committee is unaware of any serious errors in that time. Nieh Yuan-tzu's abuse of the Mayor is therefore unfounded. As for her claim to represent Chairman Mao, that is a false rumor, fostered by the Rebels.

Nevertheless, Nieh became the rallying point for the Rebel forces. Around her there gathered an alliance of dissident workers, local left-wing Red Guards, and Rebels from the North. This was a much better organized and more experienced coalition than the one that had tried to overthrow the Municipal Committee at the end of August. It was also more conscious of the need for unity on the left.

In fact, Nieh's most important speech was on the subject of unity. At a 15,000-man rally on November 25—the very day that Chang Ch'un-ch'iao threw in the sponge and returned to Peking —she reminded her listeners that 6 whole months had elapsed since her wall poster of May 25 and that it was fully 3 months since the first wave of Red Guards from the North, yet the Shanghai Municipal Committee was still brazenly peddling its reactionary line. The only way to bring it down, she said, was for all the revolutionaries of Shanghai to unite and strike together (RG 3:1.1). This rally, which had the bellicose title "We Swear We're Going to Rain Down 10,000 Bombs on the Bourgeois Reactionary Line of Ts'ao Ti-ch'iu and His Municipal Committee!" (RG 3:1.1), marked the beginning of the two most turbulent weeks Shanghai had seen since 1949.

The trouble arose over a student newspaper. The Red Revolutionaries—Shanghai's largest radical student organization, with a membership in the tens of thousands—ran a hard-hitting tabloid called *Red Guard Dispatch*. They had put out eight highly controversial issues since the students had won the right to have their own newspapers. In their fourth issue, they had attacked Ch'ang Hsi-p'ing by name; the Municipal Committee had held up publication for a day, on the basis of a passage from the Sixteen Points: "Criticism of anyone by name in the press should be decided after discussion by the Party Committee at the same level, and in some cases it should be submitted for approval to the Party Committee at a higher level." Their fifth issue had continued the campaign against Ch'ang, and the sixth had included a scathing attack on Mayor Ts'ao himself. It, too, had been delayed a few hours by the authorities (RG 5:4.3).

But the ninth issue really struck sparks. This report of the November 25 rally contained articles inspired by Miss Nieh's rousing speech that day. There was a detailed account of how the Municipal Committee had impeded the Cultural Revolution from the very beginning. The facts were interpreted in a most biased way, but there were enough of them, and they were persuasively presented. This article alone was a serious threat to the establishment, but there was worse. In another vitriolic piece, it was alleged that Shanghai's Party newspaper, *Liberation Daily*, had consistently been used to suppress the left wing (RG 3:1.1).

The irony here is that the first eight issues of the Red Revolutionaries' tabloid had been printed on the presses of *Liberation Daily*, not from choice, but because the Central Committee had ordered that all student groups should have access to publishing facilities. *Liberation Daily* could, therefore, hardly refuse to print the ninth, even though it contained material that was extremely damaging to its own prestige.

But, when the ninth issue was ready to be printed, the Red Revolutionaries demanded 650,000 copies. When the astounded officials asked how they intended to circulate so many, the students replied that, since this issue contained most important material, it should be sent out with *Liberation Daily* to all subscribers (RG 6:3.2). Needless to say, the Party Committee of *Liberation Daily* refused. The Municipal Committee backed this decision, as did the newspaper distribution office of the postal department.

The Rebels persisted for 2 days without success. In their accounts of the negotiations, they made fun of the bureaucrats:

> At about 10:00 P.M. on November 29, a dozen or so Red Revolutionaries again went to try to persuade the officials in charge of the newspaper distribution office to change their minds. . . .
> They refused, for the following "reasons":
> 1. A lot of the postal workers were against sending two newspapers out together. They wouldn't fit in the one wrapper, and they'd make the postal bags too heavy. Furthermore, the men would have to work overtime.
> 2. The readers might think the two papers were a joint publication. There was no comparison between a Party organ like *Liberation Daily* and a student tabloid like *Red Guard Dispatch*. The Party organ would therefore suffer a loss of prestige. (RG 3:1.1)

The students had little trouble demolishing these arguments. They pointed out that special issues of *Liberation Daily* occasionally ran to ten pages. In this case, the two papers together would amount to only eight. While admitting opposition among the workers, they quoted from a statement by the Shanghai newspaper retailers, which said that if the Party would not allow joint distribution of the two papers, then let them send out *Red Guard Dispatch* and throw *Liberation Daily* away. As for the readers confusing the two publications, there was little fear of that: *Red Guard Dispatch* was clearly a student paper. Anyway, the prestige of a Party organ could not be harmed by association with a Red Guard tabloid; the important point was whether it upheld the ideas of Chairman Mao. "To this," the Rebels went on, "the officials had no answer; but, because they were under orders from the Municipal Committee, they continued to refuse our request" (RG 3:1.1).

If one read only the Rebel wall posters, one might have been sympathetic toward the Red Revolutionaries. Here they were, patiently reasoning with the stubborn Party officials, trying to persuade them to give *Red Guard Dispatch* some publicity. In the context of the Cultural Revolution, their demands were not excessive and their tactics were admirably nonviolent.

The posters put up by the Moderates told a different story:

On November 29, more than 500 so-called Rebels raided the post office. They stayed from 10:00 P.M. to 2:00 A.M., during which time they disrupted the work of the postal employees and even went to the extent of searching mailbags.

This is intolerable! The post office is a semimilitary organization, since it ensures communications throughout the country. Its work is of crucial importance and must not be interrupted.[2]

The truth of what happened at the post office that night lies somewhere between these extremes. What is certain is that the "visit" or "raid" was part of a "revolutionary action" by a large number of Red Revolutionaries who were tired of waiting for Party approval and set out to force *Liberation Daily*'s hand. Here is a rather euphemistic account of "the *Liberation Daily* incident":

At about 1:00 A.M. on November 30, we Red Revolutionaries marched in the teeth of a cold wind to *Liberation Daily*. Representatives were sent in to parley, while most of us stayed outside, reading the Chairman's quotations and singing revolutionary songs.

After 2 hours, it became clear that the authorities were still refusing to send our paper out with *Liberation Daily*. To break this hopeless deadlock, we entered the building. The operation was carried out in an orderly way. Some comrades occupied the loading-ramp, to stop the day's issue going out. Others stood guard at the entrance, to prevent any incursion by misguided opposition forces who might have tried to confuse the issue, as well as to make sure no hooligans broke in and damaged state property. (RG 3:2.1)

Shanghai woke up that morning without its major daily. A city of 10 million inhabitants gets very used to reading the morning paper, and Shanghai is no exception. For a long time, people were bewildered and rumors were rife. When the truth was known, the popular reaction made the Anting affair look like a practical joke.

November 30 was quiet. Only a few people came to see what had happened. As the Rebels put it: "People came because they were concerned to know the truth about such an important

2 Copied from a wall poster.

matter. We explained the situation in detail, and there was no
fighting. At that stage, the whole affair could easily have been
settled by the normal methods of debate and discussion" (RG
3:2.1).

Inside the newspaper offices, the Rebels did not have it all
their own way. It seems they occupied only part of the building
at first and met with strong opposition. They were counting on
the support of sympathizers among the employees of the paper,
but, according to an account by some of these pro-Rebel workers,
the Party officials did what they could to keep the two forces
separate:

> On that first day, we put out a four-point statement in support of
> the Red Revolutionaries. Ma Ta [editor and Party Secretary of
> *Liberation Daily*] immediately got the Party Committee's office to
> broadcast an appeal to all Party members, Youth League members,
> and revolutionary workers and cadres, calling on them to unite under
> the Party Committee's leadership and "hold fast to principle."
>
> We retaliated by broadcasting a poster we had written, demanding
> that the Municipal Committee find a prompt solution to the ques-
> tion of the student newspaper.
>
> That night, we were approached by some Party officials, who took
> a very tough line with us and even made threats: "You will be held
> responsible for the consequences of your broadcast!" they warned
> us. They also tore down our wall posters and kept them as evidence.
>
> We suffered real persecution. People under the spell of the Party
> Committee called us "traitors." One of our comrades went to the
> general office to buy meal tickets and was surrounded and held for
> an hour. We were not permitted to attend Party conferences, and
> some of us were prevented from doing our normal work. . . . (RG
> 5:2.2)

The next day, December 1, there was still no *Liberation Daily*
on the newsstands. Large crowds gathered at the newspaper
building, and the mood was distinctly hostile. Propaganda against
the Rebels appeared on the city's walls. Nor was there any shortage of charges to hurl at them. On November 27, only 3 days
before the raid, Premier Chou En-lai had made an important
speech to Red Guard representatives in Peking. Among other
things, he had said:

We do not want disturbances in *People's Daily, Liberation Army Daily,* or any other newspaper that has the endorsement of the Central Committee. The same goes for the New China News Agency, Radio Peking, and other propaganda organs. People all over the world hear the voice of Peking.

If you feel such organizations are at fault, you have only to mention it in a wall poster and we will investigate. But you must not interfere with their operation. You are not to stop newspapers publishing or radio stations broadcasting. This could have widespread international repercussions.

You now have a great degree of democracy and freedom. This must be accompanied by discipline.[3]

Copies of this speech appeared on the walls, with angry posters declaring that *Liberation Daily* was the organ of the Municipal Committee and the East China Bureau, that it served not only greater Shanghai but also the six provinces of East China and subscribers all over the country. The Rebel raid, the posters concluded, was a flagrant violation of the Premier's injunction.

The Rebels countered with propaganda of their own. Chou's speech, they claimed, referred only to Peking papers. *Liberation Daily* had peddled a bourgeois line and therefore did not deserve the name of a Party organ. This was a thinly veiled attack on Chou En-lai, and the moderates said as much in another round of posters.

Meanwhile, at the newspaper offices, a crowd of indignant citizens, people sent by the authorities, and curious onlookers was by now large enough to worry the Rebels:

People with ulterior motives spread lies about us and plastered the building with thousands of sensational posters and slogans that read: "Root out the tiny handful of people who have closed down *Liberation Daily!*" and "The occupation of *Liberation Daily* is a counterrevolutionary act!"

They also mounted a lot of loudspeakers and set up a chant of "We want to read *Liberation Daily!*" Processions of people shouting this slogan began to form, and public opinion was gradually turned against the Red Revolutionaries. The crowds swelled until the building was fairly besieged.

3 Copied from wall-poster accounts of Chou's speech.

Then some sections of the crowd started chanting "We want to debate!" Actually, they would not listen to any opinion but their own. We ran off a flier entitled "The True Story of the *Liberation Daily* Affair," but the same people who had been yelling "We want to debate!" simply tore our leaflets up without a glance.

That evening, seven workers who were doing propaganda for us in Nanking Road were set upon by a group led by a certain Fang, the same man who had led the attack on the Peking Red Guards in September. The workers were detained for more than 2 hours, until one girl fainted. Their propaganda van was damaged, all their paper and ink was ruined, their glue was poured out in the street. . . . (RG 3:2.1)

This reference to workers is important, for it shows that the students were not acting alone. Although the actual take-over of the paper was carried out by the Red Revolutionaries, the Rebel workers gave them strong support. The absence of workers from the building in the early stages, however, would suggest that there was no fully elaborated student-worker alliance.

The next day, December 2, the unity of the left became a fact. A large force of workers, accompanied by student Rebels from outside Shanghai, managed to join the Red Revolutionaries inside the building. The Rebel account put it more precisely:

From the evening of December 2 on, Workers Headquarters began to join in. Then further reinforcements turned up group by group— revolutionary teachers and students from Shanghai, Peking, Tientsin, Nanking, Harbin, Sian, Lanchow, and elsewhere. They came because they wanted to protect state property, ensure the security of the *Liberation Daily* building, maintain revolutionary order, protect the lives of the Red Guards, and, of course, defend the proletarian revolutionary line represented by Chairman Mao. The Revolutionary Rebels were then united as one against the bourgeois reactionary line of the Municipal Committee. (RG 3:2.2)

Another account waxed lyrical: "From the factories, from the villages, from the schools and universities, from every walk of life the Rebels came, merging into one great force to overwhelm the bourgeois reactionary line" (RG 6:1.1).

These reinforcements were sorely needed. It seems that on

December 2, about 100 moderate workers climbed into the building through a small window. Though they were immediately captured, their exploit persuaded the Rebels to strengthen their defenses.

By December 3, the place was bedlam. Both sides now realized that this was to be the decisive engagement of the Cultural Revolution in Shanghai and redoubled their efforts to win over public opinion. Besiegers and besieged alike mounted all the loudspeakers they could muster, and the "true story of the *Liberation Daily* incident" blared out from both camps at once. The Rebels have left us a graphic account:

We had only three small speakers going, but the opposition had six big ones and drowned us out. Not content with this, they got ten more—brand new they were, with the wrapping still on them! They strung the whole eastern end of Nanking Road with speakers, so that we were literally surrounded by noise. This is how they used their material superiority to keep the unenlightened masses from hearing our voice.

Meanwhile, our supporters were using propaganda vans to get our views across, but the minute they appeared on the street they were deprived of their right to free speech. On December 3, about ten comrades from East China Normal College, Futan University, Peking Aeronautical Institute, and the Shanghai Workers Headquarters were surrounded by several hundred people and detained for 10 hours. Their big picture of Chairman Mao was taken, their speaker wires were cut, and finally even their van was stolen from them.

We did everything we could to present our side of the story. But, at the height of the struggle, people only had to *see* someone wearing a Red Revolutionaries or Workers Headquarters arm band, and they would crowd around him, call him a counterrevolutionary or a little monster and expose him to the ridicule of the people. One student from East China Normal College Middle School was held for 6 hours and eventually fainted when someone yelled "Let's throw him in the river!" Another comrade was called an "active counterrevolutionary," had a high hat stuck on his head and a placard on his back, and was hauled off to the Security Police. They refused to hold him.

In these battles, countless arm bands, Mao buttons, pictures of Mao, college badges, and student cards were stolen, and the Red

Revolutionaries of the Engineering College even had their flag ripped to pieces.

With all this going on, how could there be any debate? Some people outside the building were yelling "If they won't debate, we ought to drag them out here and *make* them debate!" But they were not interested in debating the issue. They simply wanted to get us out of the building. Afterward, repeated attacks were launched in an effort to evict us. (RG 3:2.1)

Few of these encounters resulted in actual bloodshed, so both sides fastened on the slightest hint of violence and wrung the last drop of propaganda from it. Here is an amusing example:

A poor peasant named Chiang came to see what was going on, and, while he was outside the *Liberation Daily* building, he happened to scratch his finger. Three men near him noticed this and immediately claimed they had "surefire proof of the Red Revolutionaries' guilt." Holding up the bleeding finger, they shouted "Look, everybody! Blood debts must be repaid in blood!" They gave Chiang a piece of paper to write a statement. Then they put him up on a platform. "Quick!" they told him. "Get up and protest against the crimes of the Rebels. Say you want revenge! You must have revenge!" (RG 3:2.1)

Had the story stopped there, it might have been credible. But the writer goes on: "They plied him with wine, chicken, and meat-filled dumplings. But Comrade Chiang saw through their trick and immediately wrote a poster supporting the Red Revolutionaries and condemning the efforts of wicked people to set the workers and peasants against the students" (RG 3:2.1).

The ridicule of the Rebels was not always directed at the establishment. Sometimes they made fun of ordinary people, calling them dupes of the Party authorities. In these caricatures, they came close to denying a pillar of Maoist theory—the perspicacity of "the masses":

We asked one middle-aged man where he worked. He started to stammer something. Then his neighbor said a word in his ear, and he finally came out with "I'm from the Shanghai machine-repair shop."

We also asked an old woman why she was shouting "We want to read *Liberation Daily!*" she replied: "We had a meeting of the people in our street. I was told to shout that."

We noticed some housewives in the crowd. When their cheerleaders yelled, "We want to read *Liberation Daily!*" the housewives yelled, "We want to read *Liberation Daily!*" And when they heard the Red Revolutionaries' loudspeakers saying, "We want to read *People's Daily!*" they started shouting "We want to read *People's Daily!*" Finally, their cheerleaders had to come and put them right. (RG 3:2.1)

Despite this superior tone, the Rebels could not deny that popular opposition to their "revolutionary action" reached overwhelming proportions. The number of defenders inside the building never exceeded 5 or 6 thousand (RG 6:3.2), while the streets outside were packed for two or three blocks. By the Rebels' own admission, more than a million people demonstrated outside the building during the 6 days that the siege was at its height. They counted no less than 120 worker, peasant, and student organizations among the crowds. This, they said, was all the work of "a tiny handful of die-hard reactionaries" (RG 3:2.1).

December 4 was a day of violence. According to the Rebels, the attackers tried to smash down the grill at the front entrance. When this failed, they used crowbars, clubs, and sticks to break the windows. They then started throwing rocks, hitting several of the defenders. As a last resort, they brought up a pair of fire engines and assaulted the building with ladders, hoses, and grappling-hooks. Some managed to get in through upper-story windows, but the main force was repulsed (RG 6:1.2).

The casualty list for this day was variously estimated. One Rebel report said 140 defenders were injured, 50 of them seriously (2 were struck by fragments of glass from broken windows), while 18 of the assault force were hospitalized (RG 6:3.2). Another count put the wounded defenders at 140, the wounded besiegers at 71 (RG 3:2.1). Yet another said *none* of the attackers were hurt.

As violence increased, the Rebels must have realized that, sooner or later, they would have to negotiate. But their propaganda never slackened for a moment. They even gloated over the trouble they had caused:

> In the brief time of a few days, Shanghai, with its population of 10 million, has been turned upside down! . . . This is wonderful! There will be no stopping the movement now! . . .
> We Rebels have been trying for 6 months to get this kind of chaos. We'd had little success up to this, but now at last we've made it! Rebellion needs disorder. Without revolutionary disorder there can be no broad democracy for the working class. . . . (RG 6:1.1)

Another reason for jubilation was the tremendous boost the siege was giving to the revolutionary consciousness of the Rebel students and workers:

> In every college, the comrades responsible for reprinting leaflets worked through the night. As soon as a poster was written at the front, it was rushed out to Red Revolutionaries all over the city. They would make copies and circulate them to all the schools. The revolutionary workers of *Liberation Daily* and *Wen Hui Pao* also worked late into the night printing leaflets in support of the Rebels. Roving propaganda teams spent all their waking hours putting slogans on the walls. This was wonderful experience in the art of propaganda.
> Others gave concerts in the factories. They were often in danger of their lives, but, wherever they performed, they made converts. . . . (RG 6:1.2)

Behind this bravado, the Rebel leaders were probably as anxious as the authorities. It was one thing to set the city agog; it was another to extricate themselves with honor from the engagement.

Backstage consultations had gone on from the beginning, and Party representatives had even been prepared to meet the enemy in his own camp. For this, they earned grudging praise from the Rebels: "Some East China Bureau and Municipal Committee officials 'responded' to Chairman Mao's call to go to the masses. They came to the *Liberation Daily* building and negotiated for whole days and nights. The inconvenience they had to undergo

was of course nothing compared to the sufferings of the Rebels
. . ." (RG 6:3.2).

It would be interesting to know the substance of these discussions. Ostensibly, all negotiations revolved around certain
demands that the Red Revolutionaries and the Workers Headquarters had drawn up during the siege. The students' demands
were the most exacting and went far beyond the original aim
of mailing their paper out with *Liberation Daily*. They insisted
that:

1. The ninth issue of *Red Guard Dispatch* be circulated along
with *Liberation Daily* to all subscribers.

2. The *Liberation Daily* Party Committee obey the Urgent Directive of the Military Committee and hand over all "black" material
relating to the revolutionary masses (including the Peking Red
Guards) and the Red Revolutionaries be permitted to examine all
original drafts and revised versions of editorials written during the
Cultural Revolution, as well as similar material, such as articles and
Party directives. During this investigation, the Party Committee of
Liberation Daily must give us every convenience, and, if we are
hindered in any way or if any material is destroyed, the Committee
will be held entirely responsible for any revolutionary action we
may have to take as a consequence.

3. The Party Committee of *Liberation Daily* must make a profound
self-criticism to the revolutionary masses. It must make a clean breast
of the grave errors it has committed, particularly in carrying out
the bourgeois reactionary line of the Municipal Committee. (RG 6:2.2)

It would have been sheer political suicide for the Party authorities to have signed these three demands—unless, of course, they
could bargain their signature against other, unspecified advantages. The thought of the Rebels poring over newspaper records,
prying into the intimacies of the Party Committee and the editorial board, must have made the Shanghai leaders sweat! There
are probably few major dailies in the world that would care to
have their relations with government submitted to the scrutiny
of a bunch of angry students. *Liberation Daily* was especially
vulnerable, for it was an organ of the Shanghai Party and had
printed what the Municipal Committee had told it to print. If
it was disgraced, the Party leaders were disgraced, and vice versa.

To make matters worse, Workers Headquarters had added some demands of its own:

1. We strongly support the demands of the Red Revolutionaries. . . .
2. The Municipal Committee must see to it that other mass organizations do not interfere with the revolutionary actions of the Rebels. . . .
3. The Municipal Committee is responsible for any consequences that may arise as a result of the *Liberation Daily* incident. . . .
4. When the workers return to their jobs, the Party authorities and the Work Teams must not make life difficult for them. They must not be harassed or forced to debate. They must not be repressed or persecuted. Otherwise, the Municipal Committee will answer for the consequences. (RG 6:2.2)

The second of these demands is perhaps the most important. The "other mass organization" referred to was one that had gained in strength as the siege progressed, until it was able to emerge as the Rebels' main enemy. This was the Scarlet Guards, a moderate workers' group that began in a small way early in November but grew into the largest organization in Shanghai. At this stage, it was directing the efforts to evict the Rebels from the *Liberation Daily* building, though it had never officially declared itself a contender and its members wore no distinguishing arm band.

By December 5, the polarization of forces and the danger of serious violence made a compromise inevitable. We will never know what happened behind the scenes, but it seems clear from Rebel accounts that Peking was consulted several times. It was claimed, for example, that twice during the siege the Party Secretary of *Liberation Daily* appealed to Peking in an effort to get the Rebels to modify their demands. Another time, on orders from the Municipal Committee, he rang the Central Cultural Revolution Group and warned Yao Wen-yuan that the Shanghai Party was "in a state of paralysis." This, said the Rebels, was equivalent to threatening Chairman Mao: "It implied that if the Central Committee remained silent while the Shanghai Committee fell, then the Central Committee would be entirely to blame" (RG 5:3.2).

No doubt there was a lot more pulling of strings than this, both in Shanghai and in the capital. As a result, on the evening of December 5, the Municipal Committee suddenly capitulated. Two of its highest secretaries, Sun Chi-wen and Wang Yi-p'ing, signed the demands of the Rebels. But, given the complexity of Chinese politics, that was not the end of it. The capitulation only triggered more protest. Ironically, most of it came from the Moderates, who felt abandoned. This being China, one side had to be in the right, and one side in the wrong. After such a serious incident, it would be no laughing matter to find oneself saddled with the blame. The only way out for the Moderate workers and students was to turn on the Municipal Committee.

The atmosphere was so tense that the Red Revolutionaries, who now actually *wanted* to leave the building, were afraid to come out. They knew that to make the most of their victory they would have to evacuate the *Liberation Daily* offices as quickly and efficiently as possible. But so much happened on December 6 that they decided to delay their retreat.

The main event that day was the formal founding of the Scarlet Guards. This was a massive affair, celebrated with all the trappings in People's Square. After the rally, the workers marched in force to the newspaper building.

Meantime, the city was flooded with angry leaflets and wall posters, protesting the Municipal Committee's capitulation.

Municipal Committee Secretaries Wang Yi-p'ing and Sung Chi-wen, unmindful of the wishes of the 10 million people of Shanghai, and without consulting the revolutionary workers and staff of *Liberation Daily* or the post office, have unilaterally agreed to the demands of the Red Revolutionaries and the Workers Headquarters. . . .

This action runs completely counter to the spirit of Chou En-lai's November 27 speech. . . .

In any case, *Liberation Daily* is an organ of the East China Bureau, and Wang Yi-p'ing and Sung Chi-wen have no authority to sign on behalf of the East China Bureau . . . the signatures are therefore invalid. . . .

We maintain, and have maintained all along, that Workers Headquarters and everyone else who is not actually employed at *Liberation Daily* must leave the building at once. . . . They were wrong to enter in the first place. . . . *Liberation Daily* is an arm of the people's dictatorship. As such, it should not be distributed jointly with any other paper. . . .[4]

The Scarlet Guards were very busy on that first day of their formal existence. They got out a tabloid of their own called *Revolutionary War Express*. Only one issue was ever printed, but it had a devastating effect. In an article entitled "The True Story of the *Liberation Daily* Incident," the Rebels were roundly denounced. They were called "irresponsible dupes of counter-revolutionary manipulators" who had "deprived Shanghai of its *Liberation Daily*, the spiritual food of the people of East China"; "resistance to them," said the article, was "even more praiseworthy than resistance to U.S. imperialism. . . ." Their newspaper also contained four demands:

1. The Municipal Committee must admit that the capitulation by Wang Yi-p'ing and Sung Chi-wen is an act of treachery, betraying the interests of Shanghai's 2 million workers.

2. The Rebels must leave *Liberation Daily* immediately.

3. The argument over the joint circulation of *Liberation Daily* and *Red Guard Dispatch* must be settled by peaceful and rational debate.

4. The Municipal Committee must not interfere in the revolutionary actions of the Scarlet Guards, nor is it entitled to "guarantee" anything on behalf of the Scarlet Guards. It must have faith in the masses and not look on them as hooligans.[5]

Not content with this newspaper alone, the Scarlet Guards had "The True Story of the *Liberation Daily* Incident" condensed into a flier. Hundreds of thousands of copies were printed, and an efficient distribution system sent them far and wide.

All this took place on December 6. It was too quick, and the Rebels, now virtual prisoners in their former fortress, began to smell a rat. They had always suspected that the Scarlet Guards

---

[4] Leaflet entitled "Urgent Notice to the People of the Whole City," dated December 6, 1966, and signed Revolutionary Staff of *Liberation Daily*.

[5] Copied from a wall poster.

were a creation of the Party authorities. Now they had "proof," and they quickly mounted a strong propaganda campaign:

> The only reason the Scarlet Guards were able to mobilize several hundred thousand men in a single night is that they were recruited by the Party branch secretaries, the Chairmen of the trade unions, and the factory managers. In some factories, the workers were even told: "If you want to take part in the Revolution, you must join the Scarlet Guards. Those who do not join are counterrevolutionaries." (RG 6:2.1)

The Rebels also insisted that the Scarlet Guards' rapid production of a newspaper was made possible only by massive Party support. They even accused the *Liberation Daily* Party Committee of having given the Scarlet Guards the press reserved for *Red Guard Dispatch*. Ma Ta, editor and Party Secretary of *Liberation Daily,* came in for much of the blame:

> Ma Ta called a secret meeting of *Liberation Daily* Party members in his home. He told them: "The demands of the Rebels are quite wrong; they are a manifestation of the bourgeois reactionary line."
>
> At another secret meeting, he examined the drafts of some documents brought by the head of the *Liberation Daily*'s news department, Hsü Hsüeh-ming. . . . His comment: "You don't need my approval before you do something revolutionary."
>
> Out of these meetings came the poisonous article entitled "The True Story of the *Liberation Daily* Incident," which was made into a leaflet and widely distributed. Copies were even found at the foreign-trade wharf, showing that this document, with its attack on Chairman Mao's own Red Guards, was intended to circulate outside the country. (RG 5:3.2)

In many respects, the Rebels were probably right. Much of the power behind the Scarlet Guards, or any mass organization with a vital part in the movement, was in the hands of high Party officials. It did not always start that way—many groups sprang from genuinely popular sentiments—but it usually finished that way. China's bureaucrats, like politicians everywhere, are reluctant democrats. The important thing is that the millions of ordinary people who enlisted in the fight, whether or not

they always knew what they were doing, had considerable freedom of political action and could gain quite an insight into the
workings of their nation.

December 6, however, was the high-water mark of confusion.
The Rebels were accusing the Municipal Committee of tricking
them. Even signing the demands was part of the plot, they said,
for the authorities had predicted the dissatisfaction that would
follow and mobilized the Scarlet Guards to give it voice. For their
part, the Scarlet Guards protested everywhere that *they*, not the
Rebels, had been betrayed by the Municipal Committee.

The situation was further complicated by the circulation of a
poorly printed leaflet dated December 6, 1966. Signed simply
"The Mao Tse-tung's Thought Red Guards," its entire text was:
"*EXTRA!* Second in Command Lin Piao proclaims the dissolution of the Scarlet Guards." I got hold of one of these, but
everyone I showed it to only laughed. "How could a mass
organization be dissolved at the stroke of a pen?" they said. I
wondered. There was every reason to consider the flier a forgery;
yet, if the Rebels were right, and the Scarlet Guards was *not* a
mass organization?

This question, like many others, must remain open, for the
Liberation Daily incident did not end neatly. The propaganda
battle raged all day December 7, and, on December 8, the
Municipal Committee belatedly ratified the signatures of its
secretaries in an "urgent notice" on Shanghai's walls:

> The Municipal Committee is in complete agreement with the
> contents of the document signed by Comrades Wang Yi-p'ing and
> Sung Chi-wen. We trust that Party organizations at every level will
> notify all cadres and see that the matter is publicized among the
> broad revolutionary masses. The document is to be conscientiously
> obeyed.
>
> The Municipal Committee hereby orders the party Committees
> of *Liberation Daily,* the postal department, and all other relevant
> bodies to ensure that the ninth issue of *Red Guard Dispatch* is distrib-
> uted with *Liberation Daily* to all subscribers and to see that the other
> demands agreed to by the Municipal Committee are met without
> hindrance.
>
> This Urgent Notice is to be publicly displayed. (RG 6:2.2)

Wherever this statement was mounted, a joyous red poster usually went up beside it, congratulating the Rebels on their victory.

Sensing that the time was now ripe to call a halt and set about consolidating their gains, the Red Revolutionaries vacated the *Liberation Daily* building. Most of the Workers Headquarters followed suit, but a small group of extremists elected to stay, in case the authorities did not keep their word.

As it turned out, this was not unwise. According to wall posters, some Rebels claimed that the Moderates began beating them up the minute they came out the door. Others said that, as soon as the Scarlet Guards had taken over the building, they held an exhibition of everything that had been damaged during the siege and invited the public to come and see what they were up against. A rally was also organized at which the Rebels were described as "fascists" and "terrorists." The song "Never Forget Class Bitterness" was sung, and someone got up and shouted "Why, this beats even what the Japanese did when they were here!"[6]

Outraged at this treachery, the Rebels swore that the Municipal Committee was behind it. But they did not deny that property had been damaged:

During the last few days of the *Liberation Daily* incident, some things were damaged, and some inconvenience was caused to the employees. But true revolutionaries, if they keep in mind that the main orientation of the Red Revolutionaries and the Workers Headquarters has been correct, should not be troubled by such details but should rather give us support and praise for what we did. Only someone with ulterior motives could attack our minor shortcomings and excesses.

We wish to point out that we did not encourage destruction. We are firmly committed to protecting state property. The damage was caused under very special circumstances and for certain specific reasons. It occurred when thousands of Rebels were fighting off repeated attacks on the building, when they were risking their lives and shedding their blood to defend the *Liberation Daily* offices from

[6] Copied from wall posters.

being wrecked! If it had not been for the Rebels, who pitted their bodies against the invaders, the crowds would have swept into the building and the whole place could have been smashed to pieces. (RG 3:3.1)

The Rebels, having survived a real siege, now found themselves besieged by defamatory posters. They were accused of a multitude of crimes—from kidnapping people off the street to keeping prisoners tied up in airless cubicles. They produced reams of evidence to prove that people who had smashed or infiltrated their way into the building were treated with respect. Every detail of the occupation was worked over in conflicting wall posters. Even the charge "They were going to squirt the crowd with fire-extinguishers!" drew a Rebel answer:

At about 5:00 P.M. on December 5, it was already dark. For some reason, the light at the side door went out. At this time, the attacks on the building were still at their peak, and some people were burning a pile of our leaflets in the doorway. The flickering of the flames was noticed from inside the building, and some comrades thought it was a real fire. The workers raced up three floors to get extinguishers, yelling "Fire! Fire!" In a matter of seconds, the equipment was on the spot. Then it was seen to be a false alarm. (RG 3:3.1)

This paper war deepened the mistrust of the Rebels. They were afraid that the Municipal Committee would somehow manage to avoid honoring its signature or that it would use its influence in the colleges and factories to see that the Rebels were punished when they went back. This would explain yet another attempt to bind the Municipal Committee to its promises. On December 10, Mayor Ts'ao signed a further four-point document:

1. The Municipal Committee publicly admits that the *Liberation Daily* incident, which has created such opposition and division among the masses, was caused by its bourgeois reactionary line. It considers it a mistake to defend the Committee and even more of a mistake to attack the Rebels.
2. The Committee looks on the actions of the Rebel workers

during the *Liberation Daily* incident as proletarian and revolutionary. Working hours lost by the Rebels are to be considered holiday time.

3. Mayor Ts'ao Ti-ch'iu will personally apologize to the wounded and their families, and the Committee will be responsible for all medical expenses.

4. The Committee is in favor of the Red Revolutionaries' uniting with the workers in the factories and joining them in the Cultural Revolution. (RG 6:2.2)

In a sense, it did not matter how many times the Mayor signed Rebel demands. The "opposition and division" mentioned above was now so deep that no piece of paper could even begin to bridge it. It was a time for action, not arbitration or legislation.

This becomes clear when we consider the fate of the very first Rebel demand—the right to send out *Red Guard Dispatch* with *Liberation Daily*. A week after the Municipal Committee's capitulation, there was still no sign of the Red Guard paper. Nor could anyone prove that the Party had reneged. The post office workers simply went on strike and refused to distribute the tabloid. In other words, there were enough angry people and enough skilled manipulators on both sides to make it a fight to the finish. The Rebels and the Scarlet Guards could not coexist in one city. The *Liberation Daily* incident gathered the previously scattered or uncommitted forces into two hostile camps. In this sense, it was the beginning of the end.

The choice of *Liberation Daily* as a battleground was not arbitrary. The Rebels believed that this paper, as the mouthpiece of the "revisionist" Municipal Committee, had actively perpetrated a bourgeois and reactionary line. Yet we look in vain for proof of this charge. The Rebels complained vaguely that the paper had "neglected" them or had "eulogized the actions of the Moderates," but the only specific allegations I saw were in a Rebel article entitled "There Is a Mountain of Evidence to Prove that *Liberation Daily* Opposed Chairman Mao!" The text was a resounding anticlimax. Its six main charges were:

1. On October 15, 1966, *Liberation Daily* published a photo that included the English words: "Long live the *vincible* thought of Mao Tse-tung!"

2. One of Comrade Lin Piao's criteria for judging a leader was "whether or not he upholds the great red banner of Mao Tse-tung's thought and whether or not he supports Chairman Mao." On November 21, 1966, a *Liberation Daily* article left out the second part of this quotation.

3. When Chairman Mao wrote the characters for "New Peking University," they were printed in red in *People's Daily*, in black in *Liberation Daily*. The following day, when the latter paper was going to publish Chairman Mao's calligraphy of the characters "Women of China," many staff members suggested publishing both titles in red, to make up for having done the first one in black. Ma Ta, the editor and Party Secretary, replied: "That would be admitting a mistake. Once we do that, the Red Guards will be hot on the trail of the Municipal Committee's 'black line.' "

4. A peasant once submitted an article in which he had written: "It's all right to go 3 days without food, but it would be disastrous to go 3 days without Chairman Mao's works." Ma Ta flew into a rage and roared: "We can't publish that sort of rubbish! The fellow should just *try* fasting for 3 days!"

5. On July 1, 1966, page 2 carried an item entitled: "We Warn U.S. Imperialism—This Escalation of the War Will Be Smashed!" The layout was done so that the characters for "War" pointed straight at a photo of Chairman Mao. One of the staff brought this to the attention of Ma Ta, who considered it insignificant and let it pass.

6. Late in May, 1966, Comrade Lin Piao made a great speech entitled: "Four Things We Must Never Forget." *Liberation Army Daily* ran the title as a huge headline. *Liberation Daily* waited 2 days before publishing it at all, and then Ma Ta said, "Make the title a little smaller." Now why on earth would he want it smaller? (RG 6:3.1)

This hair-splitting strikes us as comic, but there are two reasons for it. One is that the Chinese have a highly developed sense of the graphic; the written word has an importance for them that it does not have for us. The other is that *Liberation Daily* was a very hard paper to criticize because it consisted mostly of reprints from Peking papers. The Rebels had to be very sharp to find discrepancies, for a general attack might cast aspersions on the men in power in the capital—the Rebels' own mentors.

There is much food for thought in the *Liberation Daily* incident. Though a Western liberal might rejoice that a few thousand students and semiliterate workers shut down a Party organ in a Communist country, yet, not once during the whole affair was there the slightest whisper of dissatisfaction with the press in general or with the strict Party control of news and information. No one challenged the right of a paper to run a line; the argument was whether the line was "progressive" or "reactionary."

The same principle applies to the Cultural Revolution as a whole. It was directed not at the Party but at *tendencies* in the Party and the men thought to represent these tendencies—the "Party authorities leading the country back to capitalism." Those who see in the turmoil of the last few years a spontaneous popular reaction against the Communist Party are victims of their own wishful thinking.

9. The December Crisis

The week that followed the *Liberation Daily* affair was one of considerable confusion. It was marked by intense debate through wall posters, increasingly spectacular rallies and demonstrations, and, behind the scenes, more and more violent clashes between the rival groups. There was also a decided swing towards the Rebel position. At the beginning, the Scarlet Guards did most of the protesting, and the Rebels found themselves on the defensive. Typical of Rebel propaganda at this time was the following complaint:

> Workers of Shanghai, think carefully! These demonstrations in the streets the last few days, who are they against? Are they against the imperialists and the revisionists? No! Are they against the capitalists and the reactionaries? No! They are against the Red Guards, your class brothers, your own flesh and blood! If this sort of thing continues, it will give encouragement to the bourgeois reactionary authorities and do great damage to the Cultural Revolution![1]

On the theoretical side, much of the debate concerned the role of the workers, especially the question of whether the Rebels were right to have left their jobs and joined in the Anting and *Liberation Daily* incidents. The Rebels said they were left no choice, but the Scarlet Guards accused them of deliberately sabotaging production. Both factions ransacked Peking editorials and official statements to justify themselves. Remarks made by

[1] Copied from a wall poster.

Mao were particularly sought after, and were often quoted
without too much regard for their relevance. A triumphant
looking wall poster appeared one day opposite our apartment
building. It quoted a warning from Mao that workers and
peasants were not to impede the student movement. On closer
inspection, it turned out that Mao had made the speech a good
three months earlier, when the workers had been resisting the
Peking Red Guards.

Statements by Chou En-lai and Ch'en Yi were also used to
bolster the Scarlet Guard position. One day, whole walls in the
busy downtown section were covered with quotes from speeches
made by the Premier and Foreign Minister on November 30.
Chou En-lai was reported to have said: "It is perfectly understandable that you workers want to join in the Cultural Revolution, but production must come first. If you really have a
problem, you can send a delegation to Peking. But please send a
small one; if you come in a great crowd, I only see faces . . ."
Ch'en Yi expounded in more detail:

> The international situation is very good, but there are certain diffi-
> culties. I know that's a word you don't like, but I have to say it.
>
> Foreign affairs have a great influence on the internal situation, and
> vice versa. Conferences held recently, such as those in Manila, New
> Delhi, and Moscow, as well as that of the Organization of African
> Unity, have a big influence on China. Naturally, we didn't attend
> any of these meetings, but just the same. . . .
>
> On the other side of the balance, the Cultural Revolution is
> having a big effect on the world as a whole, and people are learning
> from us. . . .
>
> We must be ready to defeat the imperialists, the revisionists, and
> the counterrevolutionaries when they come. The Soviet Union has
> a quarter of a million troops in Mongolia. We have the Russians to
> the North and the Americans to the South.
>
> Of course, we are ten or twenty times stronger than we were. But
> everything depends on our production. There are tens of millions
> of workers in our country, and 500 million peasants. How would it
> be if they all stopped work and joined in the Cultural Revolution?

Unofficial posters like these might have won some waverers
to the Moderate cause but had little effect on the already-con-

vinced. Even the Central Committee's official statements could not defuse Shanghai. When the Center spoke, it had to address itself to the whole country; its directives were therefore necessarily so vague that almost any faction could find support in them.

This dilemma was clearly illustrated in some remarks made by Chou En-lai on November 27 to student representatives who had come to Peking seeking answers to their problems. The Premier said:

> You'll have to settle these local questions for yourselves . . . the Central Committee can't sit down and solve all your problems. . . . Have you stopped to think that if we did nothing else but receive representatives from the hundreds of universities and high schools all over the country, we would never get to the end of them? If the Central Committee had to settle every dispute that cropped up, it would simply be paralyzed. . . .[2]

This is not to say that Peking had no influence in the provinces. On the contrary, it had at least two very powerful levers: One was the Central Cultural Revolution Group, whose members included people with strong local interests (we have seen how Chang Ch'un-ch'iao used the power of this group to settle the Anting incident); the other was the Peking Red Guards with their liaison centers in all the important cities.

The strength of the Peking Rebels grew rapidly during December, and news of events in the capital began to take priority on Shanghai's walls. Every day, hundreds of posters and leaflets told of new successes by the Peking students, of huge rallies at which prominent men, now seen to be enemies of the Central Cultural Revolution Group, were exposed and denounced.

This activity was immediately reflected in Shanghai. The Scarlet Guards put out an anxious warning on December 9: "Things have been moving very quickly in Peking these last few days. Comrades Chou En-lai, Ch'en Po-ta, and Chiang Ch'ing

2 Copied from a wall-poster account of Chou's speech.

have made most important statements. .... Everyone should study these carefully."[3]

The most active Peking Rebel group was called Third Headquarters. Almost unknown in Shanghai in November, it shot to the top of the popularity (or notoriety) poll in mid-December. Rumors claimed it was loyal to Chiang Ch'ing (Mao's wife), who seemed to be winning inordinate power in the capital.

The meteoric rise of Peking Third Headquarters was bound to have a similar effect on its liaison center in Shanghai. Chou En-lai's praise of the group on December 9 must have worried the Moderates, as must the news from Peking on December 12:

> A struggle meeting against the counterrevolutionary and revisionist clique of P'eng Chen, Lo Jui-ch'ing, Lu Ting-yi, and Yang Shang-k'un was held today in the Peking workers' stadium. . . .
>
> The fact that this clique was handed over to Third Headquarters, and not to either First or Second Headquarters, shows that the Party Central Committee and Chairman Mao support the revolutionary left wing. . . .
>
> The morale of the rally was high, and more than 100,000 people were united as one under the leadership of Third Headquarters.[4]

The key words here are "the revolutionary left wing." Until December, the rank and file of every Red Guard group naively imagined themselves to be "the revolutionary left wing." But it was becoming increasingly and painfully clear that only certain groups had the right to this title—the ones who took their orders from the Central Cultural Revolution Group or from its liaison centers in the provinces. In other words, the Mao group was winning, and the Central Committee, having seesawed for months, was gradually lining up on the side of the Rebels.

It was not long before this dramatic change produced results. At Futan University, for example, which had all along been a bastion of Peking influence, the atmosphere was explosive. The

---

[3] From a leaflet entitled "Scarlet Guard Dispatch," printed by Tungchi University Brigade of the Scarlet Guard Headquarters of Shanghai Schools and Colleges.

[4] Copied from a wall poster.

Red Revolutionaries, stronger than ever as a result of the *Liberation Daily* affair, but thoroughly disgusted with the Municipal Committee for continuing to suppress their newspaper, staged a 50,000-man rally in Hongkew Stadium on December 10. Their target was Yang Hsi-kuang, the power behind the Shanghai Party Committee's Propaganda Department. After 9 days inside the *Liberation Daily* building, with access to many of the Party's secrets, they had plenty of ammunition.

Significantly, Rebels from Peking University and Third Headquarters were invited to attend the proceedings, as were Party dignitaries like Ts'ao Ti-ch'iu and Wei Wen-po. The audience heard Yang Hsi-kuang accused of crimes dating back to his term as Party Secretary of Futan, as well as more recent ones committed during the Cultural Revolution. The main charge against him was that he had tried to suppress the study of Mao Tse-tung's thought, under the pretext that too much Mao would lead to "vulgarization, formalism, scholasticism, and oversimplification" (RG 2:4.1).

This rally all but finished Yang Hsi-kuang, who had long been considered one of the plums of the Cultural Revolution. The Rebels made Ts'ao Ti-ch'iu and Wei Wen-po (for the Municipal Committee and the East China Bureau, respectively) sign a statement agreeing to report the whole matter to the Central Committee, with a view to having Yang Hsi-kuang dismissed from all his posts, and to follow this up with a thorough investigation of his crimes and the publication of the full story in the press.

The Rebels were now within sight of their 7-month-old ambition: to bring down just one high official on the Municipal Committee. One, they reasoned, would lead to another, and the fall of the Shanghai power structure would be assured.

To celebrate the achievement, a vast rally was held the next day, December 11. This was by far the biggest gathering of Rebels ever seen and gave dramatic evidence of their strength. From early in the morning, workers and students, in groups of a few dozen to several hundred, converged on People's Square. At the head of each contingent was a bicycle cart with a two-piece band—cymbals and drums—beating out a martial rhythm, but there was nothing military about the participants, who strolled along gossiping and laughing. Despite the masses of red flags and the slogans of activists alongside, the mood was decidedly amateurish. They were, at best, a motley lot, with more or less equal numbers of men and women, old and young, gay and bored.

If the purpose of the rally was to make a show of strength, it was a great success. After the speeches, it broke into triumphant columns, which made their way simultaneously down every main street east to the Whangpoo River, so that downtown Shanghai could see their numbers.

I asked a Chinese colleague, a stanch supporter of the Moderates, what she thought of the Rebels now. She did not answer for a while, then said: "It's quite complicated. In some ways we can learn from them—their revolutionary spirit, for example. In other ways, they can still learn from us." "They seem to have become very numerous," I said. "Are they now in the majority?" Again she paused before answering. "There is really no way of knowing. . . ." Before, she had consistently dismissed them as a minority. "By the way," she went on, as if it would explain everything, "did you know Miss Nieh Yuan-tzu spoke at the Rebel rally?"

So Miss Nieh was still in town, keeping her vow not to return to Peking until Mayor Ts'ao and his Municipal Committee came tumbling down. It looked as if she might have her way.

There was a deceptive lull toward the middle of the month. Street demonstrations and processions lessened noticeably, though the poster war continued unabated. Reports of violence, with headlines like "Bloodshed in No. 17 State Cotton Mill!" "Scarlet Guard Worker Killed in Glass Factory Skirmish!" and "Down with Hooligans Who Break into Houses and Steal!" showed that a bitter struggle was going on behind the scenes.

The schoolchildren imitated the language of their elders, and some of their posters added, by their very extravagance, a touch of comedy: "Horrible bloodshed has occurred at our school . . . the little revolutionary soldier Lu Feng-ying was attacked in the dead of night by an unknown assailant. . , . At 11 o'clock, Lu got up to go to the lavatory. Someone was lurking in the dark and whacked him on the head with a club. . . . This was no random assault but a deliberate plot on the part of the class enemy. . . ."[5]

As the charges and countercharges multiplied, tricks as old as Chinese culture were played. The names of enemies were often written upside down or on their sides, as a semimagical symbol of their imminent fall. A few brushstrokes might alter a name to suggest "pig" or "dog"; sometimes both the names and pronouns were crossed out or ringed in red. I saw a fine distortion of the name Ch'ang Hsi-p'ing; the character *ch'ang* means "constant," but it had been artfully transformed into the shape of a tortoise (the symbol of a cuckold).

The language itself, as it was called on to express stronger and more telling insults, resorted increasingly to the classical heritage. Proverbs, lines from old poems, aphorisms, puns, and esoteric jokes from the history books became commonplace, so that Shanghai had something of a literary renaissance, as group vied with group in wit and invective. This was a corollary of the Cultural Revolution that few would have predicted.

As December wore on, a minor civil war seemed more and more possible. Both the Rebels and the Scarlet Guards were issuing proclamations and ultimatums demanding the total surrender of the opposition. Their posters were often signed by a dozen or more organizations in conjunction, as though each side were trying to outbluff the other.

A crisis was inevitable, but no one knew when or where it would occur. Shanghai had been held together so far by the remarkably persistent unity of the Party hierarchy. Now, with the head of Propaganda teetering and the people openly divided, something had to give within the Party itself.

The most likely place for a break was Propaganda. For one thing, there was a tradition of rebellion in this department that dated back at least to the publication of Yao Wen-yuan's article of November, 1965. For another, the *Liberation Daily* incident had galvanized everyone connected with Shanghai's publishing world into unprecedented political activity, and the administra-

[5] Copied from a wall poster.

tion of the Propaganda Department could not help but be affected by the prevailing atmosphere of doubt.

The fact that the Moderate faction in Propaganda was forced to strike out at its own department heads was an indication of how bad things were. At a rally on December 17, the Moderates denounced the "bourgeois reactionary line" of certain officials. The Rebels laughed this off as a charade, pointing out that the criticisms were really innocuous, that the men attacked were still referred to as "comrades," and that no mention whatever was made of the arch-enemy, Yang Hsi-kuang. The purpose of the rally, they scoffed, was to save Yang's face by hitting his subordinates. One speech from this rally has survived. It certainly seems mild in comparison with Rebel exposures:

A worker in the Shanghai rubber factory noticed a long time ago that a photo entitled "Long Live the People's Republic of China!" published by the Fine Arts Publishing Company, had serious faults of a political nature. He wrote strong letters of protest to the Central Propaganda Ministry, the Shanghai Propaganda Department, *Liberation Daily*, and Fine Arts Publishing Company. . . . No one took any notice. . . .

In September this year, the worker called the Shanghai Propaganda Department's bluff and threatened to debate the matter on the Bund. . . .

The Vice-Director of the department took a most un-Communist attitude, which could best be described as "You don't slap a tiger on the backside with impunity!" . . . He called a meeting in the department, displayed the photo in question, pointed out the worker's criticisms one by one, and explained how to refute them. . . . He then organized the department's Red Guards to go incognito to the Bund and join in the debate. . . . The result was an argument that lasted a whole afternoon, finally involving 300 or 400 people. . . . (RG 4:2.1)

The following day, December 18, a rally with far more serious implications took place. The Rebels congregated in force; two intra-Party publications were the target: *Party Branch Life* and *Rural Party Branch Life*. They claimed that these two papers were the only ones in the whole country that had not reprinted Yao Wen-yuan's article of November, 1965. This was "sure proof" that the Shanghai Propaganda Department under Yang Hsi-kuang had been working to suppress the revolutionary Party line of Chairman Mao (RG 9:3.1).

According to the Rebels, this rally posed such a serious threat to the authorities that the highest representative of the Party in East China—Ch'en P'ei-hsien—who had hidden behind the Shanghai Committee as long as he could, was now forced to reveal himself as the leader of the opposition to the Mao group in Shanghai (RG 9:3.1). Ch'en, said the Rebels, took a drastic step: Calculating that Yang Hsi-kuang was too far gone to save, he decided to sacrifice him.

The Rebels then produced statements previously made by Ch'en in Yang's defense, such as: "Comrade Hsi-kuang worked in the Education and Public Health Department for many years. True, he made some mistakes, but on the whole he remained faithful to the sixty points of higher education. My feeling is that if we start talking about *Yang* Hsi-kuang, then *Ch'ang* Hsi-kuang and *Wang* Hsi-kuang will also come under fire, and pretty soon we'll find that everyone has made mistakes. . . ." The same source also quoted Ch'en as having said: "Yes, everyone should bring out what they know about Yang Hsi-kuang. For myself, I have an empty magazine. I have no bullets to fire at him. . . ." Yet now, the Rebels continued, here was Ch'en P'ei-hsien saying things like: "Well, we all had a fair idea of how the Yang Hsi-kuang thing would turn out" and "Why, that Education Department was a veritable independent kingdom!" The Rebels finally lashed out at him mercilessly: "We tell you straight, Ch'en P'ei-hsien, you needn't imagine that when Yang Hsi-kuang is caught you'll slip through our net!" (RG 9:3.1).

According to this same source, Ch'en tried one other gambit. He arranged a giant rally for December 23, at which a brand new Moderate organization (the Scarlet Guards had become too risky) would publicly denounce Yang Hsi-kuang and two other high officials chosen as scapegoats. The new group, to be known as Protect Mao Tse-tung's Thought Revolutionary Rebel Committee (a name whose radical cast showed Ch'en knew which way the wind was blowing), got every assistance from the Party authorities. Top men were assigned to write speeches, issue equipment, and organize public relations. The group's leaders were briefed to get 100,000 people to attend the rally, which was to be "dramatic" and "pretty hard" on the victims. No state secrets were to be revealed, and if Ch'en P'ei-hsien had to be criticized at all it should be for nothing more specific than "bureaucratism" (RG 9:3.1).

There is no evidence that the Party concocted this plot; it could merely have been the febrile imaginings of the Rebel propagandists. But the story shows the profound mistrust that the Rebels felt for the Party authorities and their childlike confidence that no attack on their own position could possibly spring spontaneously from the masses.

As it turned out, the establishment was too slow. The Rebels anticipated their move by 2 days. On December 21, there was a rally entitled "The Shanghai Press Pledges an All-Out Attack on the Bourgeois Reactionary Line of the Municipal Committee!" It was sponsored by Rebels from Shanghai's press circles, Rebel forces from Peking, and the Futan University journalism department. Between them, these three groups knew a great deal about Shanghai's Party administration.

Many revealing speeches were made that day. Representatives of *Liberation Daily, Wen Hui Pao, Shanghai Evening News,* Shanghai radio and television, the Red Revolutionaries, and the Peking Rebels made scathing attacks on the heads of the mass media. All the top East China Bureau officials—with the significant exception of Ch'en P'ei-hsien—were "invited" and sat through a torrid afternoon, where they heard the one charge expressed in a variety of ways: Shanghai's propaganda officials had obeyed Yang Hsi-kuang; Yang Hsi-kuang had obeyed Mayor Ts'ao Ti-ch'iu; Ts'ao Ti-ch'iu had obeyed Ch'en P'ei-hsien. The Great Ancestor of this anti-Mao lineage was left unspecified, but by now everyone suspected that it was Liu Shao-ch'i.

This rally brought many issues to a head. It also united the Rebels and clarified their aims, which they then summarized in ten points:

1. Protect Chairman Mao.
2. Protect the Central Cultural Revolution Group.

3. Root out the "time-bombs"—the members of Ts'ao Ti-ch'iu's Municipal Committee who have been leading us back to capitalism.

4. Use these battle cries:
   a. Bombard the Municipal Committee!
   b. Roast Ch'en P'ei-hsien!
   c. Bring down Ts'ao Ti-ch'iu!
   d. Bring back Shih Hsi-min! [former head of the Shanghai Party's Propaganda Department promoted to the Ministry of Propaganda in Peking]
   e. Fight Yang Yung-chih! [nominal head of the Shanghai Party's Propaganda Department]
   f. Hit Yang Hsi-kuang until his name stinks!
   g. Smash Ch'ang Hsi-p'ing!

5. Follow Chairman Mao and his Central Committee, not the Shanghai Municipal Committee.

6. Support the Rebels—they have been right from the start. Support the Red Revolutionaries and their actions during the *Liberation Daily* incident.

7. Unless the administrative heads of the Party press change their ways, bring them down.

8. Expose and denounce the bourgeois reactionary line of the Propaganda Department during the Cultural Revolution.

9. Long live the combined efforts of the Rebels and these first fruits of their struggle!

10. All Rebels in the press, unite under the banner of Mao Tse-tung's thought and fight the reactionaries together! (RG 5:2.1)

Another question brought into the open was that of *Red Guard Dispatch*, which had not been printed since the *Liberation Daily* incident. The representative of the Red Revolutionaries complained of this at the rally:

We prepared three issues of *Red Guard Dispatch*, explaining what really happened at *Liberation Daily* and describing the developments in the struggle against Yang Hsi-kuang. . . . We wanted to get these quickly to our readers, who were impatient to know the truth.

But Ts'ao Ti-ch'iu and other loathsome people on the Municipal Committee were so afraid of our paper and considered it such a threat that they would not print it.

We went to the East China Bureau for help. Secretary Wei Wen-po seemed friendly, but actually he tricked us. He sent us to Nanking, where the Kiangsu Provincial Committee and the *New China Daily* officials turned out to be as bad as their Shanghai counterparts and would not print our paper either. . . .

We reported the matter to the Central Committee. Chou En-lai supported us: "Chairman Mao knows about you," he said, "and is on your side." He personally rang Wei Wen-po and told him: "You must see that *Red Guard Dispatch* is printed and that the Municipal Committee makes a clean breast of this whole affair to the workers."

. . . Ma T'ien-shui had to go to *Wen Hui Pao* and say: "We have committed a serious crime by refusing to print *Red Guard Dispatch.* If we don't print it now, our guilt will be so much greater. This paper represents the correct line for Shanghai's Cultural Revolution." (RG 5:4.3)

Yet another old score to be settled at the rally was that of the original Shanghai Red Guard federation—the First Headquarters—which had opposed the Rebels all the way through. The Rebels were now strong enough to begin closing down the offices of the more conservative Red Guard groups—by force, if necessary. Futan University, the First Medical College, and Chiaotung University Rebels had already suppressed their opposition, and at dawn on the morning of the rally, a combined force of Rebels sealed the main office of First Headquarters and declared the organization defunct.

The rally ratified these actions, and the next day 3,000 former members of First Headquarters gathered in Shanghai Stadium, under slogans that read, "A Revolutionary Knows that Peking Is Near; a Rebel Knows that Chairman Mao Is Dear!" and branded their original organization "an active arm of the bourgeois reactionary line" (RG 7:4.2).

Also on December 22, *Shanghai Evening News,* the paper that had printed tabloids for the moderate Red Guard groups, was occupied by Rebels and closed down. The raiding party complained of fierce resistance, alleging that a right-wing group had run off a protest "Message to all Shanghai Revolutionaries" that had been widely circulated. It is interesting that this right-wing group called itself "Rebel Headquarters." Before long, there would not be a group in Shanghai that did not wave some kind of Rebel banner.

On December 23, the Moderates finally held their 100,000-man rally in People's Square. It was held at 6:00 P.M.—that is, after working hours—a crack at the Rebels for luring men from their jobs.

The Scarlet Guards put on a performance in the best traditions of the Cultural Revolution. After railing for hours at the evil doings of the Municipal Committee, they presented Mayor Ts'ao Ti-ch'iu with eight demands, which he obligingly signed. When the Rebels heard, they mocked the whole rally mercilessly, pointing out that these "eight stinking points" were no threat whatever to the Municipal Committee but were patently designed to weaken the Rebels and strengthen the Scarlet Guards. I managed to find three of the demands in a Rebel paper; if they are accurate they seem to bear out the Rebels' charge:

1. The Municipal Committee must acknowledge the Scarlet Guards as a popular revolutionary organization.

2. In any action affecting both the Scarlet Guards and the Rebels, the Municipal Committee must not negotiate with one side to the exclusion of the other.

3. The Scarlet Guards have the right to take whatever revolutionary action may be necessary against those who infringe the discipline of the Party or the laws of the state. (RG 7:4.1)

Whether the rally was a brainwave of the authorities or not, the Mayor cannot have been too reluctant to sign the Scarlet Guards' demands. On the old principle of "divide and rule," pressure from two violently antagonistic forces would be preferable to surrendering to the Rebels alone.

The Rebels' reaction bordered on the obscene: "No doubt Ts'ao Ti-ch'iu was only too glad to agree to the demands. The revolutionary people of Shanghai, on the other hand, do *not* agree to them. . . . As far as the Rebels are concerned, the Lord Mayor's signature is not worth a fart!" (RG 7:4.1).

On the day of the Moderates' rally, I was invited to Futan University, where I heard a long and breathless account by the Red Revolutionaries of how they had "brought down the counterrevolutionary revisionist Yang Hsi-kuang." He was now, they assured me, "sweeping floors."

I met many of my friends from the Institute that day. At the time, I knew nothing of the raids on moderate Red Guard groups and the disgrace that had befallen First Headquarters. I was therefore baffled to find that my friends, many of whom had been bitterly opposed to the Rebels, had turned into Rebel sympathizers overnight. It was now clear to them that the Party Secretary at our Institute had been on the wrong course from the beginning and that the radical students deserved the credit for exposing him. When I asked the source of this sudden enlightenment, they mentioned only that the Futan Rebels had managed to find some "black" material, which proved that the Party Committees of Shanghai's colleges had indeed carried out the hierarchy's orders to repress the student movement.

There was obviously much more to this abrupt swing. If Shanghai's entire power structure was crumbling, it was not because of a few students at Futan. It was more likely that events in Peking were beginning to have their effect. At about this time, every wall poster bearing news from the capital told of victory for the Mao group. Ho Lung had been accused of plotting guerrilla war against the Chairman's clique; P'eng Te-huai had been arrested; Lo Jui-ch'ing had been denounced by the army; Wang Jen-chung had been branded "a political pickpocket."

Everyone who fell pointed yet another finger at the ultimate targets of the movement—President Liu Shao-ch'i and party Secretary-General Teng Hsiao-p'ing. This was the time when Madame Mao was beginning her campaign against Madame Liu Shao-ch'i and when the whole Party hierarchy loyal to Liu and Teng was weakening under Rebel bombardment. There was several scandals: The Peking West Wall Inspection Brigade was found to have had police support in its activities against the Mao group; the sons and daughters of high officials in the Liu-Teng clique were accused of controlling the Moderate Red Guard groups; the Peking offices of the Provincial committees, including that of Shanghai, were raided, and "evidence of contact with foreign countries" as well as "arms and transmitters" were seized.

Odds against the survival of Shanghai's Party leaders were lengthening rapidly. The only high official who had any cause for rejoicing was Chang Ch'un-ch'iao, who, with his friend Yao Wen-yuan, was safely ensconced in the bosom of the Central Cultural Revolution Group in Peking. From this stronghold, he seems to have been watching events in Shanghai with great attention. A Red Guard paper contained this snippet of news: "In Peking, on December 23, Chang Ch'un-ch'iao received a delegation from the Shanghai Workers Headquarters . . ." (RG 19:1).

Two days later at a rally in Culture Square, a huge crowd of Shanghai Rebels forced Mayor Ts'ao Ti-ch'iu to make yet another concession. In a prepared speech entitled "An Apology to the Party and the People," he confessed that he had "committed a grave error" in signing the Scarlet Guards' demands on December 23 without "discussing it first with the Secretariat." He finished his address by formally declaring the signature "null and void."

The Mayor had now gone about as far as he could go without abdicating entirely. He had given in to both factions yet satisfied neither. The Scarlet Guards were naturally furious at his treachery, while the Rebels, almost before the December 25 rally was over, called the Mayor's speech "worthless" and maintained that Ch'en P'ei-hsien had ordered him to make it for the precise purpose of spurring the Scarlet Guards to violence (RG 9:3.1).

And violence followed almost at once. There is no proof that the Scarlet Guards started it, but, if they did, they were only taking a leaf from the Rebels' book. On December 26, both factions seem to have made abortive attempts to close down each other's headquarters. Then real trouble began on December 27.

Rebel wall posters claimed that the Scarlet Guards had broken into Chang Ch'un-ch'iao's house and had searched it thoroughly for a day and a half. They also accused the Scarlet Guards of raiding the house of the late Mayor, K'e Ch'ing-shih, who had, since his death in 1965, been posthumously sanctified as Mao's man in Shanghai and a bulwark against revisionism. The Scarlet Guards consistently denied having occupied either house and got Chang Ch'un-ch'iao's wife to state over Shanghai radio that she had indeed received a visit from the Scarlet Guards, who had politely asked her some questions and then gone away.

Someone was lying, but the important thing was not so much

what really happened as whose house was visited. It proves, if proof were needed, that Chang Ch'un-ch'iao held the key to the events of late December. The most probable explanation is that he had reneged on some agreement with the leaders of the Scarlet Guards—perhaps a promise of amnesty if they went along with his plans to depose Mayor Ts'ao. They had sent men to his house to find evidence against him.

The Scarlet Guards were also active elsewhere. On the same day, December 27, an urgent Rebel poster claimed:

> Several tens of thousands of Scarlet Guards have illegally raided and occupied Hengshan Hotel. There they barbarously beat up some Red Guards from Peking Aeronautical Institute. . . .
> The ringleaders of this affair are Ts'ao Ti-ch'iu and his Municipal Committee. . . .
> The situation at the Hengshan Hotel, and also at the East China Bureau Secretariat in Kangping Street, is still critical. We therefore issue this desperate appeal to all Shanghai's Revolutionary Rebels and their supporters and to the revolutionary comrades-in-arms who have come from all over the country to help us in Shanghai—mobilize immediately and stop these Scarlet Guards. . . .[6]

That night and the following day, the East China Bureau Secretariat became the center of attention. This massive building, set in a vast garden with a hedge around it, had once been the pride of the old French Concession. Its importance now was as a hideout for the Party leaders.

The Scarlet Guards knew Ts'ao Ti-ch'iu was there, and they went to flush him out. They had little choice, for the dialectic that totally justifies or totally condemns was tightening its grip on them: "If Ts'ao Ti-ch'iu gives his support to the left-wingers, we Scarlet Guards will automatically become right-wingers and even counterrevolutionaries overnight. We are not going to let anyone brand us as counterrevolutionaries! That's why we've come to settle our account with Ts'ao Ti-ch'iu!" (RG 7:4.1).

On December 28, they staged a demonstration in the Secretariat gardens. The Rebels then turned up in force, and there

[6] Copied from wall posters.

was fighting. In all their propaganda to justify this intervention, the Rebels claimed that they went "to prevent violence." We can take this with a grain of salt—the role of peacemakers had not been their forte in the past:

On the afternoon of December 28, a bunch of Scarlet Guard generals induced a whole gang of their men to enter the "Gates of Hell"—the Kangping Street Secretariat. They pretended that their aim was to denounce Ts'ao Ti-ch'iu and to demand that he stick by his signing of their eight points on December 23. They made it look as though they were out for his blood, but in fact the whole performance was rigged. It was all a last-ditch scheme by Ch'en P'ei-hsien, a way of getting Ts'ao off the hook by setting him against the Scarlet Guards and making him seem a left-winger. . . .

The Rebel workers and their comrades-in-arms began sending propaganda teams and loudspeaker vans. They took up positions on the four street corners around the Secretariat and started telling the Scarlet Guards a few home truths about the Municipal Committee. . . . (RG 7:4.1)

Elsewhere, the Rebels openly admitted that extremist elements in their own ranks did cause violence:

Ch'en P'ei-hsien and Ts'ao Ti-ch'iu manufactured the Kangping Street incident. They wanted the workers to leave their jobs and damage Shanghai's production, for this would put pressure on Chang Ch'un-ch'iao and the Central Cultural Revolution Group.

The proper course for the Rebels at this stage was to launch an all-out propaganda campaign to expose this plot of the authorities and get the Scarlet Guards to return to work. Their job was also to fill in for the Scarlet Guards in the factories and keep the machines running. This was the best way to make revolution and boost production simultaneously.

Workers Headquarters and other Rebel groups consequently set up a frontline command post at the Hengshan Hotel, to coordinate the operation. But others established a second command post in Kangping Street and carried on independently; they refused to obey orders and pushed an opportunistic line that seemed left wing but was in fact right wing.

In this way they played into the hands of Ch'en P'ei-hsien and Ts'ao Ti-ch'iu. By getting a large force of Rebels to leave their jobs and surround the Scarlet Guards, they only widened the breach between the two factions. This was exactly what Ch'en P'ei-hsien, Ts'ao Ti-ch'iu, and the Scarlet Guard ringleaders wanted. It had a most damaging effect on attempts to win over the Scarlet Guards and unite the people. It also gave the man in the street a very bad image of the Rebels and did great harm to the reputation of Workers Headquarters. (RG 17:3.1)

This· was quite an admission for the Rebels to make, for it implied that they were unpopular with the people of Shanghai (an intolerable position for self-styled representatives of the masses) and that their unpopularity stemmed from their use of violence (which had been strictly forbidden by the Sixteen Points). They saved some face by ascribing the violent tactics to a breakaway group, but one can scarcely blame the Scarlet Guards for denouncing the whole Rebel faction. All they saw was people with Rebel arm bands descending upon them swinging punches.

The fighting seems to have reached a peak of ferocity on December 29, despite a bland Rebel statement that read, "As a result of our propaganda, the great majority of Scarlet Guards realized by December 29 that they had been duped and began to leave the Secretariat and return to their homes and their jobs" (RG 7:4.1).

An "Urgent Appeal" from the Scarlet Guards brings the picture more clearly into focus:

It is a wonderful thing that, at the height of the Cultural Revolution, 800,000 Shanghai workers have united to form the Scarlet Guards. But, in the 3 short weeks since their founding on December 6, they have seen many of their district headquarters attacked by Rebels, their brigade offices closed, their meetings disrupted, their members arrested, publicly humiliated, even tortured. . . .

This came to a head in yesterday's classic case of factionalism and bloodshed in the grounds of the East China Bureau Secretariat, where, according to a first count, at least eight Scarlet Guards were beaten to death and untold numbers wounded. (We hear there were casualties on the other side too, but it must be clearly understood that the Rebels attacked first, and it was only after some Scarlet Guards had been killed and wounded that we struck back in self-defense.)

This battle is not over yet. . . .

In the past 3 weeks, we have upheld the great red banner of Mao Tse-tung's thought; we have kept strictly to the main line of the movement; we have launched a furious assault on the bourgeois reactionary line of the Municipal Committee and the East China Bureau. Not once have we directed our attack against any popular revolutionary organization that included in its ranks Rebel workers.

Yet a few diehards in Ts'ao Ti-ch'iu's Municipal Committee, in order to cover up their own guilt, have repeatedly slandered us in public. They have openly declared all 800,000 of us "counter-revolutionaries." This attempt to elevate the Rebels at the expense of the Scarlet Guards has resulted in serious fighting and bloodshed.

What crime have we committed in denouncing the bourgeois reactionary line? . . .

Who is spreading all the lies and causing the bloodshed? Who is killing and wounding so many class brothers?

Can't you Rebels see that you are simply being used as a shield for Ts'ao Ti-ch'iu?

Chairman Mao teaches us never to accept things slavishly but always to ask the question "Why?" So we ask: Why do we not unite in a combined attack on the bourgeois reactionary line of the Municipal Committee? Why do we not join forces to root out and punish the people who are doing all the manipulating from back stage?

The murderers of the December 29 incident must be punished! Salute to the martyrs of the December 29 incident![7]

Perhaps the most amazing thing about this Scarlet Guard document is its striking similarity to Rebel propaganda. If the names of the groups were interchanged, it could in fact pass for a Rebel text. For this reason alone, it was impossible to tell which side was truly revolutionary. No wonder the "masses" of workers, students, housewives, old folks, and children frowned and scratched their heads as they toiled through the yards of contradictory wall posters.

If the motivations of the contending forces were unclear, a few facts nevertheless emerged. Both sides agreed that the harmony of Shanghai's working class had deteriorated to the

[7] From a leaflet entitled "Urgent Appeal," signed The Workers Scarlet Guards for the Defense of Mao Tse-tung's Thought, dated December 31, 1966.

point where two massive organizations—each consisting of people who believed they were fighting for Chairman Mao and the best interests of the revolution—could stage a 2-day free-for-all on the grounds of the East China Bureau Secretariat. Both sides also agreed that the Scarlet Guards lost the engagement and then took steps that led directly to the January Revolution.

10. The Battle of Kunshan and the January Revolution

After their defeat at Kangping Street, the Scarlet Guards made a dramatic but disastrous move. They decided to stage a mass exodus from Shanghai. Their plan was to reach Peking and protest to the Central Committee about the violence they had suffered at the hands of the Rebels.

The Rebels had used the same tactic in November and gone 20 miles in a hijacked train. The Scarlet Guards went by road and had gone about 30 miles to the town of Kunshan when a strong pursuit force of Rebels caught up with them. The resulting battle was the most disgraceful and the most decisive of the Cultural Revolution in Shanghai.

In their own propaganda, the Scarlet Guards painted themselves as the victims of aggression: "On December 30 and 31, some 60,000 or 70,000 Scarlet Guards set off on foot and in trucks for Peking. When they reached Kunshan, they were attacked by a numerically stronger force of Rebels and subjected to the most brutal treatment. . . ."[1] The Rebels had their own version of what happened:

A few Scarlet Guard leaders, in an effort to regain the initiative, plotted to cut off Shanghai's water and electricity and to paralyze

[1] Copied from a wall poster.

communications. They also organized more than 100,000 unenlightened Scarlet Guards to lay down their tools and head for Peking.
The men were told it was a mission of protest, whereas, in fact, it
was to be a direct attack on the Central Committee, a blow at the
very headquarters of the proletariat. (RG 10:3.1)

Rather than guess what took place at Kunshan, it might be
simpler to quote from both sides' wall posters. Here is a fairly
detailed account from a Rebel source:

More than 2 weeks have passed since the Kunshan affair, yet all
sorts of rumors are still circulating. . . . "The Rebels killed a lot of
people at Kunshan," "The Rebels searched the houses of poor and
lower-middle peasants," "The Rebels threw girls in the river," "The
Rebels hanged a woman Scarlet Guard from a tree." Let's see what
really happened.

On the morning of December 31, thousands of Scarlet Guards
drove off in trucks to Kunshan, where they started putting up posters
and doing propaganda. They got gasoline from a factory store, and
the Kunshan County Committee gave them 100,000 yuan. They
told the local people they were going to Peking to "protest." Units
kept coming in, until they reached a strength of 70,000 or 80,000.

At 2:00 P.M., more than 100 Rebels went in two trucks to Kunshan.
Their purpose was to persuade the Scarlet Guards to return to their
jobs in Shanghai. As they approached the Chengyang Bridge, they
met organized resistance from the Scarlet Guards, and fighting broke
out. The Scarlet Guards mauled a group of students from the Peking
Third Headquarters; they also mistook some local people for
Rebels and beat them up. A reign of white terror ensued. Later,
when Rebel reinforcements arrived, the bridge was taken. The Scarlet
Guards broke and fled in all directions, with the Rebels in hot
pursuit.

That night, the Rebels confiscated many Scarlet Guard arm bands,
but some Scarlet Guards put their arm bands in their pockets, while
others slipped into private houses to hide. This gave rise to the
rumor that the Rebels had arrested local people and broken into
their homes.

The same night, in a telegram from the Central Committee, Chou
En-lai ordered the workers on both sides to return to Shanghai and
continue the Revolution without jeopardizing production. If there
were still grievances, the message went on, the Scarlet Guards could

send a small delegation to Peking. The Rebels were urged to persuade all workers to go back to Shanghai.

When this telegram was made public, the Rebels prepared to leave. But the Scarlet Guards scattered and hid in the town, where they continued to agitate. They went around destroying Rebel posters and leaflets and assaulting revolutionary students. They also masqueraded as locals and jeered at the Rebels, yelling at them to "go home." Finally, a handful of Scarlet Guard leaders got a gang together, made a detour around the town, and pushed on toward Peking.

. During this whole affair there were no deaths nor even any serious casualties. . . . (RG 10:3.1)

To balance this rosy picture of Rebel righteousness, here is an extract I copied from a Scarlet Guard account:

Some Scarlet Guards were sitting in a restaurant, peacefully eating their dinner, when the Rebels carried out a military-style raid, punching people and making arrests. One girl member of the Scarlet Guards was even dragged from the toilet with her pants around her ankles.

The Rebels boasted that this was good military training for them, though the main justification they gave for the operation was that the Scarlet Guards had entered and searched the homes of Chang Ch'un-ch'iao and K'e Ch'ing-shih.

They searched everyone they apprehended in Kunshan, even setting up checkpoints on key bridges and roads. Nor were they above stripping women to do a thorough job. One peasant remarked: "The Japs used to search us on that bridge. Who would have thought that 17 years after liberation we'd get the same treatment?"

During the fighting, many were wounded, and some were even killed. Most of the casualties were on the Scarlet Guard side, for they were far outnumbered. A Kunshan peasant was asked to estimate the strength of both sides. "First tell me roughly how many Scarlet Guards there were," he said. Hearing there were about 70,000, he went on: "Then I'd say there were half a million Rebels, because every time I saw a Scarlet Guard he had at least six Rebels around him!"

From the conflicting reports, it would seem that the Scarlet Guards enjoyed the support of the local inhabitants, while the Rebels got the cold shoulder. This was very embarrassing for the Rebels, who went to great lengths to explain the antipathy of the Kunshan people toward them. They blamed the local County Committee for aiding and abetting the Scarlet Guards:

> Early on the morning of December 30, when the Scarlet Guard advance reached Kunshan, the County Standing Committee, the heads of the local Cultural Revolution Office, and the directors of the Red Guard reception centers made preparations to cater for the main body. . . .
> The County Committee stopped production in several wineries, converting them into kitchens for the Scarlet Guards. In one dining room alone, the Scarlet Guards were issued 60,000 pounds of rice. They also got 75 gallons of gasoline and a large quantity of broadcasting equipment. . . . (RG 10:3.1)

Often, in the very act of rationalizing the resistance they met, the Rebels made it sound worse:

> Every time we went out on the street to do propaganda and to urge the Scarlet Guards to go back to Shanghai, we were abused by crowds of ill-informed people, who called us "malicious agitators," and "political sneak thieves." "Shanghai students are not welcome in Kunshan!" they yelled, and "Get the hell out of here!"
> The County Committee reception centers would not admit us and the high-school dining rooms would not serve us food. . . . Posters against us had titles like "Exploding the Myth that the Shanghai Rebel Workers Are in the Mainstream" and "Beware of a Tiny Handful of Troublemakers!". . .
> We were insulted by being referred to as "a bunch of clowns" and "self-righteous swashbucklers." Our revolutionary actions were interpreted as "an invasion of pirates, designed to stem the revolutionary upsurge of the Kunshan people." (RG 10:3.1)

In an interesting footnote to this indignant complaint, the Rebels described what happened when Peking came out on their side: "Yet, a few days later . . . these same people did a right-about-face, pretending to be penitent, writing fake self-criticisms, and letting off a lot of horse-fart about 'the great Rebels.' This political somersault showed they had no shame whatever . . ." (RG 10:3.1).

Rebel material implied that the Scarlet Guards won the sympathy of the locals because of superior public-relations work:

As soon as the Scarlet Guards arrived . . . they spread the word that they had been "beaten up" by the Rebels in Shanghai and that they were going to Peking to "protest." This was a "revolutionary act," they said, for they were really rebelling against the East China Bureau and the Shanghai Municipal Committee.

They also put up slogans that read "Respect the People of Kunshan!" and "Learn from the People of Kunshan!" They glamorized themselves with catchcries like "The Red Guards and the Scarlet Guards of Shanghai will never die!" and "The Scarlet Guards have been on the right track from the beginning!"

At the same time, they spread lies about the Rebels, saying such things as "The Shanghai Rebels are out to foment another Hungarian uprising!" and "In the Kangping Street incident, the Rebels killed eleven Scarlet Guards!"

And when they went to buy things in the Kunshan shops, they would even let the people go ahead of them, saying "We are not like those Rebels!" (RG 10:3.1)

Accounts like these can only have earned support for the Scarlet Guards, for they emerge as masters of the Maoist techniques of liaison. Another factor in their favor was the Rebels' own admission that they had used violence. As in the Anting, *Liberation Daily*, and Kangping Street incidents, this was blamed on a group of extremists within their ranks:

The Workers Headquarters issued an order that all Rebel workers were to remain at their jobs, except for a small force, which, in conjunction with student Rebels from Shanghai and other cities, was sent to Kunshan, Soochow, and Wuhsi to do propaganda work and try to get the Scarlet Guards back. . . .

But one group ignored this order and, on its own initiative, sent more than 10,000 men in trucks to Kunshan. When they got there, they did no public-relations work; instead, they played on the hatred some Rebels felt toward the Scarlet Guards and the indignation aroused by the massive walk-out and got them to make arrests and confiscate arm bands, in an effort to force the Scarlet Guards into total surrender. These people even struck Kunshan peasants by mistake, thereby earning the Rebels a foul reputation. It got so bad that this group could not buy food in the town, for the local shopkeepers would not serve them. . . .

Such behavior damaged the prestige of the Workers Headquarters and won the Scarlet Guards a lot of sympathy. The absence of these 10,000 men from Shanghai's production lines aggravated the situation and in fact played right into the hands of Ch'en P'ei-hsien and Ts'ao Ti-ch'iu. . . . (RG 17:3.1)

The Kunshan affair dragged on for several days, despite attempts by the Central Committee and the Shanghai authorities to stop it. At one stage, Ma T'ien-shui, Shanghai's Party Secretary of Industry, went in person to try to settle the issue. Paradoxically, it was the Rebels, bitter critics of Ma in the past, who supported him this time; the Scarlet Guards, who were supposed to be toadies of the Municipal Committee, held a joint rally with the Kunshan County Committee and forced Ma to admit publicly that he was "interfering with their revolutionary action." The Rebels said that they had tried to defend him but were pushed bodily off the platform. They also claimed that the Scarlet Guards then "kidnapped" Ma and were all for taking him with them to Peking, but the arrival of Rebel reinforcements made them abandon this plan (RG 10:3.1).

By January 4, most rank-and-file Scarlet Guards had returned to Shanghai, though there were still remnants in Kunshan as late as January 6, and some Rebel students remained in the town until January 11, organizing a "Kunshan General Headquarters of Revolutionary Rebels." On January 12, I copied a poster that warned that the Kunshan affair was far from over:

The Scarlet Guards, who attempted to reach Peking and force Chang Ch'un-ch'iao to make a self-criticism, were defeated at Kangping Street and again at Kunshan. But their leaders have by no means given in. They have gone underground in the Soochow area and are still busily spreading their poisonous doctrine.

The force of Scarlet Guards that managed to elude the Rebels and head for Peking seems to have made it. Even when the term "Scarlet Guards" was a dirty word in Shanghai, posters I saw were still exclaiming:

The protest delegation, with the help and support of more than a million Scarlet Guards, affiliated combat teams, and the broad masses of revolutionary people all over China, overcame every obstacle and reached Peking. The rumors and slanders that are going about will not last for long. The truth will certainly win out in the end.

Another that I copied read:

Good news! The Scarlet Guard delegation to Peking, after indescribable hardship and suffering, has finally succeeded in reaching the capital. Our dearly beloved leader, Chairman Mao himself, sent a man to welcome the Scarlet Guards, who are at present being well looked after in a reception center attached to the State Council.

The chances are that this group was not as "well looked after" as they made out. Certainly, when they got back to Shanghai, they were treated harshly. Three months later, a poster written by some Rebels in a foundry admitted:

We did not take a comradely attitude to our former opponents; we did not try to help them see the light. Instead, we used coercion to make them toe the line. In our attitude to the Scarlet Guards, for instance, we failed to make a distinction between the organization and its members. We jumped to the conclusion that, if an organization was bad, its members were bad also. So, when the Scarlet Guards returned from Peking, we issued a peremptory order that "All those who took part in the Scarlet Guards' northern expedition are to report to us before 8:00 A.M. Anyone who fails to show up will be severely criticized."

As the movement progressed, we realized that this was no way to achieve unity; it only prevented us from expanding our forces and weakened our strength for the struggle. (RG 22:2.1)

This last observation was profoundly true. Much of the sectarianism that subsequently plagued the Rebels was traceable directly to their ruthless treatment of the Scarlet Guards. "Where there is oppression, there is resistance," says Mao, and the case of the Scarlet Guards was no exception. At first, this resistance was flagrant; posters kept popping up throughout January, hastily scrawled messages that read "The Scarlet Guards are a revolutionary organization!" and "The Scarlet Guards are in the right!" And there were fraudulent ones, signed "Lin Piao," which said "I never ordered the dissolution of the Scarlet Guards. They are genuine revolutionaries." But these overt acts of defiance were comparatively few. What most of the Scarlet Guards did was what the Moderate students had done: They simply changed sides and became Rebels! One could say that they "infiltrated" the Rebel ranks, but this would not be fair, for they had little choice in the matter. Most of them were ordinary workers who had done what they thought was correct; when it became clear that they had been duped by their leaders, they looked around for other groups to join. Since every group was by now called "Rebel," they became Rebels. The leaders, on the other hand, could be said to have infiltrated, for they knew what they were doing. It was they who gave the Rebels so much trouble when the going got rough. Months later, when Shanghai had a new government, they were still a threat:

> The Scarlet Guards are still active. If only they would come out into the open and discuss the issues, if they would put on their Scarlet Guard arm bands and debate with us on television, then we would prove them wrong. In this way, they could be a help to the Cultural Revolution instead of a hindrance.[2]

The Kunshan affair therefore had a lasting effect on Shanghai, but to say that it was a victory for the Rebels would be too simple. In the short term, it was a decided drubbing for the Scarlet Guards, who suffered a "military" defeat and then had to endure a propaganda pounding that lasted for months. But in the long run, the Scarlet Guards were never suppressed, for, although Kunshan catapulted the Rebels into power, they no longer had a clear-cut enemy to fight. The Party authorities, of course, were fair game. But there was no *popular* organization that would openly declare itself anti-Rebel. The opposition disappeared, merging chameleon-like into the Rebel landscape. From then on, it became impossible to tell the exact composition

[2] From a wall poster describing a speech by Chang Ch'un-ch'iao, dated March 26, 1967.

of any particular group. Everyone said radical things, because it was fashionable to do so, but many of the most outspoken Rebels were former Scarlet Guards. Deep down, these people remembered the battle of Kunshan not as a trial of strength won by the Rebels but as a moral battle, a confrontation of principles, won by the Scarlet Guards.

The Kunshan affair led to the fall of the Municipal Committee, but, though it was the dominant factor in the Shanghai coup d'état, it was not the only one. Almost simultaneously, there was a massive American-style sit-in at the junction of Tibet and Nanking roads, the city's busiest intersection, that snarled up urban transport for fully a week.

It all started on December 27, when 116 organizations, composed mainly of Shanghai students who had been sent to work in the surrounding countryside after graduation, held a mass rally in People's Square. They claimed to represent every province and major town of East China, and they had come to Shanghai, they said, to demand that they be permitted to return to the city of their birth. They had already waited a fortnight, but the East China Bureau had refused to receive their petition. After the rally of December 27, they took nonviolent revolutionary action by simply sitting down in the heart of the city.[3]

I went downtown to get a photo. By then the intersection looked really lived-in. Dozens of bright red silk banners flew from the elevated police traffic-control box; straw mats were spread everywhere, and Red Guards were sleeping in broad daylight; monitors patrolled the perimeter, debating the issues with the crowd and keeping an eye out for troublemakers.

The banners and arm bands said "Rebels." Certainly, the Scarlet Guards treated them as such; one of their last acts before going off to Kunshan was to march a column of strike-breakers clear through the sit-in. But the students regrouped, and the Scarlet Guards were soon too busy with the Kunshan affair to bother them. Mayor Ts'ao himself came and spoke to them, also

[3] From a leaflet entitled "Another Message to the People of Shanghai," signed Temporary Headquarters of United Protest Brigade from Every Province of East China, dated December 28, 1966.

without success. It was not until January 6 that the sit-in broke up.

Whether they were genuine Rebels is a moot point. They were rebelling, certainly—against a long-standing policy of the Party to relieve the population pressure of Shanghai and help the surrounding districts by siphoning urban youth over to the rural areas. But this was also a policy of the Mao group, so these "Rebels" were probably simply taking advantage of the current disorder to air their desire to return to Shanghai. They were later accused by the Rebels of deliberately causing chaos in an effort to support the establishment, but in fact the paralysis they caused in Shanghai's transport system hastened the fall of the old guard.

Another contributing factor was the *Red Flag* editorial for New Year's Day. This editorial in the central Party journal warned that people who said the Cultural Revolution would interfere with production were "muddle-headed" and would be "swept onto the rubbish heap of history by the revolutionary masses." The Shanghai Party authorities and all the moderate organizations that supported them had constantly warned of the need to maintain the quantity and quality of industrial production and the *Red Flag* editorial thus left them ideologically defenseless. Chang Ch'un-ch'iao and the Rebel groups loyal to him had insisted that the Cultural Revolution would actually *increase* production in the long run, by getting rid of the bureaucrats and revisionists who were holding China back. Their image was therefore enhanced by the editorial.

Chang Ch'un-ch'iao was still waiting in the wings. On January 3, a wall poster I copied reported the text of a telegram from him: "The Central Committee knows that the railways are seriously blocked in East China. Passengers who were stranded along the lines sent telegrams to Peking, some asking for medical attention. This is all the fault of the Municipal Committee and a handful of Scarlet Guard ringleaders. . . ."

He would not have to wait long, for Shanghai was now ripe for change. The Party leaders who had held out so long against the onslaughts of the left were now very vulnerable. With the city in a state of partial paralysis, they were ideally placed to get the blame. And, with the Scarlet Guards discredited, the authorities had no one to use or hide behind. Even in Peking, their alliances were crumbling; it was rumored that Liu Shao-ch'i had made a confession.

The climax began on January 3, when Mayor Ts'ao Ti-ch'iu was arraigned before a mass rally in Culture Square and humiliated. In the days that followed, leading cadres in Shanghai's schools, universities, factories, and offices were subjected to a merciless barrage of criticism, with only token resistance from the former Moderates.

The foreign teachers were invited to attend the denunciation of Party leaders at our Institute. This was the first such rally I had witnessed, and I was not prepared for the intensity of it. On the stage, under a huge portrait of Chairman Mao, was a red lectern. On the right sat six student chairmen; to the left stood the three "defendants," their heads bowed.

It was an inquest rather than a trial. All day long, people from the audience succeeded each other at the lectern. They made a shallow bow to the portrait of Mao before and after speaking, and their testimony was consistently directed against the three unfortunate members of the Institute's Party Committee. There was no list of witnesses; the evidence of one person led to someone else, and if a member of the audience wanted to intervene, he simply threw a piece of rolled-up paper on the stage. One of the chairmen would read it from the lectern, and the whole meeting could switch direction as in a "happening." The "defendants" were often called to answer specific charges, and the audience shouted them down at the slightest hint of a lie or a delaying tactic. Nevertheless, simple denial was the commonest form of defense, and the enraged chairmen could do little but bellow slogans, which were immediately taken up by the whole auditorium.

It was a highly theatrical performance, but this did not seem to worry the audience in the least. In fact, they came away delighted; in one day, they had elicited an enormous amount of information about the way the Party Committee had suppressed the students in the course of the movement. And the inquest would go on the next day and the next.

I found it depressing. No attorneys, no constitutional rights, no judge, no body of law, no court of appeal. It was the justice of emotion. In retrospect, I probably was closer to unadulterated democracy that day than I will ever be again. The people ran the inquest, and the people got the answers they wanted. As happens in the democratic process elsewhere, mass sentiments prevailed over individual opinions, but everyone felt that he had really participated. The students' bark was worse than their bite, for the only punishment inflicted on the Party Committee members was a few days of kitchen duty.

With similar denunciations going on all over Shanghai, it could only be a matter of hours before the Mayor and his corporation shared the fate of their subordinates. The only thing holding up the final act of the drama was that the Rebels had no large distribution newspaper to voice their demands. Even *Liberation Daily,* after all the turmoil of December, had refused to come out with a truly Rebel stance.

Finally, *Wen Hui Pao* cracked. From conversations at the newspaper's offices, I learned that a group of Rebels within the newspaper, who went by the name "The Spark that Sets the Prairie Grass on Fire," had sent representatives to Peking on January 1. After negotiations involving the Central Cultural Revolution Group (and Chang Ch'un-ch'iao, no doubt), Chou En-lai himself approved the "Spark" group's plan to take power in *Wen Hui Pao.* The delegation was back in Shanghai on January 2; the Rebels took the paper over on January 3, and, on January 4, the "revolutionary" *Wen Hui Pao* reprinted a 1957 article by Chairman Mao, in which he had specifically stated "the bourgeois orientation of *Wen Hui Pao* should be criticized."

Shanghai radio, "after a struggle," broadcast the news of the takeover, and the Rebels now had an organ. On January 5, they published a strong condemnation of the Scarlet Guards, referring for the first time in public to the Kunshan affair. This was the famous "Message to All the People of Shanghai," drawn up and signed by eleven Rebel groups, which could all be considered allies, if not instruments, of Chang Ch'un-ch'iao. It is interesting to note that four of the eleven groups were not from Shanghai.

The Message to All the People of Shanghai charged that, by leaving their jobs, the Scarlet Guards had disrupted production and threatened the people's livelihood. It did not mention that the Rebels had done the same thing (though with far fewer men) in November and that they had done it again during the *Liberation Daily*, Kangping Street, and Kunshan incidents.

It also claimed that the Scarlet Guards were plotting to cut the city's water and electricity and throw the transportation system into chaos. This was an old charge; it had originally been leveled at the Rebels on December 9. It probably referred less to an actual sabotage plot than to the disorder that would follow if employees of essential services walked off the job.

With the publication of this highly one-sided document, the stage was set for the triumph of the left. Chang Ch'un-ch'iao made a dramatic entrance, flying down from Peking on January 6. He met with the Rebel groups and assured them of Chairman Mao's personal approval of their actions.

The next day, a mammoth rally was held in People's Square. It was televised closed circuit to eighty cinemas and theaters and twenty-seven colleges in Shanghai and broadcast to the city and the ten neighboring counties.

I watched it on television. It was not pretty. In the first snowfall of the winter, the old-guard Party leaders, dressed in greatcoats and looking thoroughly dejected, were led onto the stage to the roar of denunciatory slogans. Ch'en P'ei-hsien, head of the East China Bureau, was followed by Mayor Ts'ao Ti-ch'iu, East China Bureau Secretary Wei Wen-po, Secretary of Industry Ma T'ien-shui, acting Propaganda chief Yang Hsi-kuang, and so on. All the old enemies of Chang Ch'un-ch'iao met their Waterloo that day.

The Rebels, particularly the students, were frantic with joy; this was a sight they had waited a long time to see. Their newspaper accounts of the rally gave full play to the profound streak of romanticism that ran through all they did:

January 6 saw Shanghai's first heavy snow of the winter. The pure white flakes filled the sky, drifting and swirling in the icy air, as more than a million Rebel warriors held their great rally. . . .

From every district, factory, school, office, and hospital, from every
corner of Shanghai, they marched to the throb of drums and the
clash of gongs, their portraits of the Chairman and their red flags
held high, to People's Square in the center of the city.

They took the snow full in their faces, the cold wind pierced them
to the marrow, but they strode with their heads high, and their spirit
was one of dignity and pride. . . . (RG 8:1.1)

The whole rally was in this vein: The good Rebels had defeated the evil revisionists. In speech after speech, representatives
of all the main Rebel groups exposed the crimes of the Party
leaders. And the scene was punctuated by slogans from a million
throats. "Down with Ch'en P'ei-hsien!" and "Down with Ts'ao
Ti-ch'iu!" were roared not once but a thousand times.

Many things came to light that had only been vaguely alluded
to before, and some had such intimate political details that they
must have been provided by men at the top. The description of
how Ch'en P'ei-hsien and Ts'ao Ti-ch'iu had usurped the highest
positions in the Shanghai government is a good example. To
hear the Rebels tell it, Shanghai had been paradise when K'e
Ch'ing-shih was Mayor and Chang Ch'un-ch'iao his loyal minister. These men had followed Chairman Mao's instructions to
the letter. But, during a visit to Chengtu in 1965, K'e Ch'ing-
shih fell ill and died. When his body was brought off the plane
at Shanghai airport, Ch'en P'ei-hsien and Ts'ao Ti-ch'iu laughed
audibly. Ch'en then cabled Teng Hsiao-p'ing in Peking and said:
"If you don't appoint anyone, I'm taking over." The Secretary-
General, content to have Ch'en in this powerful position, did
not interfere.[4]

The charges against Ch'en and Ts'ao ranged from moral degeneracy to high treason. The Mayor, for example, was accused
of the following "crime": "Once, at an exhibition of Shanghai-
made clothing, Ts'ao was asked what he thought of a translucent
blouse. 'I don't know,' he muttered, 'ask my wife.' His wife said
'Oh, it's all right.' These blouses were then sold in Shanghai
shops."[5]

4 From notes taken at the rally by the author.
5 *Ibid.*

The Mayor was an old enemy, but, because Ch'en P'ei-hsien had only recently been revealed as the arch-fiend, the Rebels threw the book at him. He was accused of having too many servants, of giving his tyrannical wife too much power, and of putting on "pornographic films from Hong Kong" in the basement of the Sino-Soviet Friendship Building. It was also alleged that during the 3 bad years, when everyone else was tightening his belt, Ch'en had spent his time dancing and playing Mah-Jongg, enjoying a TV set, a refrigerator, and a piano and using government cars for pleasure jaunts and hunting trips in the mountains.[6]

As the rally wore on, the charges became more serious. The main theme was that Ch'en had acted as "the black lieutenant of the Liu dynasty" in Shanghai. Here are three extracts from the speech by the representative of the Red Revolutionaries (RG 8:2.2). They refer to Ch'en P'ei-hsien's admiration of Liu Shao-ch'i's policies and his rejection of the line laid down by Mao Tse-tung. In agriculture, for example:

In August, 1964, Liu brought his vile wife to Shanghai, and Ch'en turned on a great welcome for them. He got Madame Liu to address a meeting of cadres above the seventeenth rank. In a long and infamous speech, she peddled her so-called Peach-Garden Experiment. What she said seemed progressive but was actually reactionary, for it contradicted the revolutionary line of Chairman Mao.

Ch'en praised this speech obsequiously: "Comrade Kuang-mei [her own name was Wang Kuang-mei], under the guidance of Comrade Shao-ch'i, is doing great things for the Socialist Education Movement. Her summing-up of this experience has a profound relevance to Shanghai." . . ."It is a long time since Shanghai has heard a speech of this standard."

Ch'en's real aim was to have the Socialist Education Movement, which had been running until then along the lines of Chairman Mao's "Ten Points," declared a failure and to use Wang Kuang-mei's "Peach-Garden Experiment" as the basis for the movement. . . . He ordered all the cadres of Shanghai to listen to a recording of her speech, and he got all Socialist Education Movement Work Team members to study it carefully before going out to the countryside. . . .

6 *Ibid.*

In education, Ch'en was accused as follows:

> He widely advertised and assiduously practiced Liu Shao-ch'i's re-
> visionist policy of "two separate systems of education.". . .
> When Liu came to Shanghai in 1964 . . . Ch'en announced: "Com-
> rade Shao-ch'i, after profound reflection and research, has suggested
> a dual system of education for our country. This could be said to
> represent the fruits of experimentation overseas."
> By "experimentation overseas," he meant of course, the rotten
> wares peddled by capitalist countries. He went on to say: "This policy
> is also significant for our national defense strategy." What an in-
> credible statement! Under the guise of opposing revisionism, he
> plugged revisionist policies. Tossing off Comrade Shao-ch'i's left and
> right, he made it perfectly clear where his allegiance lay.

The third quote referred to administration policy:

> At the beginning of 1965, when Ch'en was transmitting the contents
> of a Politburo working conference, he said: "Liu Shao-ch'i wants
> Shanghai revolutionized. He wants a lot of new cadres, as in the
> period after 1949. The whole country and the whole world hopes
> Shanghai can produce large numbers of cadres."
> . . . What Liu wanted, of course, was large numbers of *revisionist*
> cadres, who would help him strengthen his control of Shanghai. . . .
> In this way, many bureaucrats . . . were sent up to P'eng Chen in
> Peking, while Shanghai bred its own nest of revisionists—men like
> Yang Hsi-kuang, Yang Yung-chih, and the treacherous Ch'ang Hsi-
> p'ing.

These accusations have little force in themselves. Liu Shao-ch'i
was, after all, President of the People's Republic, and it was only
natural that the highest officials in the East China Bureau and
the Shanghai Municipal Committee would be loyal to him and
respect his policies, just as it was natural for them to listen to
Teng Hsiao-p'ing on matters concerning the Party. The whole
case against Ch'en P'ei-hsien and the others rested on the assump-
tion—not explicit at this stage—that Liu and Teng had actively
plotted against Mao and his allies, for the express purpose of
softening China's internal and foreign policies and thereby leading the country through a period of revisionism to a bourgeois

restoration. One has the impression that few Shanghai people swallowed this interpretation whole. The Rebels, on the other hand, tended to believe their own propaganda. Though they did not know the full story of the Shanghai Party's connections with an anti-Mao clique in Peking, they knew enough to suspect the worst.

For this reason, the January 6 rally ended with three formal commands (RG 8:4.1). First, Ts'ao Ti-ch'iu was ordered to prepare a full confession of his crimes, do manual labor under Rebel supervision, and be available for denunciation by any group that requested his presence. He was also informed that his authority was no longer recognized by the Rebels and that they would ask the Central Committee to dismiss him from all his posts. Second, Ch'en P'ei-hsien was told that he would be held responsible for any further disorder in Shanghai; he, too, was to write a confession, revealing his manipulations of the Municipal Committee and his exact relations with the Liu-Teng headquarters. Third, four Municipal Committee secretaries (Ma T'ien-shui, Wang Yi-p'ing, Liang Kuo-p'in, and Wang Shao-yung), two East China Bureau secretaries (Wei Wen-po and Han Che-yi), and every member of the Party's Standing Committee were ordered to write confessions. A request was to be submitted to the Central Committee, asking for a complete reorganization of the Shanghai Municipal Committee. In the meantime,

> All Municipal Committee secretaries, Standing Committee members, and officials in charge of departmental committees will continue to do their usual work. They will be supervised in this by the Revolutionary Rebels and will not be permitted to adopt a negative or go-slow attitude. During this period, if they contribute to the welfare of the Party and the people, it will mitigate their crimes; if they continue to harm the Party and the people, it will add to their crimes. (RG 8:4.1)

This final paragraph was the only sign of a possible compromise with the Party hierarchy. Otherwise, the actions, attitudes, decisions, and demands of the Rebel rally were unrelievedly harsh. One might have imagined that such stringent measures would usher in a period of "revolutionary order" and that Shanghai would knuckle under to a new administration. But the city was, in fact, on the threshold of its most troubled time. *Red Guard Dispatch,* even as it reported the triumphal rally, warned of the power still possessed by the establishment:

> They have begun a policy of "peaceful evolution." They will tempt the leaders of Red Guard groups, both local ones and those from other cities, with offers of cars and foreign-style houses, thus luring them from the masses, from the workers and peasants, from the truth. They will keep out of the limelight but strike bargains behind the scenes. And they will try to expend the energy of the mass movement by encouraging endless debate.
>
> They will use the workers' groups still under their control to create sectarian division; they will wield their short-lived power to cause work stoppages and walk-outs, thus putting pressure on Chairman Mao's Central Committee and jeopardizing the Cultural Revolution.
>
> They will induce some temporarily unenlightened people to pose as Rebels; they will persuade workers sent to the rural areas to agitate for a return to the city and people assigned to jobs elsewhere in the country to request a transfer to Shanghai; they will stir demands for higher wages, more private housing, and other impossible things. And their purpose in all this will be to turn a crucial political struggle into a free-for-all, divert the main current, and postpone the attainment of socialism. (RG 8:1.2)

No gift of prophecy was needed here, for these things were already happening. The disgrace of the Party leaders triggered an immediate, widespread, and organized reaction. On January 7, one day after the rally, a Rebel flier described the situation in these terms:

> Shanghai has been in a turmoil lately; the whole city has been overwhelmed by the storm of revolution. Chairman Mao's revolutionary line has gained ground daily, while the Municipal Committee, the revisionist headquarters of the Liu dynasty, has been brought down.
>
> But the representatives of the exploiting classes have had long experience in counterrevolution, and they will not simply walk off the stage of history. They are still among us; they have not changed their ideas. They are still up to their tricks, plotting with all their might to stop the Cultural Revolution.

At this very moment, members of the Municipal Committee, hand in glove with a few political sneak thieves from the Scarlet Guards, are planning to cut Shanghai's water and electricity, deprive the city of coal, paralyze communications by land and water, and stop all postal and telegraph services. They have also conspired with some Party Committee bosses to be very generous with state funds, thus opening the way to economic anarchy.

They have done this in an effort to divert the movement from politics to economics. They have even encouraged people to take over private houses and steal bicycles. These side effects have built into a full-scale reaction. In some places, production has stopped altogether, and the national economy is thereby endangered. If things go on like this, the situation could get very serious. . . .

The Rebels now found themselves in much the same position as the former "bourgeois reactionary authorities"; having "jumped on the tiger's back," they began to discover that the exercise of power was not so pleasant.

Their first reaction was not very Maoist. Instead of relying on the masses to sort out their differences, they called on "the dictatorship of the proletariat"—that is, the police. On January 7, the first of a series of security regulations appeared—a five-point statement warning that the police would from now on actively support the "revolutionary left" against those who tried to sabotage the Cultural Revolution and those who said or wrote anything critical of Mao Tse-tung or Lin Piao. The document, as reported by wall posters, went on to announce that acts of violence, such as assault and robbery, would incur severe punishment and that capital crimes would receive the death penalty.

Ts'ao Ti-ch'iu would never have dared use such methods, for fear of incurring the charge of "repressing the masses." That Chang Ch'un-ch'iao, one day after his return from Peking, resorted to the police is a measure of the urgency of the situation as well as a sign that he would brook no resistance.

It was largely bluff, anyway; the police force was as divided as any other organization, and there was no guarantee that it would back Chang Ch'un-ch'iao in an emergency. The tightening of security certainly had little effect on the growing economic disorder, as the following wall poster shows:

Some Party officials have been urging workers to demand higher wages and to ask that this be made retroactive and paid in a lump sum. They have also encouraged agitation for better conditions. Such people are altering the thrust of the movement. They should be denounced to the local Rebel headquarters and handed over to the police.

What was happening all over Shanghai was that the cadres in charge of the purse strings were suddenly being very free with the state's money. Up to this time, the Party had refused, at the risk of being branded "bourgeois and reactionary," to meet the demands of certain workers. One of the main bones of contention was that "temporary" employees did not receive the same pay and welfare benefits as "permanent" ones. Another complaint was that workers had not been issued travel vouchers and funds to go off on "long marches" as the students had been. Now the cadres suddenly capitulated. As a result, vast sums were withdrawn from the banks; thousands of workers left Shanghai to "make revolutionary liaison," and those who stayed behind had a field day converting their windfalls into furniture and household goods.

There can be little doubt that the run on the banks was organized. Whether the orders came from Liu Shao-ch'i himself is debatable; but they seem to have come from as high as the Municipal Party Committee, which still controlled the loyalty and sympathy of the Shanghai Party. The timing and the extent of the phenomenon precluded spontaneity. In this case, the Rebels, who saw plots everywhere, were probably right in blaming the Party leaders.

Before this, Peking, at least in its official publications, had never come out in support of any Shanghai group, preferring to wait until one side or the other emerged victorious. But, on January 9, the Peking *People's Daily* reprinted the Shanghai *Wen Hui Pao*'s January 5 Message to All the People of Shanghai and added its editorial approval of the contents. Also on January 9, *Wen Hui Pao* and the "reformed" *Liberation Daily* both ran a new appeal to the people of the city. This one, entitled simply "Urgent Notice," lashed out at "the ill wind of economism"—

that is, the sacrifice of revolutionary principles for economic advantages. Peking picked this up immediately and published it in all the major papers and broadcast it over every station in the country.

This open recognition and approval by the Central Committee was exactly what the Rebels had wanted for months, and many rank-and-file members must have wondered why it had not come sooner. Only a few can have realized the risk that Peking was running, even now, by declaring itself in favor of one faction in a city as complex as Shanghai.

The Urgent Notice simply *had* to be publicized, for there was no other way to get Shanghai back to work. It revealed the extent of the dislocation, accusing the Shanghai Party authorities of

> . . . colluding with the capitalist forces in society . . . making use of economic benefits to distort the general direction of the struggle and to incite one group of people against another, causing breakdowns in factory production and railway and road transport. They have even persuaded dockers to stop work, thereby clogging the port and damaging China's international prestige. They have liberally distributed state funds and property, arbitrarily increasing wages and welfare, granting all kinds of extravagant allowances and subsidies, and even encouraging people to forcibly occupy public buildings.[7]

The way to solve all this, said the Rebels, was to implement a ten-point plan, which could be summarized as follows:

1. The Rebels must keep on with the revolution but set an example by not leaving their jobs.
2. They should do everything in their power to get the white- and blue-collar workers who have left Shanghai to return.
3. The travel vouchers are henceforth invalid, and the large sums of money involved must be paid back (if necessary, by installment).
4. All state funds are now frozen, except for normal running expenses.
5. The question of wages, back pay, and welfare will be dealt with later.
6. Students who have gone to factories to unite with workers are not to be paid high wages.

[7] *Peking Review*, January 20, 1967, p. 8.

7. People who have illegally moved into houses confiscated from capitalists must be out within a week.

8. The Public Security Bureau will punish those who commit crimes, those who oppose Chairman Mao, Lin Piao, or the Central Cultural Revolution Group, and those who harm the Cultural Revolution or sabotage production.

9. These points are to be publicized and practiced immediately by all Rebel groups.

10. Those who disobey these points will be punished for undermining the Cultural Revolution.

Thirty-two Rebel groups signed this Urgent Notice, as compared to the eleven who had attached their signatures to the Message to All the People of Shanghai. This might seem to indicate a threefold increase in strength, but the very multiplicity of groups represented a fragmentation. For example, the Message had carried the signature of one large workers' organization, Workers Headquarters. The Urgent Notice was signed by Workers Headquarters and no less than five other groups, all of which had originally been affiliated with Workers Headquarters but which, in the space of a few days, had grown independent enough to require separate signatures. The purpose of multiple signatures could conceivably have been to make the Rebel alliance look bigger than it was or to disguise the fact that groups from *outside* Shanghai made up much, if not most, of its strength. But, in fact, the groups that signed independently were bitterly attacked later for "fostering disunity."

Even with the overt support of Peking, the Rebels were not immediately able to restore order. Despite the power of the official press and written evidence of Peking's support—a congratulatory telegram signed by the Central Committee, the State Council, the Military Committee, and the Central Cultural Revolution Group—Shanghai could not be brought to heel.

The transport system remained in a tangle, partly because of the Kunshan affair and partly because the railways were a stronghold of former Scarlet Guards. This led in turn to a serious shortage of coal, Shanghai's main source of power.

The trouble at the port was slow to improve. I talked to dockers later, who told me the cadres had been so busy signing the workers' demands and handing out money (there were no less than fifty-seven separate Red Guard headquarters at the wharves!) that precious little work was done. One ship cabled its home port that Shanghai was crippled by a great strike and asked permission to return without unloading; another flew the Chinese flag upside down as a mark of protest; a Japanese freighter waited 4 days in the river and finally sent a curt telegram to the Chinese State Council.

All over the city, it seemed as if Shanghai's entire system was convulsively rejecting the Rebel takeover. Chang Ch'un-ch'iao knew that the people would accept his administration only if he could quickly restore order. He therefore kept his propaganda machine at full volume, while, behind the scenes, he intensified Rebel infiltration of the factories. The Chiaotung University All the Way Rebels told me of their part in this, revealing that Chang Ch'un-ch'iao was their mentor:

> On January 9, we had a discussion about whether or not we should go and help Rebel workers seize power in their own factories. Some of our members said we should not, for only a group within the factory could truly take power; we should not interfere, they said, because we had no way of knowing the facts about any particular factory Party Committee.
>
> But many factories had asked us for help and we decided to go. On the night of January 1, after a debate lasting most of the afternoon, we went out to the factories.
>
> Chang Ch'un-ch'iao helped us a lot in this matter. He first received us on January 6 and told us that Chairman Mao supported the Message to All the People of Shanghai. On January 10, he received us again and talked about this idea of going to the factories. . . .[8]

The deployment of students in the factories did not, in itself, bring peace. The Party officials were quick to exploit long-standing antagonisms between workers and students, and for a time the situation was only exacerbated. But Chang Ch'un-ch'iao had little choice; the dissatisfaction among the workers was so widespread that it had to be tackled at the roots. This meant getting people loyal to Chang into the factories, so that they could iso-

[8] From notes taken by the author during conversations with the All the Way Rebels.

late the officials opposed to him and get the Rebel workers to take power.

This would perhaps have succeeded if the police had been reliable, for they could have supervised the punishment of recalcitrant cadres. But, according to a wall poster, the whole Police Department was turned upside down on January 11 by a group that raided the central offices of the Public Security Bureau and every single one of its district and county branches. The raiders called themselves Rebels, which should have pleased Chang Ch'un-ch'iao, but there was strong opposition to the takeover from Chang's own men, and he seems to have been outmaneuvered by some former conservatives.

This general turbulence was made worse by some very persistent groups of malcontents, who took this opportunity to air their grievances. According to various wall posters, Shanghai workers assigned to rural areas launched a well-organized campaign to get back to the city. Students sent to far-off Sinkiang complained of shocking conditions and staged a hunger strike; their parents in Shanghai organized on their behalf and sent representatives to Chou En-lai, who was at first skeptical of their reports but ordered an investigation. Finally, the student protest was upheld, and the Sinkiang Party authorities were punished.

All this put pressure on the new power-holders in Shanghai. Of course, they could blame these injustices on the old Party leaders and say that this sort of thing was exactly what the Cultural Revolution was meant to correct. But they were nevertheless bombarded with "revolutionary" requests and demands.

They also had to cope with a serious loss of confidence among the people. Every day, there were new tales about the "white terror" of the former authorities. The inhabitants of Shanghai read these accounts on the walls and had to decide for themselves whether they were true. Some no doubt dismissed them as fabrications; others believed them. Either way, their view of new China would never be the same again. Evil *did* exist under socialism. The millennium had not arrived. Conversely, the gains that had been made—and they were still undeniable—seemed more precarious than they had since the new world began in 1949.

11. The Rebels Rebel

All this time, Chang Ch'un-ch'iao still had not surfaced as the leader of the Rebels. It was generally known that he had returned from Peking on January 6, and it was widely assumed that he was directing operations; yet, he had made no open declaration of his power. He had played no public role in the rally that brought down the Municipal Committee, nor had he emerged in person to call a halt to the turmoil that followed. For the most part, the people of Shanghai had no idea where he was or what he was up to.

There were fleeting glimpses of him during that first crucial week. From conversations with Red Guard groups, I learned that he and his "comrade-in-arms"—the writer and ideologue Yao Wen-yuan—had received the Chiaotung University All the Way Rebels on January 6 and 10. He gave three audiences in 7 days to Rebels from *Wen Hui Pao,* and, on the third occasion, actually went to the newspaper offices to congratulate them, on behalf, he said, of Chairman Mao himself, for their great work in seizing power and publishing the Message to All the People of Shanghai and the Urgent Notice. Mao, he maintained, had been delighted with their success; he had shouted "This is a great Revolution! One class has overthrown another!" The Chairman himself, according to Chang, had ordered the national press to reprint these documents; he had even called the Message to All the People of Shanghai the nation's "second revolutionary wall poster," thus putting it on a par with the May poster of Miss

Nieh Yuan-tzu. His joy, said Chang, was so great that he had exclaimed: "Just because the butchers have laid down their knives doesn't mean we'll have to eat pork with bristles!" This was Mao's way of saying that the workers at *Wen Hui Pao* were perfectly capable of turning out a revolutionary newspaper without the help of the bureaucratic "experts" on the editorial board.[1]

Chang Ch'un-ch'iao invoked Mao's name as if the Chairman were his close friend. He was not the only one to use this tactic, but he did it with more assurance than others. This was a great success with those who were convinced of his mandate but must have infuriated the people who did not trust him.

As January wore on, it became increasingly obvious that he had enemies, not just a few disgraced Party leaders or former Scarlet Guards, but massive opposition from the administration down to the grass roots. He was going to need more than the magic name of Mao to impose his will on Shanghai.

He had big plans. It seems the Central Cultural Revolution Group wanted to establish a brand new form of government in Shanghai and other major centers. According to various wall posters, as early as December 27, at a rally against Liu Shao-ch'i and Teng Hsiao-p'ing in Peking Stadium, Miss Nieh Yuan-tzu, just back from her turbulent month in Shanghai, suggested combining the various Peking Red Guard headquarters into a single administrative unit to be known as the Peking Commune. This was to have democratically elected office-holders and was to resemble the Paris Commune of 1871. Chang Ch'un-ch'iao's job was to organize the Shanghai Commune. But first he had to weld the Rebels into some kind of unity.

By mid-January, Shanghai was still so unsettled that he had not even dared declare himself in power. This secrecy hid his greatest asset—support from Peking—and made him appear just one more contender jostling for power.

Yet, at one point he seemed to be on top. The Rebels excelled at propaganda, and the campaign launched against "economism" was a classic. Hundreds of posters went up on the walls of Shang-

---

[1] From conversations with *Wen Hui Pao* Rebels.

hai, and Rebel workers and students took the message into every corner of the city. In essence, it was an appeal to the better instincts of those who had been deceived by gifts of money and privileges. Slogans like "Have you forgotten the bad old days?" "The money of the bourgeois reactionary authorities is sugar-coated poison!" and "Is money the ultimate aim of our Revolution?" had a powerful effect on the workers, who seemed quite susceptible to the pangs of guilt. Examples of people who had refused higher wages got widespread publicity. I was told at the wharves about an old docker who had written a poster against economism and attached his windfall to the bottom of it, with the words: "This money came from the devil, and it can go *back* to the devil!"

In this respect, Chang had some success, and the Rebel take-over of the railways on January 14 and the docks on January 17 helped considerably to get the city back to normal. But he also made mistakes. He had sent Rebels into the factories to find out who had been so generous with state funds. By the middle of the month, this method produced results, but results that, by their spectacular harshness, alienated whole sections of the population that might otherwise have supported him.

For about 10 days, from January 15 on, all Shanghai witnessed the punishment of the guilty officials. The malefactors were paraded through the streets on 4-ton trucks. Each vehicle carried about fifty Rebels, who, crammed in as they were, somehow managed to beat drums, wave flags, and raise their little red books in response to slogans. At the front of the load would be anywhere from one to three victims, usually wearing placards and dunce caps. It was a degrading sight at first, but so many people were exhibited in this way that the horror lost its edge, for both the spectators and the victims. I saw a poster complaining that some of the cadres were not taking their punishment seriously, going so far as to smile or wink at a friend when two trucks passed.

Chang Ch'un-ch'iao was wrong to imagine he could unify Shanghai by humiliating so many minor officials. These men commanded a lot of sympathy among the masses. They were also susceptible to influence from the old Party hierarchy. More important, they were essential to the smooth functioning of Shanghai's industry and administration; together, they made up the only class of people who knew by experience how the city worked. He would have done well to court their allegiance instead of driving them further into opposition.

There is reason to believe that he would have had his hands full even if he had proceeded with the patience of a saint, for he had powerful rivals, not only within the ranks of the Shanghai Rebels but also among the contenders for power in the capital. It was no foregone conclusion that he would rule Shanghai; all through January the position was open, and several bids were made besides his. By the end of the month, he had five major enemies, who controlled between them far more people than he did. Rebel newspapers have left us detailed accounts of how these opposition groups came into being and the methods they used to try to oust him.

Chang's own group, his political instrument, was Workers Headquarters; it had been loyal to him since the Anting affair. But it had also contained the seeds of division since then. We have seen how some 500 extremists disobeyed him on that occasion, pushing on to Soochow and forcing him to sign their demands. The leader of these dissidents, Keng Chin-chang, had won considerable prestige as a result of his defiance. Keng had also gained a degree of independence from Chang and Workers Headquarters, earning his group the right to wear arm bands stamped "The Soochow Brigade."

On his return to Shanghai after the Anting incident, Keng Chin-chang won control of three separate organizations, which called themselves the First, Second, and Third Regiments of Workers in the Northern Expedition. Of these, the Second Regiment was by far the strongest, and it was this group that Keng officially led.

The Second Regiment grew to be Chang Ch'un-ch'iao's greatest bugbear. Several times during December, he was acutely embarrassed by its actions. It was the Second Regiment that gave the Rebels a bad name at Kangping Street, and again at Kunshan, by downing tools and going off to fight the Scarlet Guards. And it was the Second Regiment that insisted on signing the Urgent Notice independently of Workers Headquarters.

This, at least, is what Chang's men said. Second Regiment propaganda claimed that *they* were the real heroes of the fight against the Scarlet Guards and that Workers Headquarters had been too ready to compromise. Yet, even in its most violent diatribes against the Second Regiment, the Workers Headquarters had to acknowledge the Regiment's major role in the defeat of the conservatives:

> In the course of the movement, the Rebels of the Second Regiment have shown the truly heroic and fearless spirit of the working class. They have not been afraid to hurl themselves into action, to make revolution, to rebel. They have made a great contribution to the defense of the mighty·Workers Headquarters, whose bright banner is certainly dyed with their blood.
>
> But Keng Chin-chang and his kind have tried to take all the credit. Glossing over their errors, they have demanded all the honor and glory; they have used the victories of Workers Headquarters, won at the cost of blood, as stepping stones for their own ambition. (RG 17:2.1)

This was the normal way to discredit a group: praise the ordinary members, the masses, and vilify the scoundrels who had led these good folk astray. It was said of Keng Chin-chang that he was "not a true member of the working class, but a man with a history of counterrevolution, who had sneaked into the Party." Other reports described him as a freebooter and a rapist who had joined Chiang K'ai-shek's army in 1948. When his unit was captured by the Communists, he had managed to talk his way into a position of trust and even into membership in the Party. He seems to have been an outspoken member, for he was quoted as having said during the 3 bad years: "The people's communes are killing the peasants. The cadres eat their fill, while the peasants are driven to drown themselves in their own wells" (RG 19).

This *curriculum vitae* does not explain how such a villain came to control so many people during the Cultural Revolution. By Workers Headquarters's own admission, he somehow succeeded in building his initial group of 500 into a veritable army of fourteen separate workers' organizations, of which the First and Second Regiments alone totaled a staggering 520,000 men (RG 19). This is not bad for 2 months of work. It also raises some awkward questions. How could such an evil person sway so many of Shanghai's heroic workers, who were, after all, "the vanguard of the Revolution"? And how, with so many lined up against him, could Chang Ch'un-ch'iao claim to represent the people of Shanghai?

The Rebels who supported Chang Ch'un-ch'iao did their best to explain these contradictions in their newspapers. Chang, it was said, had tried several times to curtail the growing power of the Regiments. As early as December 23, upon receiving a delegation of Workers Headquarters leaders in Peking, he had declared:

> There is no legitimate basis for the continued existence of the Regiments as an independent force. They were not formed in the crucible of struggle, nor do they share a common bond by virtue of their jobs. They are not even all from Shanghai: Some are from Anting, some from Soochow, some from Nanking. They united at the instigation of a few bourgeois reactionary authorities in the Railways Department. (RG 19)

Here we have the story of the Scarlet Guards all over again. Chang was saying that the Regiments were not a genuine flowering of the mass revolutionary spirit but a deliberate creation of the Party authorities. This does not explain, as the Regiments themselves pointed out, why the Regiments had been the most ferocious *enemies* of the Scarlet Guards and contributed more to their destruction than any other Rebel organization.

Chang's propaganda also mentioned that Keng Chin-chang "just happened" to be in Peking on December 23. He was not among the Workers Headquarters representatives but was leading a delegation of his own. This gives some idea of the continuous negotiations between Shanghai and Peking. We do not know who Keng went to see in the capital, but we can guess that he was seeking support for a move against Chang Ch'un-ch'iao (RG 19).

Workers Headquarters claimed that when Chang came to

Shanghai on January 6, one of his first acts was to ring Keng
Chin-chang and order him point-blank to unite his Regiments
with Workers Headquarters. Keng is said to have refused and to
have told his delegation: "Chang Ch'un-ch'iao is against our
independence. I have put it to the men that they should join
Workers Headquarters. They say they would rather stay in the
Regiments. Can I help it if we have the power and Workers
Headquarters is a cipher?" (RG 19).

Realizing he could not bend the Regiments to his will, Chang
must have decided early to break them. He was wise enough,
however, to maintain some semblance of Rebel unity, at least
until the spate of economism was reduced and Shanghai was
functioning more or less normally again.

When he struck, it was with the same old charges. The manipulators of the Regiments, Chang's propagandists claimed, were
the leaders of the Municipal Committee and the East China
Bureau. Ch'en P'ei-hsien had attended a meeting of Rebels in
the Railways Department on December 31, with the specific purpose of urging the Regiments to leave their jobs and pursue the
Scarlet Guards to Kunshan. Then, after the January 6 rally, men
like Ch'en P'ei-hsien, Ts'ao Ti-ch'iu, Wei Wen-po, and Ma T'ien-
shui, the disgraced leaders of Shanghai, had been placed under
the Regiments' "supervision." During this time, they had plotted
together to oppose Chang Ch'un-ch'iao and Workers Headquarters (RG 19).

Little evidence was adduced to prove this rather fantastic
charge that the extreme left of the Rebel movement had sold out
to the extreme right of the Party hierarchy. It was claimed that
Ma T'ien-shui, the Party Secretary of Industry, had given the
Second Regiment 3,000 yuan as "expenses" on December 23;
but, as all Red Guard groups were entitled to financial and material aid from the Party, this did not necessarily imply collusion.
Another "proof" was that, after the fall of the municipal authorities, the Regiments got the use of a huge house at 922 Huashan
Street, where the dethroned Party bosses were also housed, "the
better to keep an eye on them." Publicity was given to stories by
students who had visited this house and seen Keng Chin-chang
and Ch'en P'ei-hsien "standing talking together" (RG 19). All

that can be said to these bits of gossip is "maybe"—and there were a lot of maybe's and deals in the "smoke-filled rooms" of the Cultural Revolution.

The important thing about the Second Regiment, and about Keng Chin-chang's rivalry with Chang Ch'un-ch'iao, was the revelation that Workers Headquarters—a group whose fame spread far beyond Shanghai and even beyond the frontiers of China—was, by the end of January, a mere shell. The power and the numbers in the Shanghai workers' movement lay elsewhere.

Four other groups besides the Second Regiment opposed Chang Ch'un-ch'iao. One was Workers Third Headquarters, led by Ch'en Hung-k'ang. Here is the Workers Headquarters' description of him, with the usual Red Guard invective:

> Ch'en Hung-k'ang was originally a worker in the No. 15 Radio Factory. His dog of a father was one of those Kuomintang police who gained prestige and wealth by oppressing the working people. His dog of a mother was a Protestant missionary, a true lackey of the imperialists. . . . When Ch'en was still a schoolboy, he organized a "Hoodlums Headquarters". . . his personal life was so corrupt that he was once sent to Chungming Island for corrective labor.
>
> During the Cultural Revolution, he lied and cheated his way to a commanding position in Workers Third Headquarters. This organization had a glorious history in the course of the movement, but Ch'en usurped the leadership. He took no part in the Anting incident but capitalized on it to deceive some workers. After the fighting at Kangping Street and Kunshan, he saw that the Scarlet Guards had lost and he grasped the opportunity to advance himself politically. He decided to split Workers Third Headquarters from Workers Headquarters.
>
> The "reason" he invented for this move was that Workers Headquarters was too big and its funds and equipment were too tightly controlled. If a Third Headquarters formed, it could demand materials and money directly from the Municipal Committee. . . .
>
> By January 2, he was ready to make the break but decided to postpone it until it was properly publicized. Finally, on January 7, his men, who numbered several hundred thousand, solemnly put on arm bands reading "Workers Third Headquarters." Ch'en swore they still belonged to the parent body, but his acts belied his words; one of the first things he did was to start his own newspaper.

The title of the new group was chosen, he said, out of admiration for Peking Third Headquarters. This was pure fraud, for there had never been any First or Second Headquarters in Shanghai.

Ch'en was a hard, ambitious man. He drove out anyone who disagreed with him and finally amassed all power in his own hands. At the same time, he was not at all fussy about accepting bad elements into his organization, and among his members were former Kuomintang policemen, revisionist Party authorities, and Scarlet Guards.

He set up an underground headquarters in the old Korean Consulate. Apart from this, he had four foreign-style houses for his use. He collected a great quantity of equipment and supplies—two small cars, two three-wheeled vans, three big trucks, a jeep, a dozen or more motorcycles, several dozen bicycles, seventy new overcoats, more than 100 boxes of biscuits, at least 10,000 bread rolls. . . . (RG 17:4.1)

The description begins to read so like a classical Chinese biography of a bandit chief that one is tempted to reject it out of hand. But Workers Third Headquarters was a fact, for I myself saw it parading through the streets. We can also be certain that it was a sizable group; if Chang Ch'un-ch'iao's men said it was "several hundred thousand" strong, then it probably was—Chang only stood to lose face by exaggerating his opposition.

A third organization that went its own sweet way was the Red Guard Army. Unlike the Second Regiment and Workers Third Headquarters, this was a national body, and its members were mostly demobilized soldiers. Strictly speaking, it was not a Red Guard organization at all, for its members had nothing in common but the fact that they had once been soldiers.

Various attempts were made to disband the Red Guard Army. Chou En-lai, who had spoken on December 21 in a way that seemed to encourage the group, came out on January 9 with a statement against it. "I am a demobilized soldier myself," he said, "but I can't leave my job to join an organization of demobilized soldiers" (RG 18).

On January 13, according to wall posters, the Central Committee and the State Council issued a directive aimed at strengthening security. It stressed that "landlords, rich peasants, counter-revolutionaries, antisocial elements, rightists, and people who have done corrective labor or completed prison sentences are not permitted to form their own organizations." This was later interpreted as a move against the Red Guard Army, which was said to have taken many reactionaries under its wing.

Finally, Mao Tse-tung and Lin Piao came out with a strong statement: "No transferred or demobilized soldier is permitted to join any independent organization such as the Red Guard Army but each is to participate in the Cultural Revolution groups formed in the place where he works."[2]

By this time, however, the Red Guard Army had become a powerful force. In Shanghai, it had been in the front line at Kangping Street and Kunshan, and it was an independent signatory of the Urgent Notice. When it came under fire from the Center, with people accusing it of "competing with the Liberation Army," it tried to save itself from extinction by uniting with the Second Regiment and Workers Third Headquarters against Chang Ch'un-ch'iao.

The two other organizations that opposed Chang were student groups. The first had its headquarters at Tsinghua University in Peking, but, like several Peking Red Guard groups, its Shanghai Liaison Center was very influential. It called itself simply Chingkang Mountains Headquarters. Its antipathy to Chang was at first indirect; like the other Rebel groups that turned against him, it had originally been one of the Workers Headquarters' allies and a bitter foe of the Shanghai Party authorities and their alleged protectors, the Scarlet Guards.

The trouble started in the capital, where a segment of Chingkang Mountains Headquarters turned against Premier Chou En-lai and the formidable K'ang Sheng, one of the top men in the Central Cultural Revolution Group. The leader of this revolt, K'uai Ta-fu, took part in organizing a "Committee to Investigate K'ang Sheng," thereby putting so much pressure on the Central Cultural Revolution Group that the director himself, Ch'en Po-ta, had to take a hand. According to a Red Guard newspaper, he and Kuan Feng, another member of the central Cultural Revolution Group, telephoned K'uai Ta-fu:

2 Copied from wall posters.

Ch'en Po-ta: I have here a "Public Statement by the Committee to Investigate K'ang Sheng." Your group is involved in this, did you know?

K'uai Ta-fu: Yes.

Ch'en Po-ta: Well, what's your attitude now?

K'uai Ta-fu: I suppose I'd better withdraw our group.

Ch'en Po-ta: Good! And you'd better put out a statement to countermand this other one. You're in the wrong, you know. What you've been doing is reactionary. It's against the Cultural Revolution Group, of which K'ang Sheng is a respected member. The Central Committee also has faith in him.

Kuan Feng (taking the phone): Well, K'uai Ta-fu, what about it? Can you talk the other groups round?

K'uai Ta-fu: I think so. If I can't, then I'll withdraw our group.

Kuan Feng: That's the spirit! If you'd gone on like this, you'd have lost the support of the Cultural Revolution Group. . . . When you were in trouble, we helped you. We don't want to see you go down now. We want you to keep on making revolution. . . . (RG 15)

I have included this conversation, not because it necessarily occurred, but because it shows how the Red Guards *imagined* behind-the-scenes negotiations to have gone on. For our purposes, the important thing is not the attack on K'ang Sheng so much as the connection between it and the subsequent campaign against Chang Ch'un-ch'iao in Shanghai. A Red Guard paper loyal to Chang admitted frankly that there was a causal link: "By devious routes, this Peking reaction against Premier Chou and Comrade K'ang Sheng affected the situation in Shanghai, where there was a similar reaction against Comrade Chang Ch'un-ch'iao" (RG 15). The same article quotes some snippets of conversation as evidence:

At the beginning of January, when the Shanghai Liaison Center of Chingkang Mountains Headquarters was preparing for the first mass rally of January 6, one of its leaders was heard to say: "Apart from Chairman Mao and Lin Piao, I don't trust anyone. I've got my doubts about Chang Ch'un-ch'iao, too."

On January 23, when this same person learned that wall posters critical of K'ang Sheng were appearing in Peking, he was overjoyed and cried: "I've known about this for ages. Why, I knew as early as

June. I've been itching to put up a poster myself for months. . . .
I wouldn't go out of my way to defend Chang Ch'un-ch'iao, either."
(RG 15)

If sentiments like these were current among Chingkang Mountains Headquarters members on January 23, then a Chingkang
Mountains wall poster that went up in Shanghai the next day
could be interpreted as an attack on Chang Ch'un-ch'iao. The
poster was directed against the "motorized humiliation" of officials that had gone on for the past 10 days. It described it as "a
shocking waste of time, money, gasoline, and vehicles" and said
it was far too serious a punishment for the cadres and should be
reserved for real class enemies. Its use in the present situation,
the poster declared, was not a revolutionary act but an extension
of the phenomenon of economism, an attempt on the part of
the reactionaries further to disrupt production and transportation by tying up hundreds of trucks and keeping thousands of
workers from their jobs. Since Chang Ch'un-ch'iao was presumably directing these operations, it is hard to imagine this poster
referring to anyone but him.

We now have an alliance of four major organizations conspiring to attack Chang Ch'un-ch'iao. To these we must add a fifth
and last: the biggest and strongest group of Rebel students in
Shanghai, the instigators and chief protagonists of the *Liberation
Daily* incident, the publishers of the city's most antiestablishment
tabloid, the sworn enemies of Ts'ao Ti-ch'iu, Ch'en P'ei-hsien,
and the rest, the victors of a dozen battles against the forces of
reaction. I am speaking of none other than the Red Revolutionaries.

This organization, which boasted of having more than 100,000
members (though a good half were only high-school students),
completely dominated the Red Guard movement in five of
Shanghai's major colleges—Futan University, East China Normal
College, the First Medical College, Shanghai Teachers University,
and the Foreign Languages Institute. It also had branches
throughout the city's schools.

During the early stages of the Cultural Revolution, the Red
Revolutionaries had been the ones who hammered away most

persistently at the Party authorities. When these men were brought down at the beginning of January, it was the Red Revolutionaries who reaped the most prestige and power from their fall. It was they who took over political control of the campuses and conducted proceedings against the college Party committees. Although they therefore contributed enormously to Chang Ch'un-ch'iao's success, they never came out with a formal declaration in his favor. Other groups, like the All the Way Rebels at Chiaotung University, made no secret of their allegiance to him.

Around the middle of January, the Red Revolutionaries began to take an increasingly hostile attitude to Chang and the groups that supported him. Beginning on January 16, they launched a campaign against the All the Way Rebels and Tungchi University's East Is Red Regiment, charging that these were Trotskyist organizations. Red Guard groups had hurled every other epithet in the book, but this was, to my knowledge, the first time that the question of Trotskyism had ever arisen. It is anybody's guess what they meant by it; nor is it particularly important for our purposes. The point is that the students are unlikely to have thought of it by themselves, which means that their attack probably was suggested by someone else.

In my interviews with them, the All the Way Rebels did, in fact, claim that the Red Revolutionaries had helped the Second Regiment to "supervise" the disgraced Party bosses after January 6; they also charged that the Red Revolutionaries had been heavily influenced by such slippery customers as Ch'en P'ei-hsien and Ts'ao Ti-ch'iu. It was even alleged that, on January 16, these two men had offered the Red Revolutionaries a bribe of 16,000 yuan. This story, though highly improbable, shows the psychological state of the Rebels at this time and the kind of charges that were bandied about.

There is some evidence that Chang Ch'un-ch'iao was concerned about the Red Revolutionaries, for on January 21 he and Yao Wen-yuan received them in a special audience. They seem to have treated the young Rebels with some paternalism. In a significant division of labor, Chang Ch'un-ch'iao passed on four instructions from Chairman Mao and Yao Wen-yuan read four from Lin Piao. Mao's were as follows:

1. The guideline for this year's Cultural Revolution will be the New Year's Day editorials of *Red Flag* and *People's Daily*—that is, open an all-round class struggle.
2. Concentrate on establishing power in four main areas: Peking, Shanghai, Tientsin, and the Northeast. The job of the Rebels is to unite a majority. Rebel forces must be more than half.
3. Shanghai seems hopeful. All the workers, students, and administrative staff have risen up. This makes the present stage of the Cultural Revolution look very good.
4. The Red Guards must be Spartan and simple. They should model themselves on the People's Liberation Army.

Lin Piao's orders were:

1. The Rebels must continue in the spirit of daring. They must see the Revolution through to the very end.
2. They must be scientific in the struggle.
3. They should strengthen their organization and discipline; cultivate the "three-eight" style; sing four songs: (a) "The International," (b) "The 'Three-Eight' Style of Work," (c) "The Three Rules of Discipline and the Eight Points for Attention," (d) "Sailing the Sea Depends on the Helmsman." (Chairman Mao suggested the first three of these but was too modest to add the fourth).
4. Some cadres are not up to scratch. The Rebels should organize, go to the people, and try to help these cadres. But their errors should not be glossed over.[3]

This kind of interview, with its emphasis on discipline and obedience, was likely to annoy the Red Revolutionaries, who had put up with months of similar homilies from the old Municipal Committee. They were also highly suspicious of Chang Ch'un-ch'iao's right to give orders in the name of Chairman Mao. They knew, from contacts with the other major Shanghai organizations opposed to Chang, that he was considered, not only by Shanghai Rebels, but also by certain segments of the Peking Mao group, as an opportunist.

[3] Copied from a wall poster.

Chang Ch'un-ch'iao was aware of his unpopularity, but he was confident of support from the Cultural Revolution Group in Peking. He decided, therefore, to clamp unity on Shanghai before it became impossible. He scheduled a meeting of the Rebels for January 26, to "prepare for the formation of a Shanghai Commune." The implication was clear: It would be a Shanghai Commune run by Chang Ch'un-ch'iao, with the assistance of his lieutenant, Yao Wen-yuan.

Various probes were made beforehand, some tactful and some repressive, to ensure success. Reporters from *Wen Hui Pao,* for example—the only newspaper Chang could really trust—were sent around the various Rebel headquarters on January 24 to ask each one for an article praising the proposed Commune. They got short shrift from Chang's main rival—Keng Chin-chang and his Second Regiment—who reportedly told the journalists: "We have no intention of writing such an article; we are opposed to the Shanghai Commune as it stands."[4]

Another contender for power, Workers Third Headquarters, was approached in a less gentle way. There is no proof that Chang Ch'un-ch'iao was behind it, but, by a curious coincidence, January 24 was also the date of a coup by some so-called Revolutionary Rebel Members within Workers Third Headquarters against Ch'en Hung-k'ang, the leader of the organization. His underground command post was raided, the hoard of vehicles and equipment confiscated, and the whole affair publicized in wall posters.

Ch'en himself escaped by the skin of his teeth but retaliated immediately by arresting the "friend" who had betrayed him. There were lurid accounts of the "fascist treatment" this unfortunate person received, one report saying he was taken to Ch'en and beaten for 3 hours by more than twenty people. When he came around at 8:00 A.M., his clothes were "saturated with his own blood, urine, and dung."[5]

Whatever the true story, Workers Third Headquarters never regained its earlier strength. It survived for a time as an organi-

4 Copied from wall posters.
5 *Ibid.*

zation, but its activities were reduced to guerrilla tactics. During the next fortnight, hardly a day went by without some street fight between members of Workers Third Headquarters and the supporters of Chang Ch'un-ch'iao.

On January 26, the day scheduled for the meeting to discuss the formation of the Shanghai Commune, it was Chang Ch'un-ch'iao's turn to suffer a setback. Keng Chin-chang assembled representatives from all fourteen of his own organizations for a briefing. They first heard speeches by members of Workers Third Headquarters and the First Regiment, complaining of persecution at the hands of Chang Ch'un-ch'iao. According to Chang's own propaganda, statements like the following were made:

> They say we are reactionary organizations. They arrest our people and parade them through the streets, sometimes for as long as 10 hours at a stretch! . . .
> Chang Ch'un-ch'iao has admitted that the First Regiment is a part of the revolutionary left wing, yet Workers Headquarters has arrested at least fifty of our members! . . .
> Since Chang Ch'un-ch'iao took over in Shanghai, why has there been so much fighting among the workers and students, so many instances of revolutionary organizations trying to shut down each other's headquarters? . . . (RG 19)

As the stormy session reached its climax, Keng Chin-chang was reported to have said: "The leadership of Workers Headquarters is rotten! We've got to take over! In just a few minutes, we're going down to this meeting. If we don't do any good there, we'll form our *own* headquarters. Our numbers are greater than theirs, anyway" (RG 19). With this, Keng's men set off to do political battle with Chang Ch'un-ch'iao's forces: "They burst into the preparatory meeting of the Shanghai Commune, making such a fuss and causing such division in the workers' ranks that the meeting was ruined and the Commune had to be postponed." The same report went on:

> On January 26, Keng Chin-chang brought his fourteen organizations and noisily interrupted the preparatory meeting of the Shanghai Commune. In front of delegates from every Rebel group in the city,

he wrangled with Wang Hung-wen and other representatives of Workers Headquarters. Because of his obstructionism, the meeting could not go on and had to be recessed.

Later, he attended a meeting of Workers Headquarters leaders, where he had the temerity to declare: "This preparatory session was actually an attempt to discredit the Second Regiment!" He then stalked off in high dudgeon to his Regiments, where he wrote an abusive telegram to Wang Hung-wen.

In this way, the preparatory meeting for the Commune was completely wrecked. (RG 19)

Even in propaganda put out by Workers Headquarters—material specifically designed to put Keng Chin-chang in the worst possible light—he emerges as a man who had ample power to make good his boasts. The following excerpt shows that it was Chang Ch'un-ch'iao, not Keng Chin-chang, who was in a precarious position:

After the preparatory meeting, Keng mustered no less than forty-eight organizations. He got them together in the Shanghai Mansions and declared the formation of a "Shanghai Revolutionary Committee of Broad Unity," as an alternative to the Shanghai Commune. He then issued a public statement to this effect and even sent a telegram to Chairman Mao, in an effort to put pressure on him and the Central Committee. Among other points, he made the following outrageous remark:

"There are more than thirty organizations in the proposed Shanghai Commune. Of these, more than twenty are liaison centers of groups from outside Shanghai! This is perfectly ridiculous!"

He was also heard to say: "Let them establish the broadest unity they can, and we will do the same. Then we shall see whose unity is genuine." (RG 19)

To make matters worse for Chang Ch'un-ch'iao, the Red Revolutionaries chose this time to come out openly against him. At a meeting held the next day, January 27, in the Sino-Soviet Friendship Building, they subjected him and Yao Wen-yuan to a 6-hour grilling. This was a far cry from their last encounter, when the students had listened to Chang and Yao give orders. This time, the students cracked the whip. They demanded that the two leaders sign a statement admitting that the groups that supported them were in fact riddled with "Trotskyist and anarchist tendencies." According to the All the Way Rebels at Chiaotung University who told me this story, the Red Revolutionaries even tried to get Yao Wen-yuan to turn against Chang.

The gambit failed, for both men refused to sign. This left the Red Revolutionaries in an awkward position; their bluff had been called, and they now had to do something drastic to save face. Chang Ch'un-ch'iao still had his back to the wall, and it was clear that the next few days would decide his fate. There was a rumor going around at this time—so delightfully catty it deserved to be true—that former Mayor Ts'ao Ti-ch'iu, overjoyed to see Chang in trouble, wrote him a letter that began: "When you were in Peking, you issued instructions left and right like a prince. Now that you're here in Shanghai, you're starting to find out how it feels!"

The Red Revolutionaries wasted no time in putting Chang to the test. That very night, according to wall posters, a select group from their headquarters at Futan University made a midnight raid on the Shanghai Writers Union, picking up three men whom they said they wanted to question.

Many such raids had occurred during the preceding few weeks. But in this case, the arrested men were special people. One of them, Hsü Ching-hsien, the Director of the Writers Union, had, as the Red Revolutionaries put it, "suddenly changed sides" a month before and started work as Chang Ch'un-ch'iao's main speech-writer and propagandist. His job evidently included drafting diatribes against the Red Revolutionaries, which gave them, they argued, every reason to "talk with him." Chang Ch'un-ch'iao, on the other hand, saw this move for what it was: a direct challenge to his power.

Chang's reaction was swift and spectacular and caught the Red Revolutionaries completely unprepared. At 1:00 A.M., when they had just put Hsü Ching-hsien in a car and started for Futan University, a detachment of armed troops from the Shanghai garrison arrived. Most wall-poster reports agreed on the size of the squad. There were eighteen three-man motorcycle outfits, four trucks—two full of soldiers, one loaded with police, and one empty (possibly for use as a paddy-wagon). There was also a car carrying a staff officer and a political commissar.

Chang's squad released the two other prisoners who had not yet been embarked for Futan, then roared off to intercept the car bearing Hsü Ching-hsien. The Red Revolutionaries, no doubt pleased with the night's catch, were rolling blithely up to the university gates when they saw the column waiting. The scene is not hard to imagine: a bitterly cold night, the soldiers huge in their padded uniforms, their breath visible in the yellow glare of headlights, their weapons making grotesque shadows on the walls. The students must have gazed open-mouthed at this sight.

They had every reason to be shocked, for the army had not previously been used in Shanghai against any Red Guard group. In fact, its role had been minimal. There had been armed guards on the banks since the spending spree earlier in the month, and sentries had been posted at a few important buildings; there were also military trucks on the streets, but still one scarcely saw three or four a week, and the soldiers in the back were armed only with flags, musical instruments, and little red books. It was rumored that the army had taken over Shanghai radio a few days previously, because of its "semimilitary status." There had been tales in wall posters of clashes between the army and the people in other parts of the country, and a Central Committee directive had warned Red Guard organizations not to interfere with military activities or raid buildings that had been occupied by the army.

But all this was a far cry from sending troops to suppress a student group, and the Red Revolutionaries, according to their own accounts, told the soldiers as much, reminding them of their orders to support the revolutionary left wing at all times. Were the Red Revolutionaries not the left wing? they argued, and had they not done more than any other organization to bring down the bourgeois authorities? They appealed to the troops as class brothers, begging them to see what a terrible mistake they were making by intervening in a revolutionary act.

The soldiers, like soldiers anywhere, remained impassive. On orders from their commander, they set Hsü Ching-hsien free, entered the university, occupied the Red Revolutionaries' headquarters, forbade all outgoing phone calls, and stood guard for 6 hours while an "investigation" was carried out. By morning, there was quite a crowd. Chang Ch'un-ch'iao and Yao Wen-yuan turned up, along with leaders of Workers Headquarters, and joined in the debate between the army and the student leaders.

Accounts differed as to what happened next. The soldiers seem to have withdrawn quite early in the morning, but, for some reason, the staff officer and political commissar stayed on. In the paper war that broke out on the walls immediately after the incident, many posters accused the Red Revolutionaries of "forcibly detaining" these men; the students denied this vigorously, claiming that the officers stayed of their own free will and that the morning was spent in peaceful discussion.

At this stage, the Red Revolutionaries still felt they had a good chance of winning the engagement. In their minds, they had been perfectly justified in arresting the three writers; Chang Ch'un-ch'iao's response was doubly wrong: first, for interfering with the actions of the masses; second, for using the army against revolutionary students.

They were in for their second shock in 2 days. On January 29, an urgent telegram from the Cultural Revolution Group in Peking got full publicity on Shanghai's walls. It read·

1. Some Red Revolutionary leaders have recently turned the spearhead of the struggle against Chang Ch'un-ch'iao, Yao Wen-yuan, and the Central Cultural Revolution Group instead of against Ch'en P'ei-hsien and Ts'ao Ti-ch'iu, the Shanghai representatives of the bourgeois reactionary line and the main Party authorities taking the road back to capitalism. This is quite wrong.

2. They have arbitrarily arrested some revolutionary comrades in the Shanghai Municipal Committee's administration. They must release these men at once, and apologize to them.

3. The action of the People's Liberation Army in defense of a mass revolutionary organization was entirely correct; that of the Red Revolutionary leaders, who forcibly detained a political commissar and a staff officer, was completely mistaken and will certainly not be tolerated.

4. Arguments between mass organizations must be settled by discussion and negotiation, not by such illegal methods as arrest and detention.

5. We trust the comrades of the Shanghai Red Revolutionaries will help their leaders correct these mistakes straight away. If the leaders persist in their errors, the ordinary members should break with them. We will do whatever else has to be done.

The leaders who provoked this incident, and those who are manipulating them from behind the scenes, will be held responsible for any consequences that arise.[6]

This telegram made things look very bleak for the Red Revolutionaries, and they were soon being bombarded with critical leaflets and posters. They put up a bold front, declaring that the Cultural Revolution Group could not possibly have acquainted itself with all the facts in such a short time. It was highly probable, they said, that the telegram was a forgery; they had therefore sent a three-man delegation to Peking to verify it. This was more than a delaying tactic; it was a broad hint that the telegram had originated in Shanghai, that Chang Ch'un-ch'iao, as a Vice-Director of the Central Cultural Revolution Group, might have imagined that he had the right to sign its name to one of his own directives. The delegation could not fly from Shanghai; it had to go by car all the way to Nanking to catch a plane. Meanwhile, Shanghai waited.

Neither side remained idle. On the night of January 29, the Red Revolutionaries crashed a meeting called by Chang Ch'un-ch'iao himself, on the third floor of the *Liberation Daily* building; a fight broke out between them and Chang's student supporters, the All the Way Rebels of Chiaotung University.[7]

Chang's own methods were more subtle. Posters began to appear in which the student Rebels became almost unrecognizable. Their occupation of the *Liberation Daily* building in December, for instance—previously seen as the beginning of the end for the Municipal Committee leaders—was now called "an ambitious act," an attempt by the editors of the Red Revolutionaries' newspaper to win prestige. Their withdrawal from the building after the siege was also criticized as "a sheer gamble," "a political

[6] From a leaflet entitled "The Five-Point Urgent Telegram from the Central Cultural Revolution Group," circulated by Rebels in the municipal administration, printed by Tungchi University's East Is Red Regiment.

[7] From a wall poster.

compromise," that had been carried out on advice from Chairman Mao's enemy, T'ao Chu. The victories of the Red Revolutionaries over the Party committees in many schools and colleges could not be so easily explained away, but they were accused of concentrating on minor officials in order to protect the ones that really counted. When they realized that Ch'en P'ei-hsien and Ts'ao Ti-ch'iu would fall, they had tried to shore them up. And one wall poster had more sinister suggestions: The head of the Red Revolutionaries' propaganda network was said to be the son of a high official in the Peking Propaganda Ministry. He had "sneaked into the Rebel ranks," the story went, and gained power by virtue of "a tongue that could raise the dead."

The effect of this change of heart on the ordinary members of the Red Revolutionaries, many of whom were very young, was devastating. It had simply never occurred to them that their fame could turn to odium so quickly. They were utterly bewildered by the ferocity of the attack and by all the conflicting evidence.

My wife's students were Red Revolutionaries. Two of them came to see us on January 30 and made no secret of their dilemma: "The telegram said the political commissar and the staff officers were 'detained,'" one of them pointed out, "but we *know* this was not the case. Therefore, the whole telegram is suspect." The other added:

Chang Ch'un-ch'iao admitted at Futan that Chou En-lai, Ch'en Po-ta, and Chiang Ch'ing were all three absent from Peking at the time, so we know *they* had nothing to do with the telegram. Furthermore, some Red Revolutionaries put through a long-distance call that day to the Central Cultural Revolution Group. Wang Li answered and said they couldn't speak to anyone because he was the only person in the office. So who could have sent the telegram?

As time went by with no word from Peking, violent clashes between Red Revolutionaries and other groups increased in frequency. At the Foreign Languages Institute, everything was ready for a siege; on the walls near the front gate were pasted defiant quotes from Chairman Mao's poems and signs saying "We are ready for you!" These preparations were not wasted, for the Institute was raided three times in 3 days at the beginning of February. On the last occasion, Peking's Third Headquarters joined in the assault and six truckloads of Chang Ch'un-ch'iao's supporters overwhelmed the defenders. This was only part of a city-wide attack on Red Revolutionary strongholds.

There is evidence to suggest that the Red Revolutionaries were hoping to get a good hearing in Peking. Tsinghua University's Chingkang Mountains Headquarters was said to have cabled from the capital, saying "It has been arranged that Chang Ch'un-ch'iao should be opposed" (RG 15). No further details were given, but there was also a rumor that the Chingkang Mountains group had issued a three-point statement that read: "(1) The Red Revolutionaries are in the right and have been all along! (2) Tsinghua's Chingkang Mountains Headquarters and the Red Revolutionaries must fight together and win together! (3) Chang Ch'un-ch'iao cannot speak for the Central Cultural Revolution Group!" (RG 15)

These dreams were dashed once and for all by the arrival of a cable from the Red Revolutionaries' delegation in Peking. It said simply that the telegram from the Central Cultural Revolution Group was genuine and that Chang Ch'un-ch'iao and Yao Wen-yuan were "revolutionary left-wingers." My wife's students rang us to announce this sad news; I sensed that they still did not fully believe it.

This broke the Red Revolutionaries, who, during the next few days, went through the painful process of denouncing the leaders who had "deceived" them so grossly. The organization itself did not share the fate of the Scarlet Guards; it survived as an "enthusiastic" supporter of Chang Ch'un-ch'iao and the revolutionary left wing. But it never enjoyed anything like its former prestige.

Chang had now pacified the students, gaining a lot of leverage in the process. It was clear, at least, that he had strings to pull in Peking. But his main test was still to come; his victory over the Red Revolutionaries had by no means satisfied the dissident Shanghai workers that he was the man to lead a new administration. On the contrary, his rivals were now desperate to press their claims, and the outlook for February was stormy.

12. The Shanghai Commune

While Shanghai awaited the outcome of the Red Revolutionaries' challenge to Chang Ch'un-ch'iao, the different factions of Rebel workers were taking advantage of the temporary uncertainty to raid each other's headquarters. The major contenders had all read their Mao Tse-tung. They had carefully avoided top-heavy or overcentralized organizations and had literally "gone to the masses," so their power was spread wide and deep through every district and county of the municipal area.

This applied particularly to the "rebellious" Rebels. Workers' organizations like Keng Chin-chang's Second Regiment were able to defy Chang Ch'un-ch'iao precisely because they had put down the deepest roots among the people. Workers Headquarters, strongest of the "loyal" Rebel groups, had also tried to establish district branches all over the city, but Keng Chin-chang's network was far superior.

Chang Ch'un-ch'iao and his rivals all knew that the key to Shanghai's allegiance lay in control of support at the grass roots. The attempts by both sides to suppress opposition in the suburbs, which began around the end of January and continued during much of February and March, were therefore in no way a subordinate or diversionary activity. They were crucial to the outcome of the struggle.

On January 30, Keng Chin-chang struck at the South Shanghai branch of Workers Headquarters, and a 2-day incident ensued. His enemies said the attack was unprovoked, but some remarks by a defector from the Second Regiment, reported in a Workers Headquarters paper, suggest that it might have been in retaliation:

> In the South Shanghai affair, Keng Chin-chang deceived us. He told us that nine of our leaders, including a Standing Committee member, had been arrested and taken to the South Shanghai branch of Workers Headquarters. . . . He ordered us to send a detachment to lay siege to the building and demand the release of the prisoners. We sent some men, but Keng later rang to say that they too had been captured and would we send another lot.
>
> Finally, he took command himself. Announcing that the fourteen organizations under his control would henceforth be known as the United Committee of Shanghai Revolutionary Rebels, he ordered representatives from each group to draw up a coordinated plan of attack. He counted on getting 200,000 men in reinforcements from the Red Guard Army alone. His intention was to smash each branch of Workers Headquarters and then take over General Headquarters itself.
>
> As if this were not enough, he personally urged us to set in motion all the propaganda machinery at our disposal. We were to run off leaflets about the South Shanghai incident, so as to win over public opinion. In this way, he instigated a classic case of internecine strife among the workers. (RG 19)

On January 31, this fight reached its peak. The same Workers Headquarters newspaper claimed that Keng Chin-chang, seeing things going aaginst him, "had the temerity to telephone Chang Ch'un-ch'iao and ask for the support of the army! Chang Ch'un-ch'iao refused point-blank, at which Keng roared into the phone: 'Aha! You sent the army to help your friend Hsü Ching-hsien. He belonged to the "revolutionary left wing," I suppose. And I don't, is that it?'" (RG 19).

Chang Ch'un-ch'iao's victory over the student Red Revolutionaries worsened the position of the dissident Rebel workers. Chang, now confident of strong backing from Peking, pressed ahead with his plans for a Shanghai Commune.

By February 3, Keng Chin-chang and his allies, certain that their organizations would not be included in the Commune, launched a campaign to outflank Chang. They spent the day cranking out propaganda about their newly formed United

Committee of Shanghai Revolutionary Rebels, painting the walls with slogans and parading in large numbers through the streets under banners reading "Welcome to the new United Committee!" and "All power belongs to the United Committee!"

The next day, Chang Ch'un-ch'iao's supporters belatedly mounted their own demonstrations. Although the Commune was not officially declared until February 5, groups loyal to Chang worked all day February 4 parading and putting up signs saying "Welcome to the Shanghai Commune!" and "All power belongs to the Shanghai Commune!"

The people of Shanghai were, understandably, confused. Gathering around the wall posters, they read that "Chairman Mao himself" had "personally selected Chang Ch'un-ch'iao to be First Secretary of the Shanghai Commune and Yao Wen-yuan to be Second Secretary."

If the man in the street was bewildered, the organized opposition to Chang wasted no time in speculation. According to a leaflet attacking Workers Third Headquarters, Ch'en Hung-k'ang, their leader, called "all committee members from the regimental and brigade level up" to a meeting at 8:00 P.M. on February 4. In his speech to them, he made the astonishing assertion that Workers Third Headquarters was "the originator of the whole idea of a Shanghai Commune" and went on to warn them that, "because of a few disagreements with Workers Headquarters," they were to be excluded from the Commune run by Chang Ch'un-ch'iao. He had, he said, "already sent off a telegram to Chairman Mao . . . he will know about this in a matter of hours. . . . I also rang Chang Ch'un-ch'iao twice, to ask him to be here tonight. There was no answer."[1]

In what the leaflet called an "electric atmosphere," he then made three proposals:

1. Each regiment of Workers Third Headquarters should send an urgent telegram to Chairman Mao.
2. Each regiment should send one negotiator to the foundation

[1] "Exposing the Secrets of the Workers Third Headquarters' Evil Leadership," signed Chiaotung University Vanguard Rebel Regiment, dated February 18, 1967.

meeting of the Commune, which was being held that very night in the Shanghai Sports Club.

3. The whole membership should go immediately to People's Square and conduct an all-night sit-in, as a way of forcing Chang Ch'un-ch'iao to include them in the Commune.[2]

These proposals were mild in comparison with others that were brought up during the discussion. Some called for massive street demonstrations, a siege of the *Liberation Daily* building (where Chang Ch'un-ch'iao had set up his headquarters), and a search of Chang's house. Such tactics were not new; they had been tried by the Scarlet Guards in December. Some of the delegates were, undoubtedly, ex-Scarlet Guards themselves and must have been alarmed to see things shaping up exactly as they had before the battle of Kunshan.

All these efforts to put pressure on Chang Ch'un-ch'iao were of no avail. The next day, February 5, the Shanghai Commune was a fact. Perhaps out of prudence, it was formed with a minimum of ceremony; but once its existence had been declared, it received the full backing of the propaganda machine. One of the more interesting slogans put up to welcome it was the double-barrelled "All power belongs to the Shanghai Commune! Long live the People's Liberation Army!" This might reasonably have been interpreted by some as a threat.

Chang Ch'un-ch'iao had now completed, at least in theory, the task he had begun on January 6. Shanghai's Rebels, under his guidance, had "taken power" from the bourgeois reactionary authorities and now stood "united" against any attempt to restore the status quo.

But this was not enough. If he had managed to establish the Shanghai Commune as originally planned on January 26, Peking might have used his success as a model for the whole country. But the 10-day delay forced on him by his rivals lost him this chance. The Mao group in the capital, alarmed by the nation-wide disorders of January, must have been anxious for a genuine Rebel victory in a key area. The first was in Heilungkiang on January 31, and the official press quickly praised it to the skies.

[2] *Ibid.*

By the time Chang Ch'un-ch'iao got his Commune going, it was already obsolescent. The Heilungkiang model was preferred, because it fulfilled the four conditions that the Center considered essential for Rebel success. These were: "(1) a three-way alliance between Rebel leaders, high Party officials who supported Chairman Mao's line, and high army officers; (2) control of the mass media and the police; (3) Rebel takeovers from *within* organizations, not from outside; and (4) a left wing armed with Mao Tse-tung's ideas."[3]

This was a new approach, for it suggested that the Center was prepared to make a deal with the cadres; it was, in fact, an acknowledgment of the power of the Party bureaucrats to create chaos.

Chang Ch'un-ch'iao's enemies in Shanghai were quick to point out that his Commune fulfilled none of these conditions. His alliance was only twofold—his own men plus the army. He did not control the police, who were fighting among themselves. He had not let the Rebels win from within their organizations but had tried to impose his Workers Headquarters everywhere. As for the "left wing armed with Mao Tse-tung's ideas," the major part of it had been excluded from the Commune.[4]

The opposition therefore felt it still had a chance of tipping Chang from the saddle. It used two tactics against him: It did everything in its power to publicize the faults inherent in the Shanghai Commune, and it worked to stir maximum discontent at the grass-roots level.

The more interesting method took the form of a massive campaign to investigate the political integrity of the lowest rank of cadres in the city—the people in charge of street and lane committees. This class, which was very numerous, had previously escaped criticism; its members had not been considered "authorities," and many were in fact ordinary residents and not Party members.

Once the idea was suggested, however, denunciations spread like wildfire, and soon the whole city was embroiled in little

[3] Peking *People's Daily*, February 10, 1967.
[4] From a wall poster.

feuds. Anyone who has watched the Chinese argue will know that even a marital dispute can involve several hundred participants and take the better part of a day to settle. It is not hard to imagine Chang Ch'un-ch'iao's horror at the thought of several million people engaged in this kind of bickering.

His answer was to get *Wen Hui Pao* to print a strong article condemning the attack on street and lane officials. But a 3-day siege of the newspaper offices ensued, in which thousands of angry demonstrators stood outside and shouted that *all* authorities had to be examined, otherwise the roots of revisionism could not be destroyed. They accused the *Wen Hui Pao* staff—and, by implication, Chang himself—of trying to suppress the mass movement.

I spoke with some *Wen Hui Pao* officials later, who described the scene as follows:

> After the publication of our article, bad elements from communities all over Shanghai came milling around the building. It was not a genuine demonstration, for most of the people were hoodlums and dropouts and ex-prostitutes and antisocial troublemakers, while the rest were just misinformed.
>
> They were well-organized, though. There were six distinct groups, and they came in 4-hour shifts all around the clock. They yelled that our article was "a poisonous weed," "an instrument of repression. . . ."

The irony of this is that Chang Ch'un-ch'iao, who had swept to power because of the repressive tactics of the old Party authorities, was getting the same charge hurled at him.

Both sides kept up the pressure. For 2 days after the founding of the Commune, there was a constant stream of processions by Chang's own groups, who marched, often in pouring rain, to the Commune headquarters to offer their congratulations. But the Second Regiment and the rest of the opposition sent all the men they could muster to protest, and there were several clashes in the streets.

By February 7, it was obvious that something had gone wrong. The Peking press had remained curiously quiet about "the great victory" of Shanghai's Rebels, and it began to look as if the Commune had fallen flat.

This was the chance for Chang's rivals to press their claims. According to a Workers Headquarters account (RG 19), Keng Chin-chang issued a statement on February 7, threatening massive disruption if his organization was not immediately included in the Commune. "We control no less than seven municipal departments and four whole districts of the city," he boasted, "yet Chang Ch'un-ch'iao carries on as if we did not exist!"

That night, according to the same source, he called a meeting of representatives from all fourteen of his groups. In a speech that he expressly ordered to be passed on to the whole membership, he struck out at Chang Ch'un-ch'iao in the strongest of terms: "The Shanghai People's Commune was set up without the knowledge of Chairman Mao and without the knowledge of the Central Cultural Revolution Group. That is why *People's Daily* has not mentioned it. This means one thing and one thing only: Chang Ch'un-ch'iao is suspect!" He was also said to have declared open war on Workers Headquarters: "So long as there is a Workers Headquarters, our Second Regiment cannot survive; and so long as there is a Second Regiment, Workers Headquarters cannot survive! . . . We must close their General Headquarters and their district branches; only then will the Shanghai Commune topple."

Chang Ch'un-ch'iao responded through Workers Headquarters. This organization had already issued four authoritative bulletins, which were generally interpreted as Chang's own voice. The Fifth Bulletin, which appeared on February 8, was a diatribe against Keng Chin-chang's regiments.

Keng promptly sent a delegation to Peking, armed with a copy of this defamatory document. Its mission, he said, was to "present Chairman Mao with indisputable proof of Chang Ch'un-ch'iao's suppression of the famous Second Regiment" (RG 19). This may or may not have been his aim. Perhaps he simply wanted to see how much support he could muster in Peking. It was also a way to tighten the screws on Chang.

Accordingly, he kept up massive protests on February 10 and 11. His slogans now directly condemned the leaders of Workers

Main building of the Shanghai Foreign Languages Institute, where the author taught. Special frames to the right were built to accommodate overflow of Red Guard posters.

Two Field Army members outside the Party's administration building a few days after they had raided it in search of "black" material.

Frames for wall posters at Chiaotung University.

Lunghai Pagoda, where the Party had ringed each floor with signs reading, "Long live Chairman Mao!"

Antirevisionist sign beneath the window of a butcher's shop.

Futan University in December, 1966—a strong center of radical opinion.

A huge crowd of students on liaison turning out to meet foreigners coming to the Shanghai Foreign Languages Institute in a made-in-China bus.

The main intersection of Shanghai occupied by dissident intellectuals during the unrest of December–January, 1966–67.

Children jumping for Red Guard leaflets dropped from above.

Tall white hats and posters mark the humiliation of factory cadres being paraded through Shanghai on the back of a truck.

Gymnasium of the Shanghai Foreign Languages Institute serving as a dormitory for students from all over China.

Students on liaison copying important posters.

The First Department Store, site of Workers' Headquarters.

Wall-poster exhortation to study Marx
(Canton, February, 1967). This was
a way of criticizing the emphasis on
the study of Mao.

Ch'ang Hsi-p'ing's name, with the character "Ch'ang" transformed
into a tortoise—the worst of insults in Chinese.

Yang Hsi-kuang's name—crossed out to imply that he is corrupt.

Wall poster urging a "nonviolent" attack on reactionaries.

Wall-poster caricatures of President Liu Shao-ch'i.

Amusing mistranslation of the Chinese for the usual "Smash Kosygin's dog head!"

Cartoons satirizing Madame Liu Shao-ch'i, painted by art-college students.

Headquarters, but he still did not dare to denounce Chang Ch'un-ch'iao in public. In private, he was more explicit. His speeches to his own men have survived in leaflets, and, in one, he is quoted as saying:

> They want to dissolve us. They want to brand all of us, several hundred thousand people, "counterrevolutionaries.". . . They will investigate every one of us. . . . Doesn't this mean we will share the fate of the Scarlet Guards? . . . They are imposing a reign of white terror on us. They are using the tactics of fascism. . . . (RG 19)

With the attacks against him reaching serious proportions, Chang Ch'un-ch'iao suddenly discovered that Keng Chin-chang had sent envoys to Peking. He must have decided that this was a real threat to his power. Everyone had friends in the capital—and enemies, too. He and Yao Wen-yuan packed their bags and flew to Peking. Keng's men had gone by train, for Chang had control of the airports. They arrived in the capital on February 12, with Chang and Yao hard on their heels. In Shanghai, Keng made the most of his enemies' absence, spreading the word that "Chang Ch'un-ch'iao set up the Shanghai Commune on his own authority. It was done stealthily, before any three-way alliance had been established. Now the Central Committee has called him to the capital, where he's going to have to eat a piece of humble pie. . . ." (RG 19).

We can only guess what happened in Peking. One report said that Keng's delegation presented the Central Cultural Revolution Group with a fourteen-page document that contained such remarks as: "We recognize that Workers Headquarters is a revolutionary organization, but we maintain that it has fallen under the control of men who are perverting it from within and leading it along the bourgeois reactionary line" (RG 19).

According to the same source, the leader of the delegation telephoned the Central Cultural Revolution Group's Secretariat on February 13. In a "rude and threatening" tone, he said: "If you can't settle this to our satisfaction, we shall return to Shanghai and set ourselves free." This was a quote from the Sixteen Points, which said: "In the great proletarian Cultural Revolution, the only method is for the masses to liberate themselves."

Meanwhile, in Shanghai, Keng Chin-chang was said to have told his men:

> I have good news for you. All the Peking Revolutionary Rebel organizations support our Second Regiment. . . . This shows we are in the right. . . . Chou En-lai has already received our delegation. . . . Chairman Mao wants to know about us. . . . That reactionary leaflet [the Workers Headquarters' Fifth Bulletin] has been handed to the Chairman. . . . (RG 19)

To his own Second Regiment, he exuded self-confidence:

> Propaganda vans are going around Shanghai broadcasting "Smash the dog Keng Chin-chang! . . ."
> It seems that our sending a delegation to Peking, without telling Chang Ch'un-ch'iao, has upset him. But why should it? He's a Party member; I'm a Party member. We're equals. I'm not upset, because I'm in the right. If he's in the right, why is he afraid of people going to the capital? What does he think they might do? (RG 19)

On the walls, too, the battle raged. Here are two posters that show the difference in approach of the two factions. The Second Regiment was content to ask awkward questions:

> 1. Why has *People's Daily* said nothing of the Shanghai Commune?
> 2. Why have Chang Ch'un-ch'iao and Yao Wen-yuan returned to Peking?
> 3. Why, on the day the Commune was formed, did Workers Headquarters break with the three regiments?
> 4. Why is the Second Regiment under attack in Shanghai, when Peking supports it?
> 5. Why has the Workers Headquarters' newspaper not mentioned that Second Regiment members have been beaten up?
> 6. Why were the Scarlet Guards formerly so bitterly opposed to the Second Regiment?[5]

Such questions were indeed hard to answer, and Workers Headquarters wisely did not attempt to. Instead, its propaganda was dogmatic and ruthless:

[5] From a wall poster.

1. We firmly support the correct leadership of the Central Cultural Revolution Group. Any dog who attacks it will be crushed!

2. Comrades Chang Ch'un-ch'iao and Yao Wen-yuan are confirmed revolutionary left-wingers. Anyone who opposes their correct leadership is a counterrevolutionary!

3. The Shanghai People's Commune represents the unity of the proletarian revolutionaries. It springs from the victory over the Party authorities who were leading us back to capitalism. This is yet another great achievement for Chairman Mao's ideas. We warmly acclaim the Shanghai Commune and wish it long life! Its decisions are correct and we are determined to carry them out. Any dog who opposes the Commune will be crushed!

4. The Shanghai Workers Headquarters is the cornerstone of the Commune. Throughout the Cultural Revolution, its banner has been one of glorious struggle and victory. Every genuine Revolutionary Rebel is obliged to carry this banner. We firmly support every revolutionary action of Workers Headquarters. Their Fifth Bulletin is excellent! We are resolved to stay united with them, to fight alongside them, and to win with them! Any dog who opposes them will be crushed! (RG 11:1.1)

From these two examples, it is not hard to pick a winner. The Second Regiment's questions seem almost plaintive alongside this bold genealogy of the Workers Headquarters, this confident claim to the Mao-given orthodoxy of the Central Cultural Revolution Group.

Around the middle of February, with Chang Ch'un-ch'iao and Yao Wen-yuan still in Peking, internal dissension appeared in the ranks of their opponents, due, perhaps, to propaganda pressure, to some deal made behind the scenes, or to unpublished news from the capital. Whatever the cause, there was a strong rumor that some top men in Keng Chin-chang's own propaganda department had demanded that Keng "examine certain faults in his orientation." Keng is reported to have branded the men "weaklings" and "capitulationists" and immediately replaced them with some of his closest friends (RG 19).

Ch'en Hung-k'ang, the leader of Workers Third Headquarters, was also in trouble. He was said to have been "deposed and downgraded" by his own lieutenants, who then approached Workers Headquarters with an offer to amalgamate. This feeler was rejected by Workers Headquarters, which claimed that Ch'en's fall was a piece of theater and that he still had as much power as ever (RG 17:4.1).

These events provoked Chang Ch'un-ch'iao's opposition to an even tougher line. Chang had been away 5 days and was obviously having trouble getting Peking to back him. This was the time to hit Workers Headquarters and take power. It had to be done quickly, especially now that the unity of the dissidents was beginning to fray at the edges.

Workers Third Headquarters struck first. After a meeting on February 15, at which "a concerted attack on Workers Headquarters" was called for, they launched lightning raids on its district branches in the south, north, and west sections of Shanghai.[6]

Keng Chin-chang threw in his Second Regiment on February 16 and 17. His enemies said he issued the order to "close down all liaison centers of groups from outside Shanghai and impound all Rebel propaganda vans." He is said to have based his actions on the argument that "The name of Chang Ch'un-ch'iao is by no means synonymous with the Central Cultural Revolution Group. This is no time to be superstitious about one individual!" (RG 19).

There is reason to believe that Workers Headquarters was at least as belligerent as its opponents. A Second Regiment account tells of an incident that occurred on February 16 at Wusung, 12 miles north of Shanghai at the mouth of the Yangtze River. It begins by using a quote from Mao to attack Workers Headquarters. Unfortunately, Mao's words applied to a lot of Red Guard literature: "People who write reams of unsubstantiated verbiage can be called immature, but those who exaggerate with the intention of terrifying others are not only immature but plain irresponsible. Lu Hsün was criticizing such people when he said: 'Slander and intimidation are underhanded ways to fight.' " The account goes on:

> We warriors of the Second Regiment have been through the mill.
> We know a thing or two by this time, and we are not to be trifled

6 From wall posters.

with. . . . We intend to present the facts, the best eyewitnesses. The facts are as follows:

On February 16, propaganda trucks from Peking University's Protect Mao Tse-tung's Thought Combat Team, the Anhwei "August 27" group, and several others, drove the 12 miles to Wusung. Under the command of the Workers Headquarters Liaison Center, they proceeded to attack every single grass-roots organization of the Second Regiment. They called it "preaching Mao Tse-tung's ideas." . . .

In fact, their propaganda had nothing to do with Chairman Mao's ideas. Their slogans were "Down with the Second Regiment!" "The Second Regiment is entirely in the wrong!" "Members of the Second Regiment, rise up and oppose your leaders!" and so on.

As soon as they started shouting this, some of our comrades told them to be quiet. Our attitude was that if they had really come to preach Chairman Mao they were welcome but that, as long as they offered no concrete proof of the Second Regiment's errors, there was no sense in talking of "opposing the leaders." If they wanted a debate, we told them, we were ready.

Some of our members climbed on the trucks to invite the visitors down but were roughly pushed off. This unprovoked violence made the masses angry. They started pulling the broadcasting equipment off the trucks. Others, to stop them escaping, let a little air out of their tires.

This seemed to make them quite hysterical, and they called in reinforcements. Soon the number of their trucks had increased to seven, then thirteen, and finally twenty-one. In the end, they had some 10,000 people, against a mere 600 of us. They mounted more than sixty high-powered loudspeakers against us.

In their statement of February 17, they say we made off with their equipment, beat them up, and imprisoned them. If this is true, why don't they bring out the wounded people and the damaged equipment and show the masses? Let the masses be the judge.

They can't do this, because the truth is that *they* started the violence. They arrested and imprisoned our men, taking them first to the Wusung Security Bureau and then to the Shanghai People's Commune offices and the Municipal Security Bureau.

No one can deny that the Second Regiment is a part of Workers Headquarters. These people say we oppose Workers Headquarters and the Shanghai Commune, but what proof have they? If they have none, they are guilty of pure adventurism. It is true that we oppose certain leaders of Workers Headquarters; we also oppose their Fifth

Bulletin. But how can this be called opposing the whole organization? Our accusers are pitiable crickets, echoing someone else's song. They are lamentable confidence men. The February 16 incident was a trumped-up affair, and the February 17 statement had been ready for a long time in advance. This farce only serves to expose the true nature of the rogues who are manipulating these people from behind the scenes. It is a perfect example of the old Chinese proverb: "The fool picks up a stone and crushes his own foot!"[7]

This long quotation is only part of the material that appeared on both sides. To show the similarity of style and content in the accusations, here is the beginning of a Workers Headquarters' account of this same clash: "After a few reactionary leaders of the Second Regiment had manufactured the unspeakable affair of February 16, they became even more hysterical and launched a furious counterrevolutionary attack on the Rebels, provoking further fascist incidents on February 18 and 19 . . ." (RG 16).

This account, like all the others, goes on to give page after page of the "facts." It is more interesting than the Second Regiment's description in one respect: It adds a list of twenty-six organizations as joint signatories. These can be considered the allies of Chang Ch'un-ch'iao. A close look reveals that only five are well-known Shanghai groups: Workers Headquarters, *Shanghai Evening News* Rebels, Chiaotung University All the Way Rebels, Tungchi University East Is Red Regiment, and Third Headquarters of Shanghai Red Guards.

On the other hand, no less than ten are powerful groups from outside Shanghai: There are Rebels from Peking Aeronautical Institute, Peking University, Peking Geology Institute, Peking School of Engineering, and Peking Foreign Languages Institute, as well as the Wuhan Red Guards, the Anhwei "August 27" group, the Tientsin Red Guards, and Rebels from the Harbin Military Engineering and the Sian Military Telecommunications institutes. From this, it would seem that the Second Regiment's main bone of contention with the Shanghai Commune—the charge that it contained twice as many outside groups as indigenous Shanghai ones—had some justification.

[7] From an undated leaflet, signed The 306th Column of the Second Regiment of the Shanghai Workers Headquarters.

Whatever the real extent of Chang Ch'un-ch'iao's support in Shanghai, his mouthpieces always claimed that it was universal. In a war waged mostly with words, this was half the battle. Take, for example, this statement signed by twenty-two Shanghai peasant organizations:

> We, the 3 million revolutionary peasants and Rebels on the Shanghai rural front, earnestly support the Shanghai People's Commune! . . .
>
> It was Chairman Mao himself who first raised the banner of Workers Headquarters, the bastion of the Shanghai Commune. Workers Headquarters has been in the right all along, and its revolutionary actions have been excellent! We support it; we are united with it; we will fight together and win together with it!
>
> Recently, the three Regiments, along with Workers Third Headquarters and other organizations, have been carrying on counterrevolutionary activities. They have tricked a lot of Rebels into opposing Workers Headquarters. Their aim is to destroy the Shanghai Commune. . . . (RG 14)

To hear these people speak, one might imagine that Chang Ch'un-ch'iao had won total allegiance from the populous suburban communes. This was far from the case. The peasants were as divided as any other segment of society, and no single group had gained their exclusive support. Each side accused the other of manipulating large numbers of peasants and putting them up in the city's best hotels, where they were available for joining demonstrations and signing petitions.

By February 20, Chang Ch'un-ch'iao had been gone 8 days, and the suspense in Shanghai was intolerable. There were rumors that the Second Regiment was cracking under the strain, with many of its members rejoining Workers Headquarters. Keng Chin-chang was said to have arrested some defectors and warned his men: "If anyone else betrays us like this, I will not mince matters!" (RG 19) He was also reported to have called many meetings of his fourteen organizations, urging a full-scale assault on the district branches of Workers Headquarters before it was too late. He seems to have received only spasmodic support in this from his lieutenants, some of whom had probably foreseen that it might be prudent to seek an accommodation with Chang

Ch'un-ch'iao's forces. This failure to gain approval for a general attack may have prompted Keng Chin-chang to use an image worthy of some ancient Chinese commander: "The enemy's foot soldiers have crossed the river," he is said to have lamented, "The general will not be far behind them" (RG 19).

His position was not helped by the rapid decline, about this time, of one of his strongest supporters—the Red Guard Army. We get some idea of this organization's struggle to survive from the following record of a telephone conversation between a member of its Shanghai branch and a representative of the Military Committee in Peking. This was supposed to have taken place on February 21:

Question: The Red Guard Army—a member of the United Committee of Shanghai Revolutionary Rebels—is an organization composed of workers, peasants, reserve and demobilized soldiers, university students, and so on. As such, can it be described as a mass organization?

Answer: The Shanghai Red Guard Army was one of the thirty-two Shanghai organizations congratulated in the Central Committee's January 11 telegram. It can therefore legitimately claim to be a mass organization.

Question: At this moment, the Red Guard Army is under terrible pressure from public opinion in Shanghai, and there is talk of disbanding it. What is your opinion of this?

Answer: Since it is not composed solely of demobilized and reserve soldiers, then, provided its orientation remains correct, it is revolutionary, and should not be disbanded.

Question: Yet its funds have been reduced.

Answer: It should receive funds in the spirit of the Central Committee's instructions to "make revolution frugally." As it is a revotionary organization, it should settle the question of finance through discussion with the Shanghai People's Commune.

Question: The Red Guard Army units in Chingpu and Chiating counties have already been forcibly disbanded by the local armed forces. What do you think of that?

Answer: I'm in Peking. I'm not familiar with the situation in Shanghai. . . .[8]

[8] From a leaflet entitled "Urgent News," dated February 22, 1967, and signed The Shanghai Electricity Bureau Brigade of the Red Guard Army—a Member of the United Committee of Shanghai Revolutionary Rebels.

Despite this deterioration of one of his main allies, Keng Chin-chang was determined to force a showdown. Even as late as February 22, when Shanghai began to buzz with rumors that Chang Ch'un-ch'iao and Yao Wen-yuan were on their way back with instructions from Chairman Mao himself, Keng calmly went ahead and organized a mass demonstration in People's Square. This was typical of the man who, according to a wall poster, had declared: "I'm in the right and I'm going to stick it out! Even if everyone deserts me, I won't be scared off!"

The demonstration was held as planned, but it was the last of its kind in Shanghai, at least while I was there. It was the last time a massive opposition party held a rally against the established authority. The purpose of the gathering was to get as much publicity as possible for the United Committee of Shanghai Revolutionary Rebels and thus to present Chang Ch'un-ch'iao on his return with the fact that a sizable, coherent, and genuinely popular force opposed the Shanghai Commune, that it was an alternative and a successor to the moribund Commune, and that it could therefore not be snuffed out, as the Scarlet Guards had been, by a simple declaration that it was counterrevolutionary or anti-Mao or a creation of the Party authorities.

With this in mind, everybody who supported Keng Chin-chang turned up that day, heard the standard fare of speeches and slogans, and then paraded through the streets of Shanghai, shouting "Down with the leaders of Workers Headquarters, who are trying to pervert it from within!"

It was a nice try. By the next morning, February 23, Chang Ch'un-ch'iao and Yao Wen-yuan had returned. From that time on, Keng Chin-chang was never again mentioned favorably in a Red Guard publication. He was always "the man who tried to wreck the Shanghai Commune."

One subsequent reference suggested that, even on the day of Chang's return, Keng was trying to strike a bargain and that, failing a compromise, he was prepared to fight on. We do not know what Keng had to bargain with, except that the disgraced Party leaders—Ch'en P'ei-hsien and Ts'ao Ti-ch'iu—were, it seems, still under the "supervision" of the Second Regiment. The fact that he held the former authorities in custody may have been what had strengthened Keng's position all along. Anyway, it did him little good this time. According to a Workers Headquarters' account, on the afternoon of February 23, a Standing Committee member of the Second Regiment, a man named Sun, telephoned Chang Ch'un-ch'iao's house but reached his secretary instead: "Sun spoke of the former bosses of the black Municipal Committee, but Chang Ch'un-ch'iao's secretary rebuked him severely. Sun then went to see the Red Revolutionaries. He was livid with rage. He told them: 'They brought you down. Now they think they can bring us down too. . . . Let's strike sparks! Let's put on Workers Headquarters arm bands and go to the trade union building' " (RG 19).

Here the trail of dissent peters out. We are left with the impression that Chang Ch'un-ch'iao's return marked the end of an era. From February 23, the city was his. The apparent ease with which he resumed control can no doubt be explained by whatever he brought back from his 12-day stay in Peking. This probably included concessions to the battered Party hierarchy, which had been instrumental in fostering hostility to him, and to the dissident workers' organizations, which had held out against him so long for fear of meeting the fate of the Scarlet Guards.

He must have had some success in arranging a compromise, for the next day he spoke to a capacity crowd in Culture Square, and the meeting was televised all over the city. I watched this telecast in our hotel lounge and found it a fascinating spectacle. The Chinese with me evidently thought so too. They had put up with months of uncertainty and reams of exaggerated, contradictory, and stereotyped descriptions of plots and counterplots, sieges, and skirmishes. Like the rest of the city, they had often been bewildered. Now, all of a sudden, here was the man who held the key to the mystery.

It was the man himself who impressed, not because he was impressive but simply because he was a *person*. Shanghai had been a battle ground of shadows for so long. Now, at last, the people had someone to focus on. It was as if an immortal had left his kingdom of clouds and was sitting in your living room dropping ashes on the carpet.

He was startlingly casual, with a long, furrowed face more like that of a peasant than a bureaucrat. He was also a born wisecracker, with the gift of deadpan, and often had his audience laughing heartily. Underneath, there was a toughness; although he drawled his words and spoke the idiom of the people, one sensed he was used to being obeyed. He inspired confidence by addressing his listeners directly, informally, without notes, and without undue political jargon. He also had the amusing and relaxing habit of fishing single cigarettes from a pocket of his rather scruffy military-style jacket and bending away in mid-sentence to light up. This was a far cry from the usual stiff atmosphere of official speech-making in China.

He spoke for about 2 hours but bored no one. The gist of his message was that, yes, he had seen Chairman Mao in Peking. Three times, to be precise. In the Chairman's opinion, it was too early to set up a Shanghai Commune, the main reason being that Shanghai was further advanced in the Cultural Revolution than the rest of the country, and if it declared itself a Commune, then other cities would want to do the same. This could short-circuit the movement by clamping a premature formula on a process that should reach its own conclusion through free and open debate between divergent opinions.

What worried Chairman Mao, he went on, was a tendency among some Rebel groups to demand the overthrow of *all* people in authority, whether revolutionary or reactionary. This had resulted in attacks on as high a body as the Central Cultural Revolution Group. The line had to be drawn somewhere, the Chairman had said, and, for the purposes of this movement, it had been drawn at the Central Cultural Revolution Group, whose members had been chosen by Mao himself and were therefore sacrosanct. (Chang Ch'un-ch'iao did not have to remind his listeners that he and Yao Wen-yuan were members of this group.)

Having dealt with his enemies, he went on to discuss the local situation. Shanghai, he said, was China's most complex industrial metropolis. It could not be governed by students or workers alone. As everyone knew, he laughed, he and the Rebels had been somewhat out of their depth trying to keep Shanghai going. To ensure that the city functioned efficiently under its new administration, two allies were essential: the high army officers, who could keep counterrevolutionary forces under control, and the top-flight cadres, who knew from long experience how to get the best from the system.

This last feature provided the element of compromise. He put the number of top administrators at 6,000. They could, he said, be replaced, but only with great difficulty and over a long period of time. But there was no need to replace them, because most were "good or comparatively good," and even those who had "made mistakes during the movement" could be rehabilitated and welcomed to the Rebel ranks. Citing Marshal Chu Teh, then under fire in the capital, as a historical precedent, he said, "After all, didn't Chairman Mao carry Chu Teh all the way from that first guerrilla base in the Chingkang Mountains?"

By the time he had finished speaking, the people of Shanghai had a different perspective on the movement. For one thing, they sensed that the worst was over, that fights between large groups were a thing of the past. On the other hand, they must have wondered how long the shaky new "three-way alliance" of Rebels, army, and cadres would last.

That night, processions in the streets welcomed the new power structure, the so-called Shanghai Revolutionary Committee. The Commune was immediately forgotten, but its demise was a great blow to Chang's prestige, and it would take more than one speech, however persuasive, and a few processions, however enthusiastic, to convince the people that the Commune had been anything but a failure.

For the rest of February, the Revolutionary Committee was snowed under with work, and Chang and Yao seem to have done little more than receive delegations in their offices. There was so much to do, so much confusion to straighten out. The former opposition had to be handled with tact. Its leaders had to be discredited without alienating the rank and file. This meant accepting the "penitent" members of such organizations as the Second Regiment back into Workers Headquarters. This could not be done without a loss in Rebel purity, for many of the "pardoned" groups sheltered people whose actions were motivated by vengeance or ambition—opportunists, former Scarlet Guards, or men with doubtful political backgrounds.

Unity was not likely to be achieved without further disputes.

In fact, before the month was out, trouble flared again in the district where I lived. It seems that the Public Security Bureau had arrested some prominent members of Workers Headquarters, perhaps on suspicion of being former dissident leaders. Whatever the case, the police station down the road from my hotel was besieged for several days, and it looked as if the whole process could begin again.

On the whole, however, by the end of February, the outlook for Chang Ch'un-ch'iao seemed favorable. A good indication was that two powerful Rebel groups from other cities were sent home. According to wall-poster accounts, the first of these was the Chingkang Mountains group from Tsinghua University in Peking, which was ordered to be out of town by February 27. This liaison center had been one of the five Rebel groups most opposed to Chang Ch'un-ch'iao and his Shanghai Commune. The other organization, the Rebel detachment from Harbin Military Engineering Institute, was told to be out of Shanghai by March 5. It is unlikely that Chang had anything against the Harbin Rebels, who had, in fact, been among his stanchest supporters. Their departure was probably a sign of Chang's confidence that Shanghai's own Rebel groups could meet any emergency.

The Harbin Rebels have left us a long description of how Shanghai looked as they took their leave:

The General Situation

The Shanghai Rebels are now welding a three-way alliance and taking back the political, financial, and Party power usurped by those who would have led us back to capitalism. They have set up the people's own political organ, the Shanghai Revolutionary Committee. But this is only the first step of a long march.

We Shanghai Rebels must undergo a rectification designed to rid us of selfishness and teach us to think only in terms of the common good. We must now make revolution in our own minds, for we are still prey to many mistaken ideas, many unproletarian ways of thinking. Some comrades think that, because we have won, we can now enjoy ourselves. They are content to rest on their laurels, and they are not prepared to do the arduous work that has to be done among the masses. They pass judgment here and lay blame there, imagining that they alone are in the right.

Others are not concerned for the Revolution, but go around seeking prestige and position. They attract admirers and form cliques. They even use the methods of bourgeois political parties.

Others hunger for an easy life. They put on airs and speak with style; they dream of sofas and sleeping cars and good cigarettes; they grow wasteful and extravagant, avaricious, and corrupt.

Others stagnate. They don't read Mao any more or directives from the Central Committee. They imagine they are old hands at the game and despise those who have made mistakes. If they play politics, it is only to maintain their position. . . .

Lin Piao says: "We must consider ourselves not only the makers of revolution but also the targets of it." We must, in other words, "wash our faces and trim our tails." Intransigence and daring were our mottoes during the struggle; they must also be our mottoes in the rectification.

The over-all situation in Shanghai is excellent. The Rebels are united under one banner and about to take power in every district and county. The cadres have taken a stand, and we must welcome them to our ranks.

There will of course be obstacles and reverses. Some leaders of Workers Third Headquarters and the Second Regiment will continue to try to divide us. But all such opposition will eventually be suppressed. . . .

Antisocial elements will be tolerated only as long as they stay quiet. . . . Any Rebel organization that has been formed in contravention of Mao Tse-tung's instructions or the decisions of the Central Committee will be disbanded. . . .

The class struggle is at present very bitter and complex. Reactionaries in the Party have combined with all sorts of bad elements to oppose the new power. They pervert legislation enacted by the proletariat; they attack revolutionary organizations; they stir up discord among the masses; they corrupt the left wing . . . they bandy slogans like "Bring down all authorities!" they provoke people to fight against the army; they encourage economism and try to ruin production. Such creatures should be treated harshly. We must remember the lesson of the Paris Commune, which did not use all the power it had.

Rebels within the Public Security Bureau, the police, and the courts must unite. This is no time to get bogged down in technicalities. They must trust the proletarian revolutionaries, obey the Committee, cooperate closely with the army, overcome their current weakness and passivity, and start to act as real instruments of the people's dictatorship, suppressing those who oppose the new Committee or attack the Central Cultural Revolution Group, the Central Committee, or Chairman Mao. . . .

The summary goes on to assess the state of each major Shanghai organization in turn. These "lightning sketches" merit inclusion here:

The Workers Headquarters

The Workers Headquarters . . . has been right all along. But now that the struggle is more complex, it too must carry out a rectification. . . .

Some members have grown selfish, vain, and ambitious; others are now apathetic and covet luxury. If these tendencies are not corrected, the banner of Workers Headquarters will one day topple. . . .

The lower echelons have lost their unity, and there have been cases of one branch raiding another. The reasons for this are: (a) sectarianism at the higher levels, (b) so much self-seeking at the top that a blind eye has been turned to opportunists further down, (c) carelessness in the screening of members, allowing former Scarlet Guards to infiltrate.

The leadership still appoints people to offices on the basis of favoritism, and friends tend to help and cultivate each other. This has permitted some Scarlet Guard leaders to get high positions in the General Headquarters and district branches. The only way to stop this is to give more elective power to the masses. The Headquarters must not simply delegate power—this is not how the mass line works.

Another dangerous tendency is the neglect of Chairman Mao's works. During the reign of white terror, the Rebels turned to Chairman Mao for help; now, after the victory, many feel it unnecessary to go on studying. Some even claim that they won through their own efforts; others say they are now "too busy" for Chairman Mao's works.

Shanghai is the only city in China that has not recently launched a mass Mao-study movement. Is this because Shanghai alone does not need to? No! It is because Shanghai does not take Chairman Mao's works seriously enough!

The Second Regiment

Keng Chin-chang and a few Second Regiment leaders have fomented a reaction against Workers Headquarters, the Shanghai Commune, and comrades Chang Ch'un-ch'iao and Yao Wen-yuan. This followed closely on the Red Revolutionaries' opposition to the Central Cultural Revolution Group.

There is no reason why the regiments should continue to exist. They are a product of division and they play into the hands of antisocial elements. Every Shanghai Rebel worker wants to see them reabsorbed into Workers Headquarters.

The Red Guard Army

Chairman Mao teaches that political power comes from the barrel of a gun. . . . The Red Guard Army (called the Red Flag Army in other parts of the country) is composed mainly of exarmy men. It is more like an army than a popular organization. If such a body eluded Party control and was used by evil people for their own purposes, it could seriously threaten the security of our country. It should be disbanded. Exarmy men must not be allowed to put their own welfare before that of the Party and the working class as a whole.

The Cadres

There are four dangerous tendencies concerning the cadres: (a) People who say either "Cadres are irrelevant!" or "Down with *all* cadres!" Most cadres are good. They are relatively well versed in politics, organization, and struggle. They are, in fact, a precious asset, for they can help us gain power and keep it. (b) People who feel they cannot ally with cadres that they were fighting tooth and nail a few weeks before. This is wrong, for unity is the only way to help them reform. (c) Cadres who say "The Rebels won't believe I've changed; they'll think I'm pretending." Cadres must not wait to be accepted but must go to the people and join in the struggle to take power. (d) Bad elements and reactionary Party leaders who say "You were wrong to attack me in the first place. I should now be forgiven." We must make sure that real class enemies do not get away with this tactic.

The Red Revolutionaries

We must acknowledge their contributions in the early stages, but we must also see that some of their leaders had been right-wing opportunists for a long time. Their attack on the Central Cultural Revolution Group was a manifestation of this.

The Red Revolutionaries are now rectifying the mistakes of their leaders. But some have become despondent, feeling they have been utterly disgraced. They will not wear their arm bands; they avoid politics by going off to work in factories and villages or they give up altogether and go home. Such people must be made to see that the actions of their organization were simply the reflection of the struggle between two lines and that this could not help but affect every group and every individual within the organization.

The Conservative Red Guards

Most of these organizations have fallen apart, but their bourgeois line has still not been eradicated. The Rebels must help them correct their mistakes, for most of them were simply deceived. They must be neither neglected nor persecuted. There must above all be no personal revenge. We Rebels are magnanimous, not spiteful. We must not fall into the trap of repressing the conservatives as they once repressed us.

The High-School Students

These were among the first to become Rebels, but the Party authorities corrupted many by peddling a reactionary line in the schools. This has still not been erased. To this day, there are many students who spend their time at home, taking no interest in affairs of state or who go gallivanting around the country and call it "revolutionary liaison." A few have even formed gangs of hoodlums and thieves and have disrupted law and order.

All students should return to school and see that those falsely accused of counterrevolution are rehabilitated; they should do military training, raise their political consciousness, and strengthen their sense of organization and discipline. (RG 17:2.1)

This, then, was the state of Shanghai, as seen by allies of Chang Ch'un-ch'iao, at the end of February, 1967. As a piece of political analysis, the summary is as thorough as anything I saw during the movement. As an explanation of the power struggle, however, it is tantalizingly vague. There must have been so much more going on than the Harbin Rebels cared to reveal. We get more than a hint of this in their closing remarks. After thanking the Shanghai workers for teaching them "selflessness and loyalty" during the time of economism, they conclude: "We also wish to thank the land, sea, and air forces of the Shanghai garrison for the help and support of their commanders."

In this polite acknowledgment must lie the key to many an unsolved mystery of Shanghai's Cultural Revolution.

13. The New Dispensation

March is a good month to wind up this story, for Shanghai then paused to take stock. It was not the end of the Cultural Revolution by any means, but it was the end of the most crucial part of it. Power had changed hands, and the nature of power itself had changed. It was a time to consolidate gains, rectify errors, discredit the remaining opposition, justify the new regime, and get the city back to something like normal.

"Unity" was the magic word. This was to be achieved, as it usually is in the politics of emergency, by a judicious blend of repression and compromise. Enemies who had been so weakened by the struggle for power that they could no longer defend themselves were crushed; those who had managed to maintain positions of strength and a whole network of alliances in the factories, the schools and colleges, and the Party and state bureaucracies could not be conjured away at the stroke of a pen. All the weapons of the people's dictatorship—the police, the army, the press—were powerless to root this opposition out, so that compromise was the only policy for Chang Ch'un-ch'iao.

I saw this policy at work in the factories. The new regime had to make the Rebel workers feel their struggle had been worth while, which meant conceding them a victory over the forces of reaction. Certain factory cadres therefore had to be delivered to the Rebels for criticism, but they were not to be treated too harshly, for they still had the power to make things awkward.

They were thus to be quickly condemned and just as quickly forgiven.

I attended a meeting at which this play was performed. It was held in an indoor sports stadium in downtown Shanghai, and the participants were all from a nearby textile factory. The stadium had obviously been used many times for this purpose, for the walls and floor were painted and papered with layer upon layer of slogans. Even while our meeting was in progress, the audience for the next one was gathering at the entrance, paint brushes and posters at the ready.

It was a curious affair. The specators, mostly women workers, sat and chattered to each other or munched food they had brought, while the victims of the denunciation—five cadres, four of whom were women—stood out front with bowed heads. The audience laughed at the slightest hint of a joke, yet the speeches, and particularly one by the factory manager, were long and dull. The chairmen, representatives of the masses, did little but announce the speakers in their proper order. This was in marked contrast to meetings I had attended at the Institute, where the chairmen dominated the entire proceedings, interrupting to cross-examine witnesses, making speeches themselves at every opportunity, and generally keeping the atmosphere at fever pitch. Here, there was little excitement during most of the morning, and some in the audience were beginning to doze off.

Suddenly, an 8-year-old girl was led to the lectern by her father, a tough-looking worker with patches all over his clothes. He placed a box for her behind the microphone, and she got up and made a most impassioned speech, complete with great thumps of her fist to emphasize the points and a constant stream of huge crocodile tears. Her main charge was that the five staff members had conspired to brand her father a counterrevolutionary, when, as everyone knew, he had always been a stanch left-winger. The accused shuffled uncomfortably and bowed their heads even lower. The audience murmured angrily, and some were moved to tears.

When she had finished speaking, one of my wife's students, who had been doing a stint of labor in the textile mill, asked: "How did you like the speech?" I said, "Fantastic!" and he beamed with pride. "I wrote that one," he said. "I've written a number of speeches for the workers. Some of them are illiterate, you know."

I came away feeling I had sat through a Chinese opera. Yet the audience seemed satisfied. The wronged workers had been formally rehabilitated; the cadres had been thoroughly denounced and then, after an abject self-criticism, pardoned and welcomed back into the ranks of the people. Face had been saved all around, and the factory could get on with production.

This is not to say that the matter was forgotten. Grievances begun or exacerbated during the movement would presumably be brought up again the next time there was a struggle in the factory. The cadres, especially, would harbor grudges against their critics, and the thought of class vengeance would never be far from the surface.

This method of pacifying the workers and factory staff was moderately successful, and Shanghai's industry began to pick up. But Chang Ch'un-ch'iao had other problems. The schools, for instance, had remained practically deserted for months, except for random visitations by flocks of children looking for places to play. Left without maintenance, many of the buildings had fallen into disrepair. Worse still, the children would not go back to school. After months of roaming the streets, they were loath to return to their lessons. Newspaper articles condemned the semi-official tolerance of truancy:

> Now that the working-class revolutionaries are uniting and taking power, some bourgeois reactionary authorities in the old Municipal Committee are conspiring to allow a lot of children to stay away from school. . . .
>
> The students previously left school to travel the country and make revolution. Now they must do just the opposite—go back to school and finish the job they started. Although the act is different, the aim is the same: to ensure the success of the Cultural Revolution. (RG 20:2.1)

The teachers were even more reluctant to resume classes, for their students' accusations and denunciations were fresh in their minds. The Rebels did their best to reassure them:

Some teachers say they are intellectually bankrupt in comparison with their students and are afraid of making mistakes should they go back. Now, it is true that the students learned far more quickly than their teachers during the Cultural Revolution, but that is precisely why the teachers must go back and learn from their students in a spirit of humility, live with them, fight alongside them, and creatively study Chairman Mao's writings with them. . . . The real shame is not in going back but in being *afraid* to go back and take their medicine. This stigma could remain with them all their lives, unless they stand up and face the test. . . .

Other teachers say: "The students will humiliate us in front of everyone. We couldn't bear it." But they must trust the students to have gained in knowledge and experience during the movement, to have become qualified to point out faults in their teachers. It is true that the students have sometimes been harsh in the past, but this should not be held against them. Nor should it goad teachers into rejecting the students' opinions or frighten them into a false submission. (RG 21:3.1)

The school situation presented such a formidable challenge to the new government that there was talk of sending in the army to help restore normalcy. The mind boggles at the thought of People's Liberation Army soldiers, many of them hardly above school age themselves, trying to steer a tactful course amidst the perplexing tangles of class struggle and personal feuds that had all but destroyed the Cultural Revolution in the schools.

Yet the army was given a lot of responsibility in March. Soldiers were sent to certain factories, to the universities, to the docks. Their job was to play their part in the three-way alliance of Rebels, cadres, and the military, to ensure that the ugly head of counterrevolution was kept down, and to inspire the people with the Maoist spirit of unselfishness and service to the commonweal.

Security was also strengthened. Around the middle of the month, slogans such as "We strongly support the suppression of counterrevolutionaries by the Public Security Bureau!" appeared, and it seemed that the police were at last calling a halt to internecine strife. Posters against hooliganism and petty crime were also plentiful, and sometimes there seemed to be little distinction drawn between political and criminal offenses. The courts also began to get tough; witness the following piece in a Rebel paper: "On the afternoon of March 23 in Culture Square, a rally was held under the title 'The Shanghai People's Court Pronounces Sentence on Counterrevolutionaries Who Impeded or Tried to Destroy the Cultural Revolution.' Six people who had harmed the movement by committing crimes of murder, arson, or active counterrevolution were severely sanctioned" (RG 21:4.1).

With the help of these repressive forces, Chang Ch'un-ch'iao's regime managed to weld some unity in the administration. The Shanghai Revolutionary Committee was little more than a name, for it lacked mass support and roots in the districts and suburbs of the municipal areas. To remedy this, the formation of local Revolutionary Committees was given top priority. By the time I left in April, two key districts had set up such committees—the downtown area of Whangpoo and the western district of Changning.

Opposition was still strong in the city. In Changning District, where I lived, it took weeks of argument and compromise to get a workable committee set up. Many local quarrels had to be patched up before the Rebels would agree to ally with the cadres. In the process, some strange facts emerged. It turned out that this seemingly respectable suburb had harbored some utter rogues, even among the Rebels. One group was said to have lived it up on the wine, food, clothes, and cigarettes it had confiscated from the bourgeoisie. According to wall posters, some of its members had even "lured low-class women to their General Headquarters and indulged in lechery with them." Presumably, "low-class" was not a political description.

The end of March brought the first signs of spring. It was not so much the budding willows that impressed as it was the appearance of goods in the city's shop windows for the first time in months. Many Shanghai shops had two display windows—one on either side of the doorway. During the movement, both featured pictures of Chairman Mao, semipsychedelic sunrises, and quotations from the great leader's poems or articles. Now, on one side only, the wares began to appear; the other side, to play safe, remained dedicated to the Chairman.

On March 26, Chang Ch'un-ch'iao felt confident enough to make a progress report, which was publicized on the walls. It ran to some thirty-four pages, but the main points were:

1. The general situation is excellent, not only in Shanghai but in the whole country and the whole world! In fact, the greatest event in the world today is China's Cultural Revolution.

2. Shanghai is doing well industrially, except that coal production, which dropped in January, dropped even further in February. This is not the fault of the Cultural Revolution but of some bourgeois reactionary authorities.

3. Some people have suggested abolishing the Party and the Youth League. They say the Red Guards should replace the Youth League. Nothing has been decided about this yet, but the Party—a Marxist-Leninist party armed with Mao Tse-tung's ideas—is absolutely essential.

4. Some members of the Party and the Youth League are trying to forget that they ever belonged to these organizations. This is a bad attitude.

5. The broad unity is progressing, but there are still a lot of cliques. In some cases, the masses have not been strong enough to prevent bad elements from taking power. The Party can help in such situations, but this must not be interpreted as repressing the masses.

6. The Scarlet Guards are still active. . . . [See page 204.]

7. The army has proved very useful in factories, mines, and commercial enterprises. But there are not enough People's Liberation Army men to go around the whole of Shanghai, so the students must do what they can for themselves.

8. There are still many unsolved problems in Shanghai. They must be settled, for this city is of great importance to the rest of the country.

9. Some of the discredited Party authorities will be kept in their jobs for a while. For one thing, Shanghai still has agreements with foreigners that need these officials. They will not, however, be allowed to make trouble.

10. Please criticize Yao Wen-yuan and me if we make mistakes. We do not want people saying we are unimpeachable here in Shanghai. Many groups and individuals want to see us, and we simply do not have time to receive everyone.

Along with this slow progress toward a kind of unity, the job of drawing the fangs of the remaining opposition proceeded. The Chinese have had long experience in demolishing the reputations of fallen leaders, and the lessons of history were not forgotten. The traditional technique was to concentrate on the enemy's moral degeneracy rather than on his political mistakes. Even in modern China's highly politicized culture, this method was still effective.

In the campaign against Liu Shao-ch'i, for example, it was not long lists of his "crimes" against socialism that persuaded the people of his villainy; it was through his wife that he lost the most prestige. In Shanghai, the walls were plastered with photographs of Madame Liu, taken during her visit to Indonesia. Some showed her dressed in a short-sleeved summer frock, with a string of pearls gracing a daring neckline. In others, she was arm-in-arm with Sukarno or dancing Western-style. And there were shots of her toying with a drink or smoking from a long cigarette-holder. These photos so outraged the people of Shanghai that they literally tore them from the walls. I myself saw youngsters of eight or ten, from no other motive than disgust, flog these pictures with thin bamboo sticks.

A similar method was used to discredit Chang Ch'un-ch'iao's enemies. Ch'en Hung-k'ang, for example, the leader of Workers Third Headquarters, was undone by showing pictures of objects confiscated from his home: his father's Kuomintang police badge, his mother's Shanghai Christian Association pennants, his passport from pre-Communist days, some old land titles, a silk-covered inner-spring mattress, bottles of brandy, cartons of good cigarettes, and so on.

Keng Chin-chang, head of the powerful Second Regiment, proved a tougher nut for Chang to crack. He seemed to have built up quite a reputation as a clean-living, somewhat puritanical Spartan. Nevertheless, by the time the propagandists had finished with him, he had become a liar and a lecher to boot:

Keng Chin-chang once said: "Some people like to gad about and play the big-shot and sleep in first-class hotels. . . . We workers are never comfortable in such places. I was once at a meeting in the

Shanghai Mansions that lasted till four in the morning. Everyone
said I should sleep right there, but I refused. I went home and slept
like a top on my old straw mattress."

This sounded great, and many people believed it. The fact is,
Keng slept all over the place. He kept hideouts in various parts of
Shanghai. Late in January, he moved into a house in the French
Concession, because, he said, there was a guardhouse at the gate
for security and a big garage for his vehicles. Actually, he lived like
a lord in that house! And this is the fellow who called himself a
Rebel. . . .

He said he never used cars, but he had at least ten at his disposal.
When he got back from Peking, there was a car waiting for him
at the airport.

And in all the places he stayed, he had plenty of secretaries and
servants. In one house, he even spent the night in the same room
as the woman who was his private secretary! That was indeed a house
of shame! (RG 19)

Although far more serious charges were brought against Keng
Chin-chang, it is unlikely that any carried more weight with the
people than these tales of immorality. In fact, it was one of the
anomalies of the Cultural Revolution that detailed accounts of
an enemy's *political* crimes may often have served to *increase*
his prestige. The following extract refers to a "crime" of Keng
Chin-chang, which many—particularly among the Rebels—might
have interpreted as an act of admirable boldness:

Keng sent one of his lieutenants to Peking, with instructions to get
hold of Chairman Mao's four principal enemies at that time, namely:
P'eng Chen, Lo Jui-ch'ing, Lu Ting-yi, and Yang Shang-k'un. Keng's
idea was to bring these four disgraced leaders to Shanghai and display them before a vast crowd in People's Square. This would be
the best proof that his own organization was truly revolutionary. . . .

Then someone said to Keng's lieutenant: "You'll have to ask Chou
En-lai before you take them; otherwise the Red Guards of the Peking
Third Headquarters will stop you." Keng's man said: "Let's take
them first and ask Chou En-lai later!" The other replied: "It is not
right to act behind the Premier's back." He then went to Chou En-lai's
office and reported the matter, so that Keng's plan was foiled. (RG 19)

While Chang Ch'un-ch'iao's rivals were being systematically demolished, the old Party leaders—Mayor Ts'ao Ti-ch'iu and East China Bureau head Ch'en P'ei-hsien—were subjected to a meticulous examination in the Red Guard press. Their moral and political errors were described in detail and always linked with those of Liu Shao-ch'i and his followers. No account of the Cultural Revolution would be complete without a summary of the complaints that the Mao group brought against these bureaucrats.

Much of the information in the following extracts was supplied by high officials in the Party establishment, men who had followed the lead of the former Party bosses but who now found it expedient to repudiate them. Part of the bargain whereby cadres were pardoned involved elaborate criticism and self-criticism. They told what they knew of the policies of the old regime and at the same time heaped all the blame on two or three highly placed scapegoats. In Shanghai, Ts'ao Ti-ch'iu and Ch'en P'ei-hsien were held responsible for the faults of the whole hierarchy. The bureaucracy could thus continue to function while its former policies were repudiated. In theory, even the two top Shanghai men could be saved, if they sincerely confessed and were willing to betray Liu Shao-ch'i, for he was a figure big enough to bear the whole nation's guilt.

A softening-up process came first. The Rebel papers ran a series of articles listing the misdeeds of the former leaders. Many of the criticisms were of revisionist economic policies. They illustrate very clearly the difference in approach between the Maoists and the pragmatists. They also show that the Cultural Revolution was the culmination of a long and bitter feud. In agriculture, for example, Ch'en P'ei-hsien was accused of these "crimes":

1. As early as the period of land reform, and again when cooperatives were being formed, he resisted Chairman Mao's instructions and followed Liu Shao-ch'i's reactionary line instead.

Liu made a speech on land reform in 1950, in which he said: "Only in the remote future, when we have achieved a high degree of mechanization and when we have organized collective farms, will there no longer be any use for an economy that includes rich peasants." This was in open opposition to Chairman Mao.

Ch'en P'ei-hsien was at that time . . . responsible for land reform in the area around Shanghai. He and his group followed Liu's instructions to the letter. Because of the region's proximity to Shanghai, they said it was a "special case," where "the struggle must be carefully controlled." . . . They therefore ran a "peaceful land reform." The peasants were not fully mobilized, and the cadres did not take the poor and lower-middle farmers as their standard. . . . The class analysis of landlords and rich peasants was made by . . . the Work Teams, with the result that many class enemies slipped through the net. . . . This had an extremely detrimental effect on the socialist revolution. . . . In Sungchiang county alone, there are now more than 1,100 known class enemies, many of whom have sneaked into the ranks of the Party or become cadres, some even attaining positions of importance.

When the cooperatives were started . . . Ch'en P'ei-hsien followed Liu Shao-ch'i . . . in crying that it was "too quick," that "the cadres are not experienced enough yet, and the political consciousness of the masses is still too low." As a result, 258 cooperatives in the region around Shanghai were disbanded.

2. He slandered the Great Leap Forward, the People's communes, and the general line of the Party, encouraging individual enterprise instead.

During the 3 bad years, Ch'en P'ei-hsien joined with the class enemy at home and abroad in attacking the ideas of Chairman Mao. "Between 1955 and 1962," he said, "we have gone off the track several times." He called the Great Leap Forward "a fever of the brain . . . a striving for quantity instead of quality." "This is not something that can be repaired in 3 or 4 years," he said." "It will take a decade to make good the damage."

3. When the Socialist Education Movement began in the villages around Shanghai, Ch'en and Liu acted like birds of a feather, opposing Chairman Mao and his revolutionary line.

In 1963, Chairman Mao issued his Ten Points on the Socialist Education Movement. . . . Ch'en P'ei-hsien preached instead the virtues of "reducing the need for controlled purchasing," "increasing rations for the commune members," and so on. These were revisionist promises.

In July, 1964, Liu brought his wife to Shanghai to peddle her "Peach-Garden Experiment." Ch'en said in a speech: "When the landlords, rich peasants, and other class enemies heard Chairman Mao's Ten Points, they were despondent. When they heard Chairman Liu's alternative Ten Points, they sensed what a difference this would mean and were deeply grateful to the Party. . . ."

Then, in January, 1965, Chairman Mao came out with his Twenty-three Points, in which he specified that the target of the Socialist Education Movement was "Party authorities leading the country back to capitalism." But Ch'en told the Work Teams: "The County Committee leaders are trustworthy . . . the Work Teams can cooperate with them." As a result, leading officials at the county level were admitted to membership in the Work Teams and even to top positions. Naturally, no reactionary commune Party authorities were exposed, and many were actually promoted! It has taken the Cultural Revolution and the Rebels to attack these people and bring them down.

In the same month, January, 1965, Ch'en P'ei-hsien said: "It is wrong to rely too heavily on class analysis. Marx and Engels did not make good class analyses, and Chairman Mao has admitted that his own was not good. On the other hand, those carried out by the social democrats and the anti-Communists were often very good." And he went on to say: "Unless we join forces with the children of landlords and other class enemies, we will never be able to unite 95 per cent of the people. . . . The total income gained through exploitation never amounted to more than 30 per cent. We can't treat all landlords as if they were *latifundistas*!"

4. He opposed Chairman Mao's call to learn from the Tachai Brigade.

Ch'en P'ei-hsien and Ts'ao Ti-ch'iu proposed that the communes around Peking would serve as a better model for China's agriculture than Tachai, and a top Shanghai official was twice sent to study P'eng Chen's capitalistic methods. . . . (RG 12)

So much for agriculture. In commerce:

A bitter struggle has been going on in Shanghai since 1949. Ch'en P'ei-hsien and Ts'ao Ti-ch'iu closely followed the line of Liu Shao-ch'i, Teng Hsiao-p'ing, and Ch'en Yün. They committed five specific crimes.

1. They allowed free markets.

During the 3 bad years, Liu Shao-ch'i encouraged free markets, saying "A little capitalism can be a good thing." In Shanghai, former Mayor K'e Ch'ing-shih was always against having them in the city.

Ch'en P'ei-hsien and Ts'ao Ti-ch'iu did nothing while Mayor K'e was in town, but whenever he left they opened more free markets.

Early in 1961, Ch'en published an article advocating free markets for peasants' sideline products. When it was tried, all sorts of criminal elements got permits to trade; they upset the market and jeopardized law and order. Western journalists came to take photos and write articles. Finally, Mayor K'e clamped down on the free markets.

Six months later, they had crept back. Ch'en P'ei-hsien said: "It seems we have no choice." And Ts'ao Ti-ch'iu: "Since there's no way of stopping them, we might as well let them function under our control." In this way, the illegal was legalized.

By May, 1962, there were 90,000 people engaged in free-market trade, and the items traded extended far beyond peasants' sideline products to include grain, oils, and industrial consumer goods. Ch'en P'ei-hsien's comment was "Given the economic situation, this was inevitable." The principle was then extended, and even secondhand shops were permitted to set their own prices. . . .

2. *They made high-priced luxuries available.*

This idea came down from Liu Shao-ch'i, Teng Hsiao-p'ing, and Ch'en Yün in 1961. Ch'en P'ei-hsien approved of it for three reasons. One, it would reassure people. Two, it would make up for the lack of other things, which were then strictly rationed. This would appeal particularly to the intellectual elite, who had got used to certain luxuries in the past. Three, it would help money circulate.

Ts'ao Ti-ch'iu's reaction: "The market is dead; it badly needs diversification. Socialism should provide more variety as it goes along."

What these people meant was that the rich would get more "variety"; the bourgeoisie, with their checkbooks, would be "reassured."

The result was that high-priced candy, cakes, foodstuffs, bicycles, and needlework began to appear on the market—things that the workers did not need and did not like but that the bourgeoisie hankered after.

This policy caused the emergence of special service in restaurants, hotels, and bathhouses. Soon there were wedding feasts, night clubs, luxurious furniture, pornographic music, "mod" styles in clothing and hairdressing, painted eyebrows, manicures, and so on.

3. *Under the pretext of improving the distribution of goods, they cultivated a privileged elite.*

In 1961, Liu Shao-ch'i said: "To overcome egalitarianism, we must see that people get goods in proportion to their labor." This sounded reasonable, but, since at that time the supply of goods was insufficient, workers on higher salaries got more than others.

Ch'en P'ei-hsien followed Liu's lead by issuing coupons for industrial goods. Workers, irrespective of what class they belonged to, received one coupon for every 10 yuan of their wages. Those who got salaries of several hundred or even several thousand yuan naturally had far more coupons than low-paid workers.

Worse still, 500,000 people got no coupons at all. These were workers in collective enterprises or street and lane production units, pedicab drivers, teachers in community schools, and so on, none of whom were paid by the state.

Ch'en P'ei-hsien remarked: "This system is a step forward and most people are satisfied with it. The only ones who are not too happy are the half million who got no coupons."

Finally, he was forced to issue coupons to these workers. In the process, he managed to commandeer several thousand coupons for his personal use and for friends.

4. They encouraged the private sector.

In 1961 and 1962, under the pretext of cutting down on staff, more than 10,000 employees of state or joint state-private shops were transferred to cooperative shops. Many of these people later went into business on their own. In Nanhuai County, for example, more than 1,400 cooperative hot-water shops[1] reverted to private enterprise.

At about the same time, some 30,000 free-market traders received permits to do private business. This boosted the private sector. Ch'en and Ts'ao also allowed teachers to be paid for private coaching, doctors to practice privately, and peasants to raise pigs for profit.

5. They encouraged locally independent economies.

During the 3 bad years, they did not care about national shortages but kept two separate books and hoarded produce.

Ch'en P'ei-hsien clamored for more grain for Shanghai, but he had a lot put away. In 1960, he concealed from the Central Committee 100,000 mou [about 16,000 acres] of land, with a yield of 50 or 60 million catties [roughly 27,500 to 33,000 tons]. The Grains Department discovered the discrepancy. It turned out that Ch'en had declared only the grain that was stored in the city granaries, not that which was kept in the suburban communes. "That belongs to us," he had said, "why should we declare it?"

In 1964, the suburban communes around Shanghai more than

---

[1] All drinking water is boiled in China. Hot water for household and other uses is sold in special shops.

filled their quota. When Ch'en found that the extra grain was going to be reported to the Central Committee, he was furious. He told the department to falsify the records, claiming that the surplus was "a reserve supply for the collective." The same thing happened with oils and industrial products.

In 1961, a 7,000-man expanded Central Committee work conference was held, at which Shanghai was criticized for impeding centralization and encouraging regionalism. Ch'en and Ts'ao both made fake self-criticisms. On their return, Ts'ao told the Standing Committee: "It would appear that Shanghai has a rather recalcitrant spirit." (RG 13)

These charges show that the Mao group was not merely tilting at windmills. The men behind the Cultural Revolution had reason to believe that the pragmatists, by continuing to favor policies that were capitalistic, intended to let the Revolution slide. With Mao an old man, those who believed in his vision of China took steps to oust the revisionists before it was too late.

What is not mentioned in the Rebel accounts is that the policies that Ch'en P'ei-hsien and Ts'ao Ti-ch'iu followed in Shanghai were introduced during a critical slump in the nation's economy. They may have been temporary solutions, to be discarded when the situation returned to normal. They may also have been successful, a possibility that no member of the Mao group would ever admit.

After these detailed attacks in the press came massive denunciation rallies, televised on closed circuit. Ch'en and Ts'ao were forced to read confessions to very angry audiences. They were continually interrupted by slogans, insults, barbed questions, and cries that they were lying. They kept remarkably cool throughout, pausing, or even joining in, when slogans were shouted against them. They looked for all the world like chairmen of a committee weathering a stormier session than usual. Their faces gave no hint that this was probably the end of their political careers.

Ch'en P'ei-hsien was the more adept of the two. He had the knack of leading his detractors into the no-man's land of "more or less" and "you might say that," often getting half an hour deep into a skillfully contrived red herring before his listeners became aware of the deception. This made the arguments difficult to follow, for they galloped back and forth over time and topic. According to notes that I jotted down in the dark, Ch'en P'ei-hsien seems to have been accused of the following:

1. When he became First Secretary of the East China Bureau, he began his administration by announcing to the heads of departments: "We must not imitate the mistakes of K'e Ch'ing-shih; instead, we must learn from them." He then proceeded to change every single policy of the former mayor.

2. He had been a parasite of Teng Hsiao-p'ing [former Secretary-General of the Party], often communicating directly with him rather than with the Central Committee.

3. On the question of Shanghai's war-preparedness, he had pre-ferred the ideas of P'eng Chen [former Mayor of Peking] to those of Chairman Mao. Mao wanted to move key industries inland, especially to Szechuan Province, where they would be less vulnerable to nuclear attack and where they would also provide the interior with the industrial boost it so badly needed. Ch'en P'ei-hsien had been the only top man in Shanghai to disagree with this plan, but he had managed to sway the others. He had emphasized the importance of Shanghai as a great industrial and trade center and suggested that, were the U.S. imperialists to invade, the factories should be handed back to the capitalists. This, said his detractors, was exactly what the capitalists had been itching for since 1962.

4. He had been closely connected with the traitors Kao Kang and Jao Shu-shih in 1954.[2]

5. He had supported the anti-Mao moves made at the Lushan Conference in 1959.[3]

6. He had been to the Soviet Union in 1961, and, on his return, had praised the administrative system of Leningrad.

7. When he was in charge of Shanghai's agriculture, he had channeled money for all kinds of projects through his department, purely to increase his personal prestige.

8. Also for his own prestige, he had spent 80 yuan per foot instead

[2] Former Party officials in Manchuria and East China. They were removed in 1954.

[3] At the Lushan Plenum of the Party Central Committee in August, 1959, Marshal P'eng Te-huai, then Defense Minister, sharply attacked Mao's radical policies, particularly the Great Leap Forward of 1958 and the growing dispute with the U.S.S.R. P'eng's position was repudiated, and he was dismissed from his post.

of the agreed 50 yuan per foot to build a road from Shanghai to the satellite town of Minhang.

9. During the Cultural Revolution, he had got the head of Shanghai's industry to prepare a report on the harm that the movement was doing to production. This he intended to present to the Central Committee.

10. He had also suppressed some decisions of the Central Committee. The 18-day working conference at the beginning of October, 1966, for instance, he had reported to the Shanghai Municipal Committee in a ridiculously short 1-hour speech.

11. When a vice-mayor of Tientsin was killed during the Cultural Revolution, a message had been sent out from the Cultural Revolution Group in Peking, complaining that the funeral service of half a million people organized by the Tientsin Committee was "using the dead to attack Chairman Mao." This key phrase was omitted from the report that was delivered to the Shanghai Committee.

12. He had turned a big Shanghai hospital into a rest home for revisionist cadres.

13. His private life was luxurious, and he had an aversion to manual labor. The workers in a factory where he had once spent a few days criticized him for using an electric stove.

14. He had been opposed to part-work part-study schools, preferring Liu Shao-ch'i's idea of two distinct systems of education.

This strange blend of the crucial and the irrelevant all came out of one afternoon's television session. A few days later, another meeting was filmed live, and some additional information was revealed:

1. In 1962, some Shanghai factory managers exchanged light industrial products for eggs and other produce from the communes. Former Mayor K'e Ch'ing-shih and Secretary Chang Ch'un-ch'iao were furious, for this sort of barter disrupted Shanghai's economy.

2. Ch'en P'ei-hsien and Ts'ao Ti-ch'iu decided that Shanghai had too many industrial workers, and many were sent to the countryside. A lot of them climbed on the free-market bandwagon and made money by transporting goods between city and country. Some 2,000 received licenses to do this.

3. Shanghai's hotels had to send people out to the communes to buy provisions, which were therefore terribly expensive by the time

they got on the menu. In the long run, it was only bourgeois people who were happy about the free markets.

4. Even now, there were 30,000 hawkers in the streets of Shanghai —remnants of the free-market system.

5. Ts'ao Ti-ch'iu's line that the workers were too poor betrayed his bourgeois standards. He also claimed that they were getting poorer under socialism. "How much longer are we going to have to worry about food distribution before every New Year?" he asked.

6. Ch'en P'ei-hsien had been very much against K'e Ch'ing-shih. He called him a Stalin and said that Shanghai should concentrate on light, not heavy, industry. In 1959, Mayor K'e had sent the Central Committee a report on the Great Leap Forward. Chairman Mao was pleased with it, but Ch'en P'ei-hsien had insisted that a *daily* report be sent to Peking. Liu Shao-ch'i read this more detailed report— which Ch'en had postscripted with a sarcastic "See what we've achieved in this Great Leap Forward!"—and returned it to K'e Ch'ing-shih with a reproach for his poor performance. The implication was that the policy of the Great Leap itself was to blame.

7. Ch'en P'ei-hsien and K'e Ch'ing-shih could not coexist in one city. K'e got Ch'en sent to the Party School for some "extra training," which Ch'en interpreted as a punishment. He got his revenge at a meeting in Peking by accusing K'e of having mislaid important documents. He made the case seem very serious.

8. Mayor K'e had set high *quantity* standards for production, while Ch'en P'ei-hsien was forever insisting on *quality*. In the years immediately following the Great Leap Forward, K'e wanted to go on opening up more blast furnaces, while Ch'en was for closing some down. In private, he had once remarked: "We were hotheaded to strive after such quantity." His listener commented wryly "All crows are black," meaning that the situation was as bad all over the country and the blame could be laid at the feet of "you know who."

9. Mayor K'e, despite a grave kidney ailment, traveled extensively all over China right up to his death. Many of his last months were spent in Szechuan, supervising the installation of industrial equipment from Shanghai. He found that many machines had been sent incomplete or without adequate instructions for assembly, so that valuable equipment had been left to rust. This was not his fault but Ch'en P'ei-hsien's.

10. Everyone knew Mayor K'e had died from a kidney disease, complicated by overwork. But Ch'en P'ei-hsien had ascribed his death to "a surfeit of peanuts."

This summary by no means exhausts the charges against Ts'ao and Ch'en. The debate could dwell on an indignant phone call from Mayor K'e's widow and then go straight on to consider whether Ts'ao Ti-ch'iu had betrayed the Party in a Kuomintang prison back in 1932.

Perhaps the most interesting part of the experience was sitting in a darkened room full of hotel-workers watching the television screen. The Chinese followed every move with rapt attention, responding to the thrusts and parries of the protagonists as if they themselves were present. Many times, as Ts'ao or Ch'en seemed to be lying or deliberately spreading confusion, they slapped their thighs and howled with frustration or turned to each other and exchanged exasperated sighs. And when their own boss, the head of the hotel system in Shanghai, got up once to give testimony, these boys literally fell out of their chairs and rolled on the floor, for this was the man they had fought tooth and nail for months. The thought of his being permitted to stand up and testify against others, and thereby clear his own conscience and perhaps get his old job back, elicited considerable hilarity.

These televised denunciations were only the top of the iceberg. Throughout Shanghai, at every level of society, endless meetings were held in an effort to achieve unity. I attended some of these at the Foreign Languages Institute and heard the self-criticisms of the Party cadres. The striking thing about the confessions was their lack of detail. There were plenty of vaguely self-deprecatory statements, such as:

> I simply obeyed the orders of the Party Committee. I believed that if I followed these blindly, I would make no mistakes. . . . I looked on myself as wise and on the masses as idiots; I never went to them to discuss things, and my decisions were often arbitrary. This was a bad habit, which resulted from always doing things for others instead of letting them do things for themselves.

Remarks such as these cut the ground from under the inquisitors. They tried to keep the initiative by interrupting the cadres with shouts of:

He is not sincere. . . . The movement has not touched his soul. . . .
He is still afraid of losing his position in the Party. . . . He says
he was *influenced* by the bourgeois reactionary line, when we know
he was actually *perpetrating* it. . . . This man was so bad in the
past that it is hard to imagine he has now swung over to the Rebels.
. . . He is shifting all the blame onto the Party Secretary. . . . He is
making himself out an honorable person, but we *know* what type he
is. . . . This self-criticism is very shallow; it can only be considered
the first step. . . .

But both the students and the cadres knew that, for the sake
of unity, the misdemeanors and "crimes" of the Party officials
simply *had* to be pardoned. With the exception of one or two
scapegoats (at our Institute, it was the Party Secretary who took
all the blame), the rest of the staff would get their old jobs back.
This added a touch of unreality to the proceedings. I sensed that
the deep factional divisions were not really bridged. The bitterness that remained would keep surfacing.

The Rebels at our Institute, who would normally have dominated the scene, were hampered by the memory of their involvement in the Red Revolutionaries' plot against Chang Ch'un-
ch'iao at the end of January. The Moderate Red Guards tried
several times to take advantage of this, but their own record
was so thoroughly blotched that they had only doubtful success.
They still insisted, however, that the Rebel position, though
admirable on many points, was far from perfect. "For one thing,"
they said, "the Rebels lack humility." This independent spirit
was remarkable, considering that these students had been arguing
for almost 9 months. I asked them how many meetings they had
attended in that time. Their reply: "An average of two a day."

About a fortnight before I left China, the Institute held a
rally to celebrate the attainment of unity. This was an occasion
of great joy, in sharp contrast to the angry, quarrelsome mood
that had predominated for so long. The stage was prepared with
meticulous care: The big portrait of Mao still hung as a backdrop
to everything, but now there were potted pines and cypresses—
symbols of longevity and hope—arranged symmetrically on either
side of the lectern. And all the posters and slogans were done

on red paper, often with "double-happiness" signs tricked out in gold paint.

I sat with a Chinese colleague, a tall, quiet teacher who had managed to survive the whole movement without taking sides. "Watch and learn" was the way he described his secret, admitting that this was close to "wait and see." He was visibly more relaxed than at our previous meeting. While we were waiting for the rally to begin, he told me how the Cultural Revolution had affected him. He stressed the bewilderment of the first few months, when there was no clear indication of the true course and purpose of the movement. He spoke of the excitement he had experienced, as it gradually began to dawn on him that this was to be a cleansing of the Party itself, his relief when he realized that he and the other teachers were not the principal targets, and the drama of exposing little by little the ways in which the Party had conspired to keep the students in the dark, to restrict the display of wall posters and stir up factionalism.

He reminisced about his trip to Peking, where he "saw Chairman Mao in Tien An Men Square but had time to do other things, visit famous places, look up friends. . . ." He was philosophical about the hardships that the movement had caused, the waste of time and energy, the damage done to the economy and to the discipline of the people. These things were inevitable, he said; he insisted on seeing the Cultural Revolution as a sign of hope, a sign that China was not going to walk blindly, as Russia had, into a future plagued by bureaucratism and the indifference of the officials to the people they served.

I reminded him of the cost of the Cultural Revolution—the parading of people in high hats, the raiding of private houses, the vengeance engendered by violence. He looked hurt. Violence, he said, had been specifically forbidden by the Central Committee. The Party had always been against violence, but it was deeply rooted in the people and their history.

This conversation was interrupted by the playing of "The East Is Red" over the public-address system. Everyone stood, while three verses of the stirring tune blared out. Then it was time for the speeches.

A new committee of revolutionary unity had been formed, its

members democratically elected from their own groups. The task of this alliance of Rebel Red Guards and Party cadres would be to guide the Institute into the post–Cultural Revolution period.

The shock came when the new committee members began to file onto the stage to make their bows, for there, at their head, walked none other than Comrade Chou, the Vice-President who had been viciously attacked in a wall poster by the Party Secretary, a man once regarded by almost the whole Institute as a malingerer and a degenerate. I could hardly believe my eyes; yet there he was, dressed in his oldest working clothes, the red arm band shining on his sleeve, marching on stage to loud applause.

I was so surprised that I barely listened to the speeches. "A joyous day," someone was saying, "half a year's struggle . . . the Rebels have won . . . a great victory for Chairman Mao's ideas. . . ."

It turned out that Vice-President Chou had himself been Party Secretary of the Institute once and that the present Party Secretary had usurped his position and used it to implement the policies of the revisionists. When the Vice-President had pounded the table and roared: "I'm not some second-rate hack! I was sent to Shanghai by the Central Committee Secretariat!" he had not been bluffing. He was, and had always been, a dyed-in-the-wool Maoist.

Chou was making his acceptance speech: "Chairman Mao the red, red sun in our hearts . . . the situation very favorable . . . a decisive victory all around . . . the three-way alliance . . . Shanghai going great guns . . . the January Revolution. . . ."

A photographer popped a flash. It was like a press conference.

The phrases succeeded one another—"the strength of unity, the danger of a comeback by the class enemy, the need for military training, for rectification of the Rebel ranks, for the utter repudiation of Liu Shao-ch'i and all his works. . . ."

Then one of the Rebels took the floor. The unity of the student left wing with the Party cadres was essential, he said, for without it the Rebels would find themselves isolated. He went on to point out, with a sense of mercy that had often been sadly absent from the Rebel ranks, that a cadre was not to be judged solely by his mistakes during the movement; his whole career should be taken into account.

A worker took the microphone, a grizzled old fellow who did odd jobs around the Institute. He said that the Cultural Revolution had changed his concept of work. He realized now that cleaning blackboards was not necessarily good in itself. He had cleaned many, only to have reactionary teachers write evil things on them! Did this not mean that he, too, had participated in the trend towards revisionism? Everybody laughed.

An element of fantasy then crept into the meeting, as representatives of various colleges, factories, and commercial enterprises took turns congratulating the Institute on its new unity. Each brought a huge red poster that he attached to the lectern or held for everyone to see. Before long, the whole stage was flowing with color, and the mood was more like an old-fashioned carnival than "a new stage of human history."

The contagion spread to the foreign teachers, one of whom got up to say a few words. The applause was more polite than ecstatic as the big European strode to the lectern. "Thank you, comrades," he said. "This is a day of great significance for us all. You have unity, and Chairman Mao's thought has once again been vindicated." A flash bulb went off. "The revolutionary masses must hold fast to the dictatorship of the proletariat. Everything smacking of capitalism must be destroyed." Another flash. The applause still restrained. "Chairman Mao says: 'We must pursue the tottering foe . . .'" Loud applause. "Do not abandon the movement now. Carry it through to the end."

Then slogans, each one taken up by the audience:

"Down with All Opponents of Chairman Mao's Revolutionary Line!"

"Down with Liu Shao-ch'i, the Man Who Had Been Leading China Back to Capitalism!"

"Down with Kosygin and Brezhnev, the Leaders of Soviet Revisionism!"

"Long Live the Great Leader of the World's People, Chairman Mao!"

"Long Life; Long Life; Long, Long Life to Him!"

The audience was now in good voice. After 9 months of repeating slogans, you get good at it.

I wished it had all been so simple for me. I could not help remembering that this foreigner had come to China with a box of Beatles records. Was that progress? Had he really completed his *personal* Cultural Revolution? Had the movement touched him to his soul?

The meeting was breaking up to a new slogan. Instead of merely wishing the Chairman long life, the toast was now one that had applied in the past to emperors: "*Wan Shou Wu Chiang!*" a cheerleader shouted through a bull-horn: "Life Without Limit." This was not repeated by the audience. Instead, everyone clapped.

With this applause ringing in my ears, I went home to finish packing, while the whole Institute prepared for an almighty concert.

Postscript

Had we been dealing with a clear-cut struggle between easily identifiable protagonists, this story would have been more quickly told. But the Cultural Revolution was a many-sided, many-centered mass movement involving millions of people in a bewildering interplay of organization and action. To have simplified it would have been to have distorted it. By its very nature, it required that we join in it, that we take up positions alongside the people who waged it, and that we go with them through the perplexing tangle of false starts, feints, back tracks, dead ends, and breakthroughs that they had to negotiate.

The alternative would have been to have sat up high in the detached empyrean of scholarship and scanned the natives, as anthropologists used to do, through the tubes and lenses of Western superiority, to construct flat maps of Chinese behavior, capturing the torques and thrusts of the new culture in neat plane geometry theorems. Unfortunately, the Chinese have a habit of smashing out of these traps and going their own way. Then people get angry. China, they say, is inconsistent and irrational; it does not conform to their image of what it should be.

This book is not meant to be a catechism; it is not meant to proffer answers at the touch of an index. It is an attempt to set the reader in the tide of China, in the continuous ebb and flow of experimentation that makes this society unique. If there is a lesson to be learned, it is that the problems of China are, in a very real sense, our problems. If China finds answers to the con-

tradictions of bureaucracy and democracy, revisionism and permanent revolution, industrialization and agriculture, moral and
material incentives, and so on, then we all find answers. This is
no fuzzy ecumenism; in a nuclear world, of which the Chinese
make up one-quarter, it is a statement of fact. With this in mind,
and having been through the mill of the Red Guard movement,
we should be able not so much to draw conclusions as to high-
light some of the dominant features of the experience.

First, it is clear from this account that the Cultural Revolution was indeed a revolution. It was not a game; it was not, in
the words of Mao, "a dinner party, or writing an essay, or painting a picture, or doing embroidery." Although its beginnings
were tinged with fantasy, it soon outgrew its "Don Quixote"
phase, passed beyond student knights tilting at the windmills of
revisionism, and became what its title said it was: "a full-scale
revolution to establish a working-class culture."

As we have seen, December, 1966, and January, 1967, were
pivotal months in this change. This was the point at which dilet-
tantism got its fingers burned. What had been a campaign waged
as much in the imagination of the participants as in hard political realities suddenly became a battle for real power at every
social level.

Both stages had a profound effect on the people. The initial
student movement blew like a refreshing breeze through the
rather staid city of Shanghai. Sooner or later, the whole population came alive; the crowds that surrounded the important wall
posters thrashed out the nation's political problems right there
on the street, and millions of people were inspired to join
groups, to take sides, to act out the drama of change.

In galvanizing the city, the students were responding eagerly
to Mao's appeal: "The world is yours, as well as ours, but in the
last analysis, it is yours. You young people, full of vigor and
vitality, are in the bloom of life, like the sun at eight or nine in
the morning. Our hope is placed on you." There was a strong
strain of romanticism in the Red Guard movement. It was ex-
citing to drop out of classes, organize a group, affiliate with allies
wherever you could find them, and wage a swinging war against
revisionism, the half-understood enemy. This enthusiasm spread

contagiously. The man in the street began to see that the Cultural Revolution was not something that could be carried out by edict from the Center, that the struggle to revitalize Chinese society could only be fought and won by the people.

The harsh reality of this struggle did not become fully clear until the radical students and workers suddenly realized that they were going to win political power. They were going to achieve what they had hardly dared hope for—the ouster of Mayor Ts'ao Ti-ch'iu and the Party bureaucrats. They then would have to step into the vacuum created by their victory and take over control of government that the Party had held. This was a different matter from sitting down and writing diatribes against the leadership; it was a fight for power, a revolution. Most Red Guards, whether students or workers, were completely unprepared for the intensity of this battle and for the responsibilities that came with victory. Some groups squabbled among themselves; some fell prey to the influence of the old Party cadres; others dropped out of the movement in disgust. Only the hard-core radicals—those who had fought as a persecuted minority from the beginning and the Red Guards from Peking and other cities—managed to maintain some sort of unity, and it was they who, under the command of Chang Ch'un-ch'iao, swept into power.

Many Red Guards, especially those who belonged to massive and famous Shanghai organizations, were bitterly disappointed at the way things turned out. They plainly felt that Chang Ch'un-ch'iao and his forces were interlopers and did not have the allegiance of the Shanghai people. Some reasoned that Chang's take-over was simply another form of revisionism and decided to treat him as they would treat any cadre who tried to impose his will on the masses. They struck out, only to find that Chang had the approval of the Center and the backing of the army. That was the beginning of the end, and the rest of the Cultural Revolution in Shanghai was largely a matter of straightening out the legitimacy of the new power, the proper balance of the three-way alliance that Chang headed, and the relations between civilian and army authority.

Out of this struggle came important changes in the political structure of Shanghai. Where previously the Party had reigned supreme, now power was shared by the Party, the army, and the Red Guards. This meant new blood in the leadership, new methods, new approaches, a revitalized government. It was not as radical a change as the initiators of the Cultural Revolution had envisioned, perhaps, but there was enough upgrading of popular forces and downgrading of tired bureaucrats to provide the city with revolutionary energy for a number of years.

The reality of the movement was also reflected at the personal level. People suffered. Cadres who felt they had served well over the years suddenly found themselves disgraced and even dismissed; students who had fought hard against the power structure in the early stages had their wings clipped when the new government was established; radical workers who had expected to play a major role in the running of factories and enterprises had to share power with the people they had opposed so bitterly. Grudges born or exacerbated during the movement will keep reappearing in the future. However, one must take into consideration the millions of people for whom the Cultural Revolution was a liberating and enlightening experience. The tension between these two groups will be a permanent factor in China's development.

The second feature that emerges from this study is that some kind of campaign against bureaucratism was necessary. Few observers in the West are willing to concede this; ironically, many commentators profess sympathy for the Party and Liu Shao-ch'i. Yet, it is clear from the behavior of Party officials when challenged, first by a handful of radical students and later by a student-worker alliance, that the power structure had grown repressive. It had lost the spirit of Yenan; it had forgotten the principle of identity with the masses, had applied a policy of paternalistic tutelage toward the people, and had shown impatience with any form of dissent.

The Red Guards have left us ample and eloquent testimony on this point. The radicals sensed at first and then proved that the Party had resorted from the start to traditional political tactics, making secret alliances with conservatives, using blackmail and intimidation to subdue rebellious students and workers, subtly and insidiously manipulating people, but never, unless left no alternative, openly taking a stance against the forces that threatened it.

Even when the movement was in its infancy, the Party, though in no immediate danger from the dissidents, reacted as though its existence was at stake. This showed that there was a strong and carefully coordinated nationwide pact between establishment cadres, who had a fair idea of the Mao group's aims and went all-out to divert them. The Party's reaction caused confusion among the college students, destroyed the movement in high schools, delayed it for six months in the factories and for even longer in the ranks of the administration. It also made the defeat of the revisionists more certain, for the anger and bitterness of the radicals swelled during the time of their repression, and when they broke free and swung at the Party, it was with all the force of pent-up rage. This is what made the later events seem inexplicably harsh and extreme to the outside observer; he could not see and did not know what the radicals had suffered, and so he did not understand their fury when it came.

The Party came through the Cultural Revolution looking rather bedraggled. Not only had it been shown up as antiradical; it had also been stripped of its trappings of pseudorevolution. It was the Party above all that churned out vast quantities of Maoist slogans, pamphlets, posters, and editorials lauding "the red, red sun in our hearts" and "the leader of the world's people" and "our beloved Chairman," although the producers of this verbiage were often the people who had the least faith in the leadership of Mao Tse-tung. This fraud, which the radicals rightly derided as "waving the red flag to oppose the red flag," gave the movement a lot of its fanatical repetitions and much of its violent tone. The Party, in effect, inflated the currency of the language, and the Red Guards were forced to extremes of hyperbole merely to keep in the running.

This reaction by the Party was the best proof that a movement was needed, that a shake-up of the power structure was essential if the mass line was ever to prevail. China's growth as a radical working-class culture was being distorted by the bureaucratism and revisionist economics that had crept into official thinking. If a move to check these tendencies had been delayed much longer, the country could indeed, as the radicals put it, have changed color, lost its revolutionary *élan,* and settled down to the building of an urban, industrial, and consumer-oriented society, with the consequent growth of an elite technocratic class and the inevitable neglect of the peasantry as the backbone of the economy.

Looking back now, it is hard to see how a revitalization of China's leadership and a reorienting of its national ideals could have been effected in any other way. The Party could hardly radicalize itself; the impetus had to come from outside, and the Red Guards were an ingenious solution. Though the recalcitrance of the authorities in the face of Red Guard criticism was a sure sign of disease in the Party, the fact of the Red Guards and the energy with which they went about their task were signs of vitality and flexibility in the Chinese body politic.

The third consideration that should be mentioned here is the possibility that the Cultural Revolution, despite its anticlimactic ending and the profound compromises it was forced to make, was, at least partially, a success.

From an economic point of view, it is still too early to be certain. The disaster predicted by Western analysts has not materialized, but neither has there been a second Great Leap Forward. China's foreign trade dipped sharply for a time, but not nearly as much as expected; it has since picked up, and the level of international business seems quite restored. Internally, China has reaped record harvests, and its industrial production is steady. The planners of the movement had allowed for an over-all drop of 10 per cent in production;[1] this was exceeded at certain times and in certain places, but, if the whole economy fell this far, it has recovered by now. The most optimistic Red Guard writings predicted unparalleled achievements by a newly awakened work force "armed with the thought of Mao Tse-tung." This could still happen, but it becomes less likely as time goes by. We are left with the impression that the Cultural Revolution has had little effect one way or the other on the economy.

[1] Radical wall posters in Shanghai used this statistic to argue against Party officials who stressed the importance of production in the fall and early winter of 1966.

Politically, China seems to be in a transition phase. Revolutionary committees, like the one led by Chang Ch'un-ch'iao in Shanghai, have now taken power in every province. There is evidence of heavy going in places, with the three-way compromise causing friction. But the fact that the country is functioning reasonably well suggests that the committees will be able to cope, at least until a new form of government—perhaps a variant of the Commune that failed in Shanghai—can be established.

More important than the mechanics of politics, perhaps, is the new appreciation of power that the masses now have. So many pepole have had firsthand experience, not only of bringing down authorities but also of trying to replace them, that it would be strange indeed if there were not a heightened consciousness of "people's power." And if the people have learned the extent of their power, how much more do the present authorities realize the limits of theirs. Having seen so many cadres criticized, those who now hold positions of leadership must be only too aware that their power is delegated by the masses and subject to recall by the masses. This could tend to make them timid, but they will be prodded by the populace into taking the initiative, nonetheless. This tension, which exists in every political system, will certainly continue in China. The situation could hardly be worse than it was before the movement, when Party cadres made most of the decisions in committee. This was elitism and deserved the hammering it got. If the leadership now goes to the opposite extreme and fears public opinion, at least that will be more conducive to democracy. In this sense, the political outcome of the Cultural Revolution, though not an unmixed blessing, is definitely promising.

Militarily, there can be little doubt that China is far stronger than it was before the Red Guards put on their arm bands. Mobilization was an ingredient of the movement from the beginning and coincided, to some extent, with the increasingly hostile actions of the United States and the Soviet Union on China's borders. It is hard to blame the Chinese for wanting their country to be ideologically at full strength should a showdown come. This has been largely achieved. The people are alert to the possibility of war; they have gone over the Party's domestic and foreign policy with a fine-toothed comb and have decided that the nation must remain united, prepared, and committed, if it is to survive. The basis for this ideological stance is the thought of Mao Tse-tung. In its military aspect, however, this commitment to Mao's thought has nothing to do with the personality cult; it is rather an adherence to Mao's common-sense ideas on the evils of bureaucratism, commandism, and yesmanship and on the virtues of self-reliance, perseverance, decentralization, and versatility. The ideal man of the future will be one who can farm, write, handle machinery, and fight, a man who would be hard to beat in the kind of a guerrilla situation in which China might find itself in a few years. From a military point of view, it is obvious that any country planning to invade China would have been wise to do so before the Cultural Revolution. This is one field, then, in which the movement has been a success.

Finally, a word about the spiritual effect of all this on the Chinese people. This is an aspect that our analysts tend to neglect, though the Mao group made it perfectly clear, by describing the thought of Mao as a "spiritual atom-bomb," that they consider the nation's material welfare to depend to a large extent on the moral and spiritual health of the people.

The Cultural Revolution has instituted the works of Mao as the guideline for China's future. We are prone to scoff at this, to consider it a tragedy that a nation of 700 million should be subjected to the totalitarianism of one man's vision. Yet the Chinese feel that Mao's vision reflects their own experience; they see, in the breadth and integrity of his writings, the key that Chinese thinkers have sought for a century, the answer to the question of how to be both modern and Chinese.

The elevation of Mao's ideas, despite the obvious dangers it involves, opens up new dimensions for the future. Under Communism, the Chinese have made great progress in most fields, but they have barely begun until now to break free from the deeply-rooted sense of obedience and respect for all authority, however paternalistic, that is their legacy from the Confucian past. Democracy, people's power, participation in government—these concepts have remained stunted while the society forged ahead in other respects. Mao knows and the leaders loyal to him know that China's progress is an illusion as long as the people tend toward passivity and self-satisfaction. Only when the masses realize their power and realize how important it is that they use this power will China have the spiritual momentum to keep ahead of its own development.

The Cultural Revolution is one stage, perhaps only the first, in this process of realization. It has not done all that was expected of it. Because the forces in Chinese society that were working against Mao's mass line are now known, it has become clear that too much was expected from one movement. But, insofar as it opened people's eyes to the beauties and the horrors of their society and showed them both the good and the evil possibilities for the future of that society, it has been a success.

In this light, it is not remarkable that the students and workers were misled, cheated, manipulated, and hurt during the Cultural Revolution. It is no wonder that people reacted spitefully, cruelly, and vindictively. The marvel is that it was not worse, that so many millions were involved for so long in so exacting a process, without the country's sliding to the brink of civil war or splitting into mutually antagonistic regions.

China has passed through a self-imposed ordeal by fire. It has emerged, not unscarred by the experience but stronger and more sure of its future. In a world where acts of political courage on a national scale are rare, the Cultural Revolution is a challenge to every society.

Appendix: Organizations Active in the Cultural Revolution in Shanghai

Chingkang Mountains Headquarters, a student organization with headquarters at Tsinghua University in Peking but with an influential Shanghai Liaison Center which was opposed to Chang Ch'un-ch'iao.

Field Army Red Guards (formerly called Red Guards, Peking Headquarters), Shanghai Foreign Languages Institute radical student group. Affiliated to the city-wide Second Headquarters (Red Revolutionaries).

First Headquarters (General Headquarters of Red Guards from Shanghai Schools and Colleges). Loyal to the Party establishment.

First Regiment (of Workers in the Northern Expedition), loyal to Keng Chin-chang. Cooperated with Second and Third Regiments and Workers Third Headquarters against Workers Headquarters (loyal to Chang Ch'un-ch'iao) and against the Shanghai Commune.

Peking Third Headquarters, a radical Red Guard group in the capital, formed to circumvent the Party's influence in the Peking First and Second Headquarters of Red Guards. Its Shanghai liaison center played a vital role in the struggle to bring down the old Party leaders.

Proletarian Revolutionary Rebels Headquarters, a group at Shanghai Engineering College.

Red Guard Army, a nationwide organization of demobilized soldiers. Cooperated with First, Second, and Third Regiments and Workers Third Headquarters against Chang Ch'un-ch'iao and Workers Headquarters.

Red Guard Regiment, Shanghai Foreign Languages Institute branch of the First Headquarters of Red Guards from Shanghai Schools and Colleges. Loyal to the Party establishment.

Red Guards, Peking Headquarters, Shanghai Foreign Languages Institute branch (see Field Army).

Red Revolutionaries (see Second Headquarters).

Scarlet Guards (Workers Scarlet Guards for the Defense of Mao Tsetung's Thought), a powerful Moderate Shanghai workers' organization. Loyal to the Party establishment and opposed to Red Revolutionaries and to Workers Headquarters.

Second Headquarters (Revolutionary Committee of Red Guards from Shanghai Schools and Colleges, or Red Revolutionaries), a radical group established to prevent the Shanghai Party Municipal Committee from dominating the Red Guard movement.

Second Regiment (of Workers in the Northern Expedition), led by Keng Chin-chang. Joined with First and Third Regiments and Workers Third Headquarters to oppose Chang Ch'un-ch'iao and Workers Headquarters; also opposed Scarlet Guards and Shanghai Commune.

Shanghai Revolutionary Committee, an alliance of Army officers, reliable Party cadres, and Rebel Red Guards. Designed to serve as the highest locus of power in Shanghai, assuming a role similar to that previously played by the Shanghai Municipal Party Committee.

Third Regiment (of Workers in the Northern Expedition), loyal to Keng Chin-chang. Cooperated with First and Second Regiments and Workers Third Headquarters against Workers Headquarters (loyal to Chang Ch'un-ch'iao) and against the Shanghai Commune.

United Committee of Shanghai Revolutionary Rebels, formed by Keng Chin-chang and allies. A confederation of workers' groups opposed to Workers Headquarters, Chang Ch'un-ch'iao, and the Shanghai Commune.

Workers Headquarters (Shanghai Workers Revolutionary Rebel Headquarters), loyal to Chang Ch'un-ch'iao. The organization finally identified as being in the mainstream of the Mao line in Shanghai.

Workers Scarlet Guards for the Defense of Mao Tse-tung's Thought (see Scarlet Guards).

Workers Third Headquarters, a dissident group led by Ch'en Hungk'ang. Cooperated with First, Second, and Third Regiments to oppose Workers Headquarters, Chang Ch'un-ch'iao, and the Shanghai Commune.

Key to Red Guard Newspapers
Cited in the Text

As is customary, the modified Wade-Giles system has been used for the transliteration of Chinese terms and personal names appearing in the text. Place names have been rendered according to established usage. A different transliteration system, however, is used in the People's Republic of China, and, because U.S. libraries holding Red Guard (RG) newspapers generally catalogue them according to the Chinese Communist system, that system is used below. Each newspaper has been numbered, in chronological order, from 1 to 22, and this is the first number in each index. The second number, following the colon, is the page number of the article, and the third, following the period, indicates the order of the article on the page.

RG 1: *Hongwei Zhanbao (Red Guard Dispatch)*, No. 6, November 15, 1966. Joint publication by Revolutionary Committee of Red Guards from Shanghai Schools and Colleges (Red Revolutionaries) and Shanghai Red Guard Headquarters. This was the best-known and most outspoken student newspaper of the Shanghai movement. Its consistent radicalism embarrassed the Party authorities no end.

    1:2.1: "We Workers Will Not Be Deceived Again." Signed: The Ever Faithful to Mao Tse-tung's Thought Combat Team from Number Seventeen State Cotton Mill.

    1:2.2: "What Does the Bloodshed at the Engineering College Signify?" Signed: The Revolutionary Rebel Committee of the Shanghai Engineering Institute.

    1:2.3: "It Was the Municipal Committee That Set Students Fighting Among Themselves." Signed: The Relentless Pursuit Combat Group from Shanghai's Chiaotung University.

1:3.1: "Bring Down Once and for All the Bourgeois Reactionary Line of the Shanghai Municipal Committee." Signed: T'an Ch'i-t'ai, a Futan University Red Guard.

1:4.1: "Ch'ang Hsi-p'ing Cannot Deny that He Tried to Wreck the Cultural Revolution." Signed: The Hit Ch'ang Regiment of the East China Normal College Red Revolutionaries.

RG 2: *Geming Zaofan Bao (Revolutionary Rebel News)*, December 15, 1966. A hard-hitting radical paper published by Revolutionary Rebel Headquarters of Shanghai Red Guards.

2:2.1: "A Rap on the Knuckles of Soviet Revisionism." Signed: Observer.

2:4.1: "Futan Roots Out the Counterrevolutionary Revisionist Yang Hsi-kuang." Dated December 10, 1966.

RG 3: *Hongwei Zhanbao* (see RG 1), Special Supplement, December 17, 1966. "The True Nature of the *Liberation Daily* Incident."

3:1.1: "Putting into Focus the Struggle Between Two Lines in Shanghai."

3:2.1: "Outside the *Liberation Daily* Building."

3:2.2: "Inside the *Liberation Daily* Building."

3:3.1: "To Dispel a Few Rumors."

RG 4: *Chuban Zhanxian (The Publishing Front)*, December 24, 1966. A Moderate publication put out jointly by Red Guards and Scarlet Guards of Shanghai's Publishing Network. It tried to take the pressure off Shanghai's Propaganda Department heads by criticizing the former Party Secretary of Shanghai Propaganda, Shih Hsi-min.

4:2.1: "A Serious Case of Stirring Up Fighting Among the Masses." Signed: The Turmoil of Wind and Thunder United Combat Team of the Shanghai People's Fine Arts Publishing Company.

RG 5: *Xinwen Zhanshi (News Warrior)*, December 26, 1966. Published by Revolutionary Rebel Committee of Shanghai Press Circles. This paper appeared at a critical time in December and provided the radicals with the material they needed to bring down the Municipal Party Committee.

5:1.1: "Press Circles Quickly Raise a Rebel Army and Courageously Bombard Ts'ao's Encampment."

5:2.1: "Statement by the Revolutionary Rebel Committee of Shanghai's Press Circles."

5:2.2: "Plenty of Proof that the *Liberation Daily* Party Committee Suppressed the Revolutionary Rebels." Speech by the representative of United Headquarters of *Liberation Daily* Revolutionary Rebels at the December 21 rally in Shanghai.

5:2.3: "Shanghai Radio and Television Were Willing Tools of the

Ts'ao Clique's Municipal Committee." Speech by the representative of Revolutionary Rebels in Shanghai People's Radio and Television at the December 21 rally in Shanghai.

5:3.1: "What Did the Shanghai Branch of the New China News Agency Do During the Cultural Revolution?" Speech by the representative of Revolutionary Rebels of the Shanghai Branch of the New China News Agency at the December 21 rally in Shanghai.

5:3.2: "Ma Ta Was the Chief Instigator of the Fighting Among the Masses." Speech by the representative of Iron Broom Combat Group of the United Headquarters of *Liberation Daily* Revolutionary Rebels at the December 21 rally in Shanghai.

5:4.1: "How the Municipal Committee and the Cultural Revolution Group of *Wen Hui Pao* Suppressed the Revolutionary Rebels." Speech by the representative of Red Hearts and Iron Bones Combat Regiment of *Wen Hui Pao*'s Spark that Sets the Prairie Grass On Fire Revolutionary Rebel Headquarters at the December 21 rally in Shanghai.

5:4.2: "Some Underhand Tricks of the Municipal Committee in Its Peddling of the Bourgeois Reactionary Line." Speech by the representative of the Spark Combat Regiment of the Shanghai *Evening News* at the December 21 rally in Shanghai.

5:4.3: "The East China Bureau and the Shanghai Municipal Committee Were the Ringleaders of the Attempt to Throttle the *Red Guard Dispatch*." Speech by the representative of Red Revolutionaries at the December 21 rally in Shanghai.

RG 6: *Hongwei Zhanbao* (see RG 1), No. 11, December 30, 1966. Ready for publication on December 11, 1966, but held up for 3 weeks by the *Liberation Daily* incident.

6:1.1: "An Experience in Martial Vigor." Editorial.

6:1.2: "When the Winds Blow, Men See the Dawn Again."

6:2.1: "How the Swindle Worked." Revised by Documentation Group of the Frontline Command.

6:2.2: "Candle in a Paper Boat Thinks It's the Sun in the Heavens."

6:3.1: "There Is a Mountain of Evidence to Prove that *Liberation Daily* Opposed Chairman Mao." Signed: Some Fighters from the Revolutionary Committee of Red Guards at East China Normal College.

6:3.2: "Let the Truth Speak for Itself." Signed: Tai Pu-p'ing, a fighter in United Headquarters of *Liberation Daily* Revolutionary Rebels.

6:4.1: "This Is the Kind of 'Party Organ' It Was." Signed: Defend the East Combat Group of *Liberation Daily*.

RG 7: *Hongwei Zhanbao* (see RG 1), No. 15, January 4, 1967.

7:4.1: "Ch'en P'ei-hsien and Ts'ao Ti-ch'iu Are the Ringleaders of the Fighting Among the Masses."

7:4.2: "The Conservative 'First Headquarters' Turns Over a New Leaf."

RG 8: *Hongwei Zhanbao* (see RG 1), No. 16, January 8, 1967.

8:1.1: "Bring Down Once and for All the Shanghai Municipal Committee Led by Ch'en P'ei-hsien and Ts'ao Ti-ch'iu."

8:1.2: "The Great Thought of Mao Tse-tung Has Condemned the Shanghai Municipal Committee to Death." Editorial.

8:2.1: "The Shanghai Municipal Committee Turned Its Guns on the Headquarters of the Proletariat." Speech by the representative of Workers Headquarters at the January 6 rally in Shanghai.

8:2.2: "Ch'en P'ei-hsien Is the Shanghai Vassal of the Liu Dynasty's Revisionist Headquarters." Speech by the representative of Red Revolutionaries at the January 6 rally in Shanghai.

8:3.1: "Smash the Shanghai Municipal Committee! It Has Opposed Chairman Mao." Speech by the representative of Revolutionary Rebels in the Office of the Municipal Committee Cultural Revolution Group at the January 6 rally in Shanghai.

8:3.2: "The Shanghai Municipal Committee Cannot Deny Cruelly Suppressing the Workers' Movement." Speech by the representative of Revolutionary Rebels in the Municipal Committee's Urban Socialist Education Office at the January 6 rally in Shanghai.

8:4.1: "A Rally to Hold High the Great Red Banner of Mao Tse-tung's Thought and Bring Down the Shanghai Municipal Committee Led by Ch'en P'ei-hsien and Ts'ao Ti-ch'iu."

RG 9: *Hongwei Zhanbao* (see RG 1), No. 17, January 10, 1967.

9:2.1: "An Extremely Important Document." The Message to All the People of Shanghai.

9:2.2: "Urgent Notice." With an editorial comment by *Wen Hui Pao*.

9:3.1: "Ch'en P'ei-hsien Is the Ringleader of Shanghai's Stubborn Promotion of the Bourgeois Reactionary Line." Signed: Revolutionary Rebel Brigade from Offices One and Two in the Municipal Committee Building.

9:4.1: "Ts'ao Ti-ch'iu Was the One Who Tried to Kill the Student Movement." Signed: Red Revolutionaries.

RG 10: Dongfanghong (The East Is Red), No. 6, January 19, 1967. Published jointly by General Headquarters of Shanghai East Is Red (Mao Tse-tung's Thought Group and Red Guard Group) and East Is Red Regiment from Tungchi University. This student paper described the part played by radicals from Tungchi in the Kunshan affair.

10:3.1: "The Truth About the Kunshan Incident." Signed: Combat Kunshan Column of Tungchi University's East Is Red Regiment.

RG 11: Huoqi (Flag of Fire), No. 2, February 12, 1967. Published by Twelve-Three Revolutionary Rebel Committee of Shanghai. Nothing is known of this group except its role in exposing the tactics of Work Teams in the administration.

11:1.1: "A Strong Statement."

11:4.1: "If You Won't Cooperate, I Have the Police." Dated November, 1966.

RG 12: Hongwei Zhanbao (see RG 1). This issue, dated February 16, 1967, was published by Shanghai Red Guard Headquarters. The sudden disappearance of Red Revolutionaries from the joint publication shows their loss of power at this time, due no doubt to their attack on Chang Ch'un-ch'iao (see the end of Chapter 11).

RG 13: Caimao Zhanshi (The Finance and Trade Warrior), February 18, 1967. Published by Liaison Committee of Revolutionary Rebels in Shanghai's Financial and Trade Circles.

RG 14: Anonymous. Dated February 19, 1967. The article referred to is entitled "Joint Statement."

RG 15: Qinghua Tongxun (The Tsinghua Examiner), February 22, 1967. Published by the Shanghai Liaison Center of the Tsinghua University Chingkang Mountains Headquarters. This paper exposed the factionalism within the Chingkang group and condemned the ultraleft line of those who opposed Chang Ch'un-ch'iao.

RG 16: Anonymous. Dated February 25, 1967. The article cited is "Strong Statement by the Frontline Command." Signed: The Make Revolution–Boost Production Frontline Command of the Shanghai Revolutionary Committee.

RG 17: Hongse Zaofan Bao (Red Rebel News), Nos. 8 and 9 combined, February 28, 1967. Published by the Shanghai Liaison Center of the Red Rebel Brigade from Harbin Military Engineering Institute. A consistently radical paper, perhaps more loyal to Chang Ch'un-ch'iao than any other publication.

17:2.1: "With Power We Must Pursue the Tottering Foe."

17:3.1: "Exploding a Few of the Myths About Keng Chin-chang."

17:3.2: "Statement."

17:4.1: "See the Gruesome Features of a Few Workers Head-quarters Leaders!"

RG 18: *Geming Lou (House of Revolution)*, No. 3, March 10, 1967. Published by Revolutionary Rebels in Shanghai Drama Academy. Little else is known about this group.

RG 19: *Gongren Zaofan Bao (Workers Rebel News)*, No. 6, March 13, 1967. Published by the Propaganda Department of Shang-hai Workers Revolutionary Rebel Headquarters. This was the organ of the largest workers' organization loyal to Chang Ch'un-ch'iao. It did a lot to discredit his opposition.

RG 20: *Dongfang Pinglun (The Eastern Critic)*, No. 3, March 15, 1967. Joint publication of Homeguard Red Guard Regiment of the Eastern Commune Revolutionary Committee and the Rock in Midstream Regiment of the Shanghai Engineering College Revolutionary Rebel Committee. Despite the fancy title, this paper was essentially moderate; like many others, it found it convenient to adopt a radical posture.

20:2.1: "Rush Back to Class and Get On with the Revolution!"

RG 21: *Hongwei Zhanbao* (see RG 1), No. 30, March 27, 1967. Pub-lished by Shanghai Red Guard Headquarters.

21:3.1: "Revolutionary Teachers, Go to Your Students!" Signed: Red Flag Combat Team Teachers from Kongjiang Middle School.

21:4.1: "National News."

RG 22: *Jidian Zhanbao (The Mechanical and Electrical Dispatch)*, No. 3, April 5, 1967. Published by Shanghai Revolutionary Rebel United Committee in the First Department of Mechanical Industry. A moderate tabloid of little interest.

22:2.1: "A Revealing Poster by the Revolutionary Little Soldiers of the 'Lu Hsun' Regiment." Signed: East Is Red Com-mune of the Rebel Regiment in the Red Flag Foundry.

Index

Aidit, D. N., 19

Central Committee (*see* Chinese Communist Party, Central Committee of)

Central Cultural Revolution Group, 41, 130, 139, 140, 141, 142, 144, 146, 148, 167, 179, 180, 193, 208, 218, 222, 230, 235, 240–43, 250, 251, 253, 254, 261, 265, 266, 283

Chang Ch'eng-tsung, 99, 148

Chang Ch'un-ch'iao, 20, 21, 34, 35, 140–48, 151, 179, 191, 192, 193, 199, 202, 206, 208, 209, 215, 222–76, 283, 293, 297

Ch'ang Hsi-p'ing, 32–34, 37, 63, 65, 73–80, 84, 110, 134, 153, 183

Ch'en Hung-k'ang, 228, 235, 246, 253, 274

Ch'en P'ei-hsien, 21, 28, 29, 37–39, 41, 142, 143, 153, 185, 186, 191, 193, 194, 202, 209–13, 232, 240, 242, 259, 276–85

Ch'en Po-ta, 139–42, 145, 179, 230, 231, 242

Ch'en Yi, 8, 178

Ch'en Yün, 278, 279

Chiang Ch'ing (Madame Mao Tse-tung), 16, 18, 21, 37, 136, 179, 180, 242

Chiang K'ai-shek, 8, 23, 40, 88, 119

Chiang Nan-hsiang, 23

Chinese Communist Party, 4, 6, 7, 31, 32, 44, 45, 48, 66, 70, 73, 74, 95, 98, 112, 113, 116, 118, 119, 120, 123–30, 133, 150, 153, 158, 186, 227, 229, 273; Central Committee of, 10, 16, 25–28, 31, 37, 41, 42, 62, 74, 84, 95, 104, 106, 107, 111, 112, 116, 128–30, 145–48, 160, 179, 180, 197, 198, 202, 206, 207, 208, 213, 214, 216, 218, 227, 264, 265, 280, 281, 283, 287; Eleventh Plenary Session of, 64–87; Work Teams, 27, 39, 40, 43, 62, 63, 66, 95, 96, 99, 100, 101, 278; Youth League, 44–49, 52, 58, 72, 78, 273 (*see also* East China Bureau; Peking, Municipal Party Committee; Shanghai, Municipal Party Committee)

Chou En-lai, 19, 50, 51, 52, 55, 62, 113, 125, 159, 160, 168, 178, 179, 180, 188, 198, 208, 220, 229, 230, 242, 252, 275

Chou Pi-tai, 147

Chu Teh, 262

Chuang Tse-tung, 23

Communist Party (*see* Chinese Communist Party)

Dulles, John Foster, 24

East China Bureau, Chinese Communist Party, 28, 37, 38, 103, 104, 134, 142, 143, 153, 160, 165, 187, 192, 194, 195, 196, 205, 209, 212, 213, 227

Index

Some other Oxford Paperbacks for readers interested in Central Asia, China, and South-east Asia, past and present

CAMBODIA

GEORGE COEDÈS
Angkor

MALCOLM MacDONALD
Angkor and the Khmers*

CENTRAL ASIA

PETER FLEMING
Bayonets to Lhasa

ANDRÉ GUIBAUT
Tibetan Venture

LADY MACARTNEY
An English Lady in
Chinese Turkestan

DIANA SHIPTON
The Antique Land

C. P. SKRINE AND
PAMELA NIGHTINGALE
Macartney at Kashgar*

ERIC TEICHMAN
Journey to Turkistan

ALBERT VON LE COQ
Buried Treasures of
Chinese Turkestan

AITCHEN K. WU
Turkistan Tumult

CHINA

All About Shanghai:
A Standard Guide

HAROLD ACTON
Peonies and Ponies

VICKI BAUM
Shanghai '37

ERNEST BRAMAH
Kai Lung's Golden
Hours*

ERNEST BRAMAH
The Wallet of Kai Lung*

ANN BRIDGE
The Ginger Griffin

CHANG HSIN-HAI
The Fabulous Concubine*

CARL CROW
Handbook for China

PETER FLEMING
The Siege at Peking

MARY HOOKER
Behind the Scenes in Peking

NEALE HUNTER
Shanghai Journal*

GEORGE N. KATES
The Years that Were Fat

CORRINNE LAMB
The Chinese Festive Board

W. SOMERSET MAUGHAM
On a Chinese Screen*

G. E. MORRISON
An Australian in China

DESMOND NEILL
Elegant Flower

PETER QUENNELL
A Superficial Journey
through Tokyo and Peking

OSBERT SITWELL
Escape with Me! An Oriental
Sketch-book

J. A. TURNER
Kwang Tung or Five Years in
South China

HONG KONG AND MACAU

AUSTIN COATES
City of Broken Promises

AUSTIN COATES
A Macao Narrative

AUSTIN COATES
Myself a Mandarin

AUSTIN COATES
The Road

The Hong Kong Guide 1893

INDONESIA

S. TAKDIR ALISJAHBANA
Indonesia: Social and
Cultural Revolution

DAVID ATTENBOROUGH
Zoo Quest for a Dragon*

VICKI BAUM
A Tale from Bali*

'BENGAL CIVILIAN'
Rambles in Java and the
Straits in 1852

MIGUEL COVARRUBIAS
Island of Bali*

BERYL DE ZOETE AND
WALTER SPIES
Dance and Drama in Bali

AUGUSTA DE WIT
Java: Facts and Fancies

JACQUES DUMARÇAY
Borobudur

JACQUES DUMARÇAY
The Temples of Java

ANNA FORBES
Unbeaten Tracks in Islands of
the Far East

GEOFFREY GORER
Bali and Angkor

JENNIFER LINDSAY
Javanese Gamelan

EDWIN M. LOEB
Sumatra: Its History and
People

MOCHTAR LUBIS
The Outlaw and Other Stories

MOCHTAR LUBIS
Twilight in Djakarta

MADELON H. LULOFS
Coolie*

MADELON H. LULOFS
Rubber

COLIN McPHEE
A House in Bali*

ERIC MJÖBERG
Forest Life and Adventures in
the Malay Archipelago

HICKMAN POWELL
The Last Paradise

E. R. SCIDMORE
Java, Garden of the East

MICHAEL SMITHIES
Yogyakarta: Cultural
Heart of Indonesia

LADISLAO SZÉKELY
Tropic Fever: The Adventures
of a Planter in Sumatra

EDWARD C. VAN NESS AND
SHITA PRAWIROHARDJO
Javanese Wayang Kulit

MALAYSIA

ISABELLA L. BIRD
The Golden Chersonese:
Travels in Malaya in 1879

MARGARET BROOKE
THE RANEE OF SARAWAK
My Life in Sarawak

HENRI FAUCONNIER
The Soul of Malaya

W. R. GEDDES
Nine Dayak Nights

A. G. GLENISTER
The Birds of the Malay
Peninsula, Singapore and
Penang

C. W. HARRISON
Illustrated Guide to the
Federated Malay States
(1923)

BARBARA HARRISSON
Orang-Utan

TOM HARRISSON
World Within: A Borneo
Story

CHARLES HOSE
The Field-Book of a
Jungle-Wallah

EMILY INNES
The Chersonese with the
Gilding Off

W. SOMERSET MAUGHAM
Ah King and Other Stories*

W. SOMERSET MAUGHAM
The Casuarina Tree*

MARY McMINNIES
The Flying Fox*

ROBERT PAYNE
The White Rajahs of Sarawak

OWEN RUTTER
The Pirate Wind

ROBERT W. SHELFORD
A Naturalist in Borneo

CARVETH WELLS
Six Years in the Malay Jungle

SINGAPORE

RUSSELL GRENFELL
Main Fleet to Singapore

R. W. E. HARPER AND
HARRY MILLER
Singapore Mutiny

JANET LIM
Sold for Silver

G. M. REITH
Handbook to Singapore
(1907)

C. E. WURTZBURG
Raffles of the Eastern Isles

THAILAND

CARL BOCK
Temples and Elephants

REGINALD CAMPBELL
Teak-Wallah

MALCOLM SMITH
A Physician at the Court of
Siam

ERNEST YOUNG
The Kingdom of the Yellow
Robe

Titles marked with an asterisk have restricted rights.